MW00561278

Postcolonial African cinema

MANCHESTER
1824

Manchester University Press

Postcolonial African cinema

Ten directors

DAVID MURPHY AND PATRICK WILLIAMS

Manchester University Press

Manchester and New York

distributed exclusively in the USA by Palgrave

Copyright © David Murphy and Patrick Williams 2007

The right of David Murphy and Patrick Williams to be identified as the authors of this work has been asserted by them in accordance with the Copyright, Designs and Patents Act 1988.

Published by Manchester University Press
Oxford Road, Manchester M13 9NR, UK
and Room 400, 175 Fifth Avenue, New York, NY 10010, USA
www.manchesteruniversitypress.co.uk

Distributed exclusively in the USA by
Palgrave, 175 Fifth Avenue, New York,
NY 10010, USA

Distributed exclusively in Canada by
UBC Press, University of British Columbia, 2029 West Mall,
Vancouver, BC, Canada V6T 1Z2

British Library Cataloguing-in-Publication Data
A catalogue record for this book is available from the British Library

Library of Congress Cataloging-in-Publication Data applied for

ISBN 978 0 7190 7202 4 hardback

ISBN 978 0 7190 7203 1 paperback

First published 2007

16 15 14 13 12 11 10 09 08 07   10 9 8 7 6 5 4 3 2 1

Typeset by Servis Filmsetting Limited, Manchester
Printed in Great Britain
by The Cromwell Press Ltd, Trowbridge

For Aedín, Ailbhe and Gabriel
Jen, Sophie and Louis

Contents

Illustrations

The illustrations can be found between pp. 114 and 115.

Acknowledgements

The authors would like to thank the following people for sharing their ideas and expertise with us and/or for looking at early drafts of the manuscript: Lizelle Bisschoff, Alison Donnell, Charles Forsdick, Gary Needham, Aedín Ní Loingsigh, Bert Ross, Andy Stafford, Michael Syrotinski. We would also like to thank the Arts and Humanities Research Council for the support it provided via its research leave scheme, which gave us both the opportunity to complete our respective sections of the manuscript. David Murphy would like to thank the British Academy and the Leverhulme Trust for their financial support, which allowed him to carry out important archival research at the Cinémathèque Afrique in Paris, where Jeanick LeNaour was always willing to share her vast knowledge of Francophone African cinema. Finally, we would like to acknowledge the support of our friends and families, in particular, Aedín and Jen, who always allowed us to put things in perspective, even in the more fraught stages of producing the manuscript. This book is dedicated to them with love.

Availability of African films

Until quite recently, it was difficult to obtain copies of many major works of African cinema, and those that were available were, in general, expensive to purchase. Researchers were thus often obliged to view even key works in archives such as the excellent Cinémathèque Afrique in Paris (www.adpf.asso.fr/cinematheque/index.html) or at the British Film Institute in London (www.bfi.org.uk). However, the DVD revolution of the past few years has resulted in the production of relatively cheap copies of important feature films by both established directors and young and upcoming filmmakers. In the United States, the following distributors have an extensive African catalogue, which is available for purchase on-line: California Newsreel (www.newsreel.org), New Yorker Films (www.newyorkerfilms.com), Kino Films (www.kino.com). In France, the Médiathèque des Trois Mondes (www.cine3mondes.com) has released important work by many African directors from both north and south of the Sahara (other distributors tend to concentrate on Francophone West Africa). In Britain, a small number of African films have long been available for screening at the British Film Institute in London. There are now signs that even mainstream distributors, most notably Artificial Eye, have regained an interest in African cinema, as recent films by Haroun (*Abouna*), Sissako (*Waiting for Happiness, Bamako*), Sembene (*Moolaadé*) and Nacro (*The Night of Truth*) have gained an automatic release on DVD just a few months after their theatrical release; while the French distributor Pathé brought out in 2004 a box set of four of Souleymane Cissé's feature films. As for Africa itself, access to these films remains a major problem, with the cost of DVDs produced in the West being far beyond the pockets of many Africans.

Of the filmmakers discussed in this volume, a range of their feature films is available from a mixture of the above sources. In some cases, such as that of Sembene, virtually the entire back catalogue is now available, following Médiathèque des Trois Mondes' release of a five-DVD box set (just a few years ago, only three or four of Sembene's films were commercially available). While the more successful films (either commercially or artistically) of directors such as Chahine and Darrell Roodt are marketed by outlets such as Amazon (www.amazon.co.uk; www.amazon.com), the same is not uniformly true of their other work. In other cases, such as that of Flora Gomes or Idrissa Ouédraogo, the picture is even more mixed, with a partial selection of films being available from various sources; inexplicably, and scandalously, the one director whose work is currently not available at all is Med Hondo.

Introduction

Representing postcolonial African cinema

Representing Africa

Despite the well-documented – and seemingly intractable – difficulties in production, distribution and exhibition that it has faced over the last fifty years, African cinema has managed to establish itself as an innovative and challenging body of filmmaking, and this volume represents a response to some of the best of those films. It is the first introduction of its kind to an important cross-section of postcolonial African filmmakers from the 1950s to the present, and its approach marks a shift from that adopted in most previous critical works. There are surveys of African cinema as a whole (Malkmus and Armes 1991) and of North African (Armes 2005) or sub-Saharan African cinema (Diawara 1992; Ukadike 1994; Barlet 2000; Shaka 2004) individually, which typically provide at best very brief analyses of the work of individual directors, and which, given their historical scope, rarely have space to engage with major theoretical issues. There are a few thematic and stylistic overviews of African film (Thackway 2003; Gugler 2003); there are collections of essays looking at the film industry in Africa or analysing one or two films by a specific director (Harrow 1999a; Givanni 2000; Pfaff 2004); and, finally, there are rare book-length studies of individual directors (Pfaff 1984; Signaté 1994; Murphy 2000a; Fawal 2001; Wynchank 2003).[1] Building on the best of this criticism, this volume will bring together ideas from a range of disciplines – film studies, African cultural studies and, in particular, postcolonial studies – in order to combine the in-depth analysis of individual films and bodies of work by individual directors with a sustained interrogation of these films in relation to important theoretical concepts.

Structurally, the book is straightforward, even slightly schematic, though the aim is to incorporate diversity and complexity of approach within the overall simplicity of format. The aim of the chapters is twofold. Firstly, we provide both an overview of the director's output to date, and the necessary background – personal or national, cultural or political – to enable readers to achieve a better understanding of the director's choice of subject matter, aesthetic or formal strategies, ideological stance. Secondly, we offer a particular reading of one or more films, in which we hope to situate African cinema in relation to important critical and theoretical debates. As will be argued below, African film criticism has, owing to the very particular nature of its development, long been subject to a form of exceptionalism, which has seen it occupy a space in-between other, more established fields, and one of the primary aims of this volume is to overcome this sense of exceptionalism. Consequently, we believe that this book constitutes a new departure in African film studies, recognising the maturity of the field, and the need for complex yet accessible approaches to it, which move beyond the purely descriptive while refusing to get bogged down in theoretical jargon.

While a volume of this nature could not hope to be comprehensive, the aim is to achieve a certain kind of representativeness. The choice of the ten directors was the subject of lengthy discussions over a period of more than a year in which we wrestled with the competing claims of various representative demands: style, nationality, gender, religion, history. In order to facilitate our task, we decided that we would have to narrow our focus in certain ways. Firstly, we decided to focus on fiction films, which ruled out the exceptional (semi-)documentary work of Safi Faye, David Achkar and Jean-Marie Téno, amongst others. We also decided to exclude directors who had not yet made feature-length films, which ruled out exciting young directors such as Balufu Bakupu-Kanyinda, director of the darkly comic masterpiece *Le Damier* (1997), and, at the time we began this project, Régina Fanta Nacro, who has since gone on to make the outstanding feature *The Night of Truth* (2004). In particular, we chose to focus on what might loosely be called the *auteur* tradition of filmmaking, closely associated with Francophone African cinema, which explicitly views the director as the 'author' of a work of art.[2] This authorial conception of cinema has been widely critiqued within film theory, and it is a particularly problematic concept in relation to African cinema, which has often had a highly political and communal vision of filmmaking. Equally, the authorial approach excludes the extremely popular video-filmmaking tradition that has emerged over the past decade in Nigeria and Ghana (see Haynes 2000; Barrot 2005): these films are, in general, hastily made on shoestring budgets and they are widely seen as disposable forms of popular entertainment. Our intention is not to endorse the *auteur* tradition as somehow superior to commercially popular cinema. On the contrary, a central aim of this volume is to re-examine the development of the authorial tradition in Africa, as well as the conception of both artist and audience that has underpinned it at various stages over the past fifty years. For, as will be argued later in this introduction, the question of whether the *auteur* tradition in African cinema can ever be deemed truly popular has been one of the most vexed questions in African film criticism.

In the end, we were forced to acknowledge the impossibility of an 'authentically' representative sample and chose instead to focus on three issues that we deemed particularly important. Firstly, we wanted to give a sense of the evolution of African cinema, from the work of Chahine, Sembene, Mambety and Hondo in the 1950s and 1960s (and beyond) to the work of important younger or more recently emerged directors such as Moufida Tlatli and Jean-Pierre Bekolo: six of our directors began their careers in the 1950s to 1970s, while the other four began in the 1980s or 1990s. Secondly, we were keen to represent as wide a geographical sample as possible, in order to trace the development of filmmaking in different contexts across this vast continent. Consequently, directors from nine countries are examined in this book, from both North Africa and sub-Saharan Africa – Egypt, Senegal, Mauritania, Mali, Guinea-Bissau, Burkina Faso, Tunisia, Cameroon, South Africa – with only Senegal represented twice (Sembene, Mambety). Although the volume cannot be said entirely to shift the focus away from Francophone African countries – the subject of most studies of African cinema – the inclusion of Chahine (Egypt: Arabophone), Gomes (Guinea Bissau: Lusophone) and Roodt (South Africa: Anglophone/Zulu) is part of a conscious effort on our part to widen the field to include other African filmmaking contexts. The fact that we include North Africa and South Africa – both routinely excluded even from otherwise generally comprehensive survey works (e.g., Ukadike 1994) – marks both our desire to reverse this pattern of exclusion, and the need to reflect the continent-wide historical context – shared, but sometimes very different – of imperialist domination: colonialism, neocolonialism, even 'colonialism of a special sort' in South Africa.

The final 'representative' issue is centred on questions of style and aesthetic. The ten directors chosen for this volume represent a broad range of approaches to cinematic expression: social realism, surrealism, comedy, didacticism, film-essay, melodrama, poetic lyricism. Many overviews of African cinema have rightly stressed the importance of a didactic, social realist tradition (associated most commonly with the work of Sembene) in the 1960s to 1970s, which is argued to have given way to a less political form of filmmaking in subsequent decades. However, this account of the evolution of African filmmaking is somewhat misleading and this volume will attempt to draw out a more complex genealogy of African cinema, which traces the development of other stylistic trajectories from the very inception of this cinematic tradition. For a start, African filmmaking of the 1960s and 1970s was never limited solely to political or protest films made in a social realist or naturalistic style, as certain critical approaches might lead us to believe. As will be shown in the chapters on Sembene, Hondo and Cissé in particular, these so-called social realist films in fact adopted a wide range of narrative and cinematic strategies, which are not always sufficiently acknowledged in critical work.

As for the likes of Chahine and Mambety, who often appear within African film criticism as unique, maverick figures, they can in fact be situated in relation to broader trends in African filmmaking: their idiosyncratic, playful style, and their focus on personal rather than explicitly political stories (although we would argue that the personal is always at some level political), was shared by directors as diverse as Mustapha Alassane and Désiré Ecaré, who are now often reduced to the role of mere footnotes in African film histories. However, if we view their work alongside that of Chahine and Mambety, we gain a sense of the sheer diversity of cinematic approaches that existed in the 1960s and 1970s. Alassane's hilarious parody Western, *The Return of an Adventurer* (1966), takes the classic motif of the 'alienated' African who returns from the West imbued with 'foreign' ideas. However, eschewing realism, Alassane grafts this story on to the Western genre (then hugely popular in Africa). His protagonist returns from the United States with cowboy outfits for all his friends and they proceed to terrorise the locals, rustling cattle and hijacking the chief of the village. Ecaré's *Concerto for an Exile* (1967) is a very elegant and atmospheric vision – clearly influenced by the *nouvelle vague* – of African university students in Paris unsure of whether to return to their newly independent homelands. The film displays an extremely mature cinematic talent but, unfortunately, Ecaré was not to make another film until the mid-1980s when he released the magnificent *Visages de femmes* (1985). Talented contemporary filmmakers such as Abderrahmane Sissako and Jean-Pierre Bekolo often explicitly situate themselves as the heirs to Mambety and other less explicitly political directors, and our volume will consistently attempt to tease out a sense of the different, overlapping strands within African cinema.

We are extremely conscious of the omissions from this representative overview but accept these as a necessary by-product of the limitations of the format we have chosen. This is in no way to disavow what this book seeks to achieve through its choices, and we stand by our selection as an illuminating cross-section of African cinematic creativity. However, it is understandable that readers might wish to engage in creating an alternative 'top ten', and we realise that an updated version of this volume ten years hence might produce a radically different set of choices. In that spirit then, what are the alternative choices that might have been made or might be made in future?

The claims of Haile Gerima and Gaston Kaboré as 'classic' filmmakers were very difficult to overlook, and the temptation to 'rehabilitate' neglected but hugely important directors such as Mustapha Alassane and Désiré Ecaré was very strong. However, in the end, the case for the inclusion of Chahine, Sembene, Hondo, Mambety and Cissé was simply too strong: we recognise that these directors have already been the object of a substantial body of critical work, and our aim is not to glorify their position in some critical pantheon but rather to explore new directions for the understanding of their films. Critical reputations fluctuate, and ten years from now certain of these choices may seem curious, but at this particular juncture we believe that the outstanding body of work created by these five directors makes a compelling case for their inclusion.

The choice of directors from the 1980s and 1990s might appear even more questionable, as critical appraisals of more recent work can be especially volatile. One could easily make the case for the inclusion of innovative, younger directors such as Adama Drabo (*Taafe Fanga*), Cheick Oumar Sissoko (*Guimba the Tyrant*), Dani Kouyaté (*Keita: The Heritage of the Griot*), Nouri Bouzid (*Bezness*), Mahamet Saleh-Haroun (*Abouna*),

Moussa Sène Absa (*Madame Brouette*) and, in particular, the much-fêted
Abderrahmane Sissako (*Waiting for Happiness*). Ten years from now, their
reputations may have soared above those of Tlatli, Bekolo and even
Ouédraogo, whose star has waned dramatically since the early 1990s.
Equally, the past few years have seen the emergence of a vibrant, young
cinema from South Africa: the awarding to South African films of the Best
Film Prize at FESPACO (the major African film festival) in 2005 and the
Oscar for Best Foreign Film in 2006 – *Drum* by Zola Maseko won at
FESPACO, while *Tsotsi*, directed by Gavin Hood, won the Oscar – seem like
staging posts in the development of a major continental player in the field of
cinema. The chapter on Darrell Roodt in this volume is an attempt to trace
the separate development of South African cinema from the apartheid era to
the birth of the Rainbow Nation: in particular, what is the status of a white,
liberal director such as Roodt in our conception of African cinema?

The most regrettable omission is that of women directors, of whom we
have included only one. Unfortunately, there have been very few women
directors from either north or south of the Sahara: for example, Keith Shiri's
Directory of African Film-makers and Films (1992) lists over two hundred
and fifty directors, of whom a mere eight are women. This situation has
improved in the course of the last decade with the emergence of directors as
diverse as Fanta Régina Nacro, Moufida Tlatli and Ingrid Sinclair, building
on the pioneering work of Safi Faye. Tunisia, for example, can now boast six
women directors, but Moufida Tlatli, with just two feature films to her
name, is the most prolific (if that is quite the word). Ten years from now, it
is to be hoped that many more African women filmmakers will have established themselves.

The final representative notion that must be considered is the very concept
of 'African cinema' itself. By using this term, we are in no way suggesting
that films produced in different contexts and at different times on various
parts of the continent are in some way expressions of a singular, ineffable
but inherently African cinematic vision. 'African cinema' is employed in this
volume as a collective term for a range of cinematic practices, in the same
way that the terms 'Hollywood' and 'European cinema' reflect a series of cinematic choices and contexts. However, there are other more compelling
reasons for this strategic use of the singular term 'African cinema'. For
African cinema was largely born in the context of the anticolonial struggle
and its immediate aftermath (Egyptian cinema has a longer and, in many
ways, separate history, as will be argued below and in Chapter 1 on Youssef
Chahine), and African film directors of the 1960s and 1970s joined together
in a corporative union, FEPACI, which set out various charters for the development of an explicitly African form of filmmaking.[3] For many critics and
filmmakers of this period, African cinema was at the cutting edge of a politically and artistically radical 'Third Cinema', which explicitly rejected the
capitalist world order of the West (Gabriel 1982). In reality, as was argued
above, this vision of African cinema was always an excessive generalisation,

which occluded the existence of other cinematic trajectories such as the playful, comic vision of the likes of Djibril Diop Mambety and Mustapha Alassane, the poetic lyricism of Désiré Ecaré or the brilliant idiosyncrasy of Youssef Chahine, and many within later generations of African filmmakers have retreated from the political idealism of their elders.

Although this would seem to point to a more individualistic vision of the filmmaking process, there are still compelling reasons for us to continue to examine something called African cinema, for the continent's cinematic output remains subject to a process of marginalisation and exclusion that has marked the development of Africa as a whole in the postcolonial era. African cinema exists but it has been and remains a precarious existence, largely dependent on the financial support of Europe, although Egypt has been the exception to this rule. As was mentioned above, Egypt has a distinctive cinematic history: it is the continent's oldest film industry, having begun production in the 1920s, and in its heyday it was a leading exporter of films throughout Africa and the Middle East; however, it has long since entered a period of slow decline and its production is now targeted chiefly at its home market. If Francophone Africa has been such a dominant presence within African filmmaking, then it is largely, if not solely, because the French authorities have invested heavily in cultural 'co-operation' – including cinema – with their former colonies, in an attempt to maintain their strategic 'presence' in Africa. Sources of funding have diversified over the past two decades with money now available from the European Union, European television channels (ARTE, Channel 4) and independent producers. However, the primary problems of African cinema remain those of distribution and exhibition, for many African films are still not screened on the continent itself, as they are viewed as commercial risks, with distributors and cinema owners preferring to provide audiences with the tried and trusted formula of Kung Fu and Bollywood melodrama. This is not to say that African films are unpopular in Africa. On the contrary, many African films encounter great success when they are screened, but this does not happen often enough. The nationalisation of the film industry that took place in Burkina Faso, home since the late 1960s to Africa's major biennial film festival FESPACO, has not been repeated elsewhere. To complete this somewhat morose picture, cinemas are shutting across the continent, as the economic context in most African countries remains sombre and audiences find cheaper forms of entertainment.

On the international film circuit, the picture is little better. In the mid-1970s, at the height of the Third Cinema movement, African cinema made its first real mark on the international stage when the Algerian director Lakhdar Hamina, won the Palme d'or at Cannes for *Chronique des années de braise* (1975). It had seemed in the late 1980s that African cinema was about to make a major breakthrough with the commercial and critical success of Souleymane Cissé's *Yeelen* (1987) and Idrissa Ouédraogo's *Tilaï* (1990). However, African films have largely been displaced by Asian cinema (from

Iran to South Korea) as the next 'big thing' in World Cinema, and the isolated success of a film such as *Moolaadé* (2004) by veteran director Ousmane Sembene serves only to underline the almost complete absence of African films from television and cinema screens in the West. (It is scandalous, but all too common, for works on 'World Cinema' to exclude African cinema completely.) Thus, in many ways, African cinema finds itself without a home and without an audience. Although this is a rather bleak picture, one of the aims of our volume is to underline the continuing richness of African filmmaking, although not in an uncritically celebratory fashion. Solely in filmmaking terms, the likes of Chahine, Sembene and Mambety deserve to be known and analysed as widely as Hitchcock, Renoir and Buñuel. Equally, African cinema constitutes a wide range of complex cultural expressions of African life in the postcolonial era, which deserve to occupy a more central role within the analysis of postcolonial African cultures.

A kind of history

Although the periodising model of the precolonial, colonial and postcolonial is not the only relevant history here, there is no way of understanding Africa, or – most importantly for our concerns – its cinema, without an awareness of the past and present effects of imperialism on the continent. An appropriate discussion of that is clearly far beyond the scope of this type of introductory overview; however, in this section we offer a glimpse of some of the relevant aspects of that history in the context of African cinema.

Film and the precolonial

There may have been no film in precolonial Africa, but precolonial Africa undoubtedly influences African filmmaking in a variety of ways. At the formal and structural level, these include the role of oral narrative, ideas regarding the nature and function of cultural practices including modes of spectatorship, and the role of the griot. At the level of content, precolonial social formations and social and cultural practices are the subject of variously celebratory or revisionist representations in contemporary African film.

One of the more frequently evoked, and occasionally controversial, topics is that of authorship (already mentioned above), which, in so far as a traditional African perspective is posited, is typically lodged in the complex figure of the griot as storyteller or bard or praise-singer. Historically, the griot was attached to the family, or even the person, of important individuals: warriors, nobles, and the like, and had the duty of simultaneously recalling the past, honouring the present and, to a lesser extent, imagining the future – all in the context of praising the individual and the family. Of these, it was the past that was of the greatest importance, and the griot functioned both as genealogist for the family and, by extension, historian for the community of which they were part. The significant deeds of the great men (and perhaps women) of the past were important not only in themselves but also in terms of the values that they embodied, and that were considered essential to cultural cohesion and stability. The identification of the filmmaker with the griot was given an early lead by Sembene in an interview in 1978 where he said: 'The African filmmaker is like the griot who is similar to the European mediaeval minstrel: a man of learning and common sense who is the historian, the raconteur, the living memory and the conscience of his people. The filmmaker must live within his society and say what goes wrong with his society' (Gadjigo 1993: 15). This was enthusiastically taken up by a number of critics and commentators, and led, for example, to the BFI calling their major 1995 celebration of African cinema *Screen Griots*, while more recently Melissa Thackway gave the same title to the longest chapter in her book on African film *Africa Shoots Back* (2003).

There are, however, a number of potential difficulties with identifying the filmmaker with the griot. A particular problem relates to the normative nature of the griot's performance: as faithful transmitter of tradition, the griot is required – on pain of death – to be factual and truthful, as Semebene remarked: 'When there were wars between tribes, griots were never killed. The griot would only be killed when he was lying. Because when the griot lies he deceives an entire people' (Gadjigo 1993: 44); that strict obligation may be lessened when what is being performed is narrative rather than history, but as a model it hardly constitutes the space of the African filmmaker as one of freedom of expression, still less of radical innovation. (There may, of course, be those who feel that ideas of freedom of expression and radical innovation are notionally too 'Western', and not necessarily appropriate for African directors.) Also, the version of the griot evoked in the comparison is the griot of the past, rather than of the present day – an all-too-often culturally impoverished figure, who appears in *Borom Sarret*, for example, as a mere street entertainer (see Chapter 2 for analysis of this sequence in Sembene's film). In addition, the conservative – for better or worse – aspect of the reinforcement of particular values and behaviours via the griot's performance may seem at odds with the nature of contemporary cultural practice. Further, for those who place a particular premium on cultural authenticity, griot is a term that relates very much to West Africa, and denotes a figure who may have no equivalent in other parts of the continent, as pointed out, for example, by Ngugi (Gadjigo 1993: 66). Finally, the comparison implies a level of individual authorship that does not necessarily correspond to the collective production of cultural texts in the societies in which the griots originated (or indeed in much of the rest of Africa). As Robert Stam comments: 'The communal expression of the *griot* paradigm might be contrasted with the more individualist "*caméra stylo*" of the French new wave, rooted in the romantic notion of the heroic individual *auteur*' (Stam 1999: 126). At the same time, some filmmakers are far from happy at being identified with the Western figure of the *auteur*, which they feel is not relevant to the way they themselves make films.

It may be, however, that the aligning of the traditional griot and the cine-matic auteur produces a kind of hybrid *griauteur*, who is an appropriate figure for contemporary African filmic practice. One way in which that might pre-sent itself is in a form that would respond to the unhappiness of filmmakers just mentioned: to the extent that the griot acts as a conduit for histories, genealogies, narratives and values, he represents a diminishment, in line with Foucauldian and Barthesian notions, of the creative authorial function, which (over-) privileges the *auteur*. As a recent work in a cognate area argues:

> The question of the appropriateness of the function of authorship in Asian cinema also needs to account for the agency of the director as someone with the lived experiences, for example, of colonialism or diasporic identification. Such an approach shifts the emphasis from the director who occupies the romanti-cised position equal to a creative role and instead, following Michel Foucault, would consider 'the name of the author' as a discourse around which the direc-tor is a filter for various lived experiences. In other words, recognising the social and cultural experiences that shape texts through the agency of the director is a crucial strategy for minor and marginal cinemas. (Needham 2006: 362)

Although African cinema is emphatically marginalised rather than 'mar-ginal', and though we would perhaps want to accept 'minor' only in the way that Deleuze and Guattari (1975) theorise it, this remains a useful statement.

One thing that certainly does unite griots and African filmmakers, however, is the need to combine a multiplicity of roles: Olivier Barlet, for example, talks about the griot as court jester, wandering minstrel, involved storyteller, mouthpiece of the powerful, counsellor, news bearer, therapist (2000: 162–5) while Sembene comments: 'But in my country the griot was at one and the same time his own author, his own musician, his own actor, and his own narrator. This made the griot a very important person' (Gadjigo 1993: 44). For their part, African filmmakers frequently find themselves required to be directors, producers, scriptwriters, publicists, accountants, song writers and more besides – though whether that makes them 'very important people' is less certain.

Whether or not Manthia Diawara is correct to claim that '[o]ne can see the influence of oral tradition in all African films' (1996: 215), the desire to see the influence as widespread in African cinema is pervasive among critics. Filmmakers themselves are less unanimous: some claim it as their deepest inspiration, others want to distance themselves to varying degrees; for Diawara, however, there is no escape for them, since

> film-makers, like novelists, are influenced, consciously or not, by the narrative forms of the oral storyteller. They have been initiated into oral tradition before going to Western schools. The way the storytellers narrate becomes their point of reference when they take their first steps at film school. During the rest of their careers, they are bound to be dealing with oral tradition. (1996: 214).

Part of the problem here is that there is no consensus on precisely what the influence of oral tradition might consist of: in formal terms, for instance,

Diawara argues that the typical narrative has a linear structure, one action, and three stages (departure, arrival and return); for Med Hondo, on the other hand, simplicity and linearity are precisely *not* what characterise the traditional tale, and (in his view) the digressive, repetitive, non-sequential nature of his film *Soleil O* comes much closer to representing the essence of African oral narrative. (These rival claims regarding the role of orality will be examined further in the section on popular cinema at the end of this introduction.) Clearly, the claim to include, or be influenced by, traditional narrative is ideologically important in relation to film, whatever the actual nature or extent of its incorporation. The debate is given a more theoretical turn in 'Towards a Theory of Orality in African Cinema' (Tomaselli et al. 1999), though in the end their argument is indeed 'towards', rather than anything like a theory of orality, and its effectiveness is blunted by its use of problematic concepts such as 'Western industrial discourse', and its polarised models of Africa and the West, or orality and literacy, which are typified by statements like 'Two entirely different ways of making sense – the literate and the oral'.

Inclusion of precolonial Africa at the level of film content, Mbye Cham argues, means that

> rather than depicting Africa as a place of perfect order and Africans as a special/unique species of humanity, these films find the following elements to be part of the reality of Africa: love, deception, lust and prejudice; father–son rivalry and fights for power; social cohesion, in relation to anti-social behaviour; adultery, violence against women, care for orphans, the indigent and the disabled, male chauvinist practices, exploitation, and oppression; religious piety and charlatanism of all sorts. (1996: 11)

Some of the most interesting African films of the last twenty years are ones that address aspects of the precolonial: African spirituality in Souleymane Cissé's *Yeelen* (1987); village life in Idrissa Ouédraogo's *Yaaba* (1989); the abuse of power in Cheick Oumar Sissoko's *Guimba the Tyrant* (1995); and, in Dani Kouyaté's retelling of the great West African epic of Sundiata, *Keita: The Heritage of the Griot* (1995), the most extensive representation of the figure of the griot to date. Once again, however, there is a lack of consensus concerning the implications of the manner in which precolonial Africa is represented. As will be seen in different ways in the chapters on Cissé, Gomes and Ouédraogo, both filmmakers and critics have strong differences of opinion over whether the use of the precolonial allows access to the reality of Africa (even if this is not necessarily glorious, or free from worrying problems and social divisions, along the lines indicated by Cham), or whether it merely panders to Western desires for images of Africa that are colourful, exotic, distanced from the unhappy contemporary condition of the continent, and generally in line with Eurocentric stereotypes. However, as Edward Said argues so convincingly in *Orientalism*, it is not the notional truth content of images, nor their degree of verisimilitude, that matters, since all representations are vulnerable to being co-opted by powerful discourses or institutions, and therefore African films are potentially liable to be misused by the West, whether they 'pander' to its inappropriate desires or not.

Film and colonialism

The colonial period brought film to Africa, and in some instances its introduction was a deliberate part of colonial policy, though it was commercial interests that provided the initial impetus, as it took less than a year after the original screenings by the Lumière brothers in Paris in 1895 for film to reach Egypt and South Africa, and some filmmaking in North Africa by Europeans followed by the turn of the century. The largest part of Africa was still, in these years following the Berlin Conference of 1884–85 and the resultant 'Scramble for Africa', being gradually colonised, and so parts of sub-Saharan Africa in particular had to wait until the 1920s before cinema reached them. From the 1920s also, as the chapter on Youssef Chahine explains in greater detail, Egypt began the process of developing the first independent cinema industry in Africa. At the same time, interest in Africa grew, as did the number of films set there, or purporting to be about the continent and its people. Among the earliest of these were works now deservedly forgotten such as *The Wooing and Wedding of a Coon* (1905) and *The Kings of the Cannibal Islands* (1908). A decade later, the first of the Tarzan films appeared, while the 1930s saw the making of such 'classic' Hollyood films of Africa as *Trader Horn* (1931), *Sanders of the River* (1935) and *King Solomon's Mines* (1937), or their French counterparts, *Les Cinq Gentlemen maudits* (1931) and *L'Homme du Niger* (1939). All of these, when not straightforwardly racist, at least confirmed colonialist stereotypes about Africans and African culture among the cinemagoing populations of the West, and as such contributed towards the ideological justification of the colonial enterprise in a period when its legitimacy was increasingly being questioned.[4]

At the same time as cinema was representing Africa to the West and beyond, it was being used in different ways to represent the West to Africa. The most colonialist and paternalist of these projects were undertaken by the British in East Africa and Belgians in the Congo. In the former, Major L. A. Notcutt, director of the Bantu Educational Kinema Experiment, saw film as a source of literal illumination for Africans: 'With backward peoples unable to distinguish between truth and falsehood, it is surely in our wisdom, if not our obvious duty, to prevent as far as possible the dissemination of wrong ideas. Should we stand by and see a distorted presentation of the white race's life accepted by millions of Africans when we have it in our power to show them the truth?' (Notcutt and Latham 1937: 23). The 'truth', oddly enough, consisted of films about farming and medical problems in Africa, as well as essential elements of the 'the white race's life' such as tax, and the Post Office savings bank. These were, however, by and large films made in Africa for Africans, with commentary in a range of African languages. Notcutt's BEKE was followed in 1939 by the Colonial Film Unit, with sections in all parts of the British Empire in Africa, and it continued the practice of paternalist and propagandist films. After the Second World War, the great documentary maker John Grierson wrote a report for UNESCO with the radical recommendation that colonised people should make their own films for and about themselves. Partly in response to this, the British set up a film school in Accra (then the Gold Coast, now Ghana), though despite self-congratulatory self-assessment it achieved relatively little.

Colonial government attitudes to Africans and film, with their heady mix of paternalism and paranoia, were shared by missionaries and commercial companies, especially in places like South Africa and Rhodesia. Films could be beneficial for Africans, it was argued, but only certain types of films, or, in the extreme, certain parts of films; and if wholesome, educational or uplifting fare were not available, then films must be censored in order to prevent Africans seeing anything other than 'good' Western culture, to avoid them becoming politically dissident or criminal, or both (Burns 2002).

An entirely different approach to representing the West to Africa was that adopted in the French Empire, which was simply to show French films to Africans, since the French colonial ideology, embodied in the notion of 'la mission civilisatrice', worked on the premise that their colonised subjects could, or would soon be able to, appreciate the products of French culture. Unlike the attitude of Major Notcutt, and the British in general, which assumed an African inability to understand film appropriately, the French approach at least allowed Africans to be considered as a proper audience for proper films. A rare example of government intervention by the French was the 1934 Laval Decree, which obliged anyone wishing to make a film in Africa to submit the script, cast list and other details to the Governor of the relevant colony for approval. Rarely invoked, it was nevertheless used to prevent Paulin Soumanou Vieyra, the first African graduate from IDHEC (Institut des Hautes Etudes Cinématographiques) in Paris, from filming in his own country of Senegal. Since, however, the law did not prevent him from filming in France, Vieyra – in collaboration with Mamadou Sarr – shot *Afrique-sur-Seine*, the first film to be directed by a black African, in Paris in 1955.[5]

Unlike a range of other cultural forms – poetry, song, music, stories – film had, for very obvious reasons, almost no part to play in the anticolonial process. Since there was almost no part of the continent in which Africans had appropriate access either to the techniques or to the technology of film-making at this time, and given the priorities of the different struggles for national liberation, it is hardly surprising that, apart from some reportage-style pieces by the FLN in Algeria, there are almost no anticolonial films contemporaneous with the period of decolonisation. One exception to this is *Jamila al-Jaza'iriyya* (*Jamila the Algerian*, 1958) by the Egyptian director Youssef Chahine. Based on the experiences of Jamila Bouhired, one of the heroines of the battle for the Casbah, which is the focus for Gillo

Pontecorvo's *Battle of Algiers* (1965), and who was captured, tortured and sentenced to death by the French, Chahine's film was made during, and about, the Algerian war of independence (1954–62). The fact that it could be made was due to the existence of a full-scale cinema industry in Egypt. The fact that it was made was due to the courage and independence of Chahine. That it was an act of courage and independence was demonstrated by the fact that the film was promptly banned in Algeria, in France and (unofficially) in Egypt.

Film and postcolonialism

As is clear from the previous section, African film, with the exception of the burgeoning Egyptian industry and a few films made in places like South Africa, is almost entirely a postcolonial phenomenon. This much is explicitly agreed on by many critics, tacitly accepted by others, and ignored by quite a few. A representative description is offered by Mbye Cham:

> African film-making is in a way a child of African political independence. It was born in the era of heady nationalism and nationalist anticolonial and anti-neocolonial struggle, and it has been undergoing a process of painful growth and development in the postcolonial context of general socio-economic decay and decline, devaluation . . . and political repression and instability on the continent. One is therefore talking here about a very young, if not the youngest, creative practice in Africa. (1996: 1)

In general, however, those working in the area of film have been remarkably resistant to engaging with the insights and the arguments of postcolonial studies. The acknowledgement of a relatively uncontentious fact – that as a matter of simple chronology African film largely belongs to the period after colonialism had formally come to an end – is as far as some critics want to go in their association with postcolonialism: any further, and we enter the notoriously and bitterly contested discursive, political or theoretical terrain that is the postcolonial.[6] Clyde Taylor, writing about African film and post-modernism, is representative of this trend of blinkered non-engagement. For him, it is just not worth going there; postcolonialism is simply a waste of time: 'One of the alternatives proposed to "postmodernism" is "postcoloniality" . . . but the losses carried by this formulation outweigh the gains' (2000: 137). Although Taylor has little time for postmodernism either, the aligning, or, in the worst cases, the identifying, of postcolonialism with post-modernism has provoked largely pointless discussions that have repeatedly been an obstacle to an adequate understanding of postcolonialism, especially in contexts such as film studies.

One film critic who is more sympathetic to postcolonialism – or at least prepared to discuss it – is Robert Stam. Even he, however, can be prone to reductive assessments that bedevil discussions of postcolonialism: 'While Fourth World peoples often invest a great deal in a discourse of territorial claims, symbiotic links to nature, and active resistance to colonial incursions,

postcolonial thought stresses deterritorialisation, the artificial, the constructed nature of nationalism and national borders, and the obsolescence of
anti-colonialist discourse' (1999: 124). Among the many points to be made
in relation to the problematic assertions here, we will mention just two:
firstly, a proper awareness of 'the constructed nature of nationalism and
national borders' in no way implies an inability or unwillingness to fight for
territorial claims; and secondly, as several chapters in this book demonstrate
(and at that level, we would argue, they are nothing out of the ordinary), a
belief in 'the obsolescence of anti-colonialist discourse' is categorically not
part of any useful postcolonial analysis. Talking about the 'blurring of perspectives', Stam continues: 'So: given that colonial experience is shared, albeit
asymmetrically, by (ex) coloniser and (ex) colonised, does the "post" indicate
the perspective of the ex-colonised (Algerian, for example), the ex-coloniser
(in this case, French), the ex-colonial settler (*pied noir*), or the displaced
hybrid in the metropole (Algerian in Paris)?' (1999: 124) The answer is, of
course, all of them – to differing degrees, and in ways that are both connected
and radically divergent, even antagonistic. Although Stam offers this as an
example of the many problems of a postcolonial approach, one could turn it
round and argue for it precisely as a positive outcome, since postcolonial
studies, despite its real and perceived failings (expressed at length in the persistent questioning of its key suppositions, which has taken place within the
field over the past two decades), has none the less permitted an important his-
toricised understanding of what Said, in *Culture and Imperialism*, calls the
'overlapping territories, intertwined histories' of all these groups, which are
simultaneously related and also profoundly different.

    In the introduction to almost the only book to highlight a postcolonial
dimension in the analysis of African cinema, Kenneth Harrow suggests that
'[p]ostcolonialism has a special meaning when used in reference to African
cinema – a meaning that arises out of the particular history of colonialism
and cinema in Africa' (1999b: ix), though the discussion which then follows
does not seem to make that 'special meaning' clear. Nevertheless, the idea
that in addition to the generally relevant meanings of postcolonialism there
are some particular ones generated by the specific history of African cinema
is useful. In the next section we briefly consider some of those meanings,
both in their wider context and in the more specific one of African filmmaking.

Film and postcolonial tasks

As Basil Davidson pithily expresses it, referring to African independence,
'the transfer of power was, above all, a transfer of crisis' (1992: 190). As a
result, various urgent tasks of construction and reconstruction, both infrastructural and superstructural, constitute the immediate postcolonial
agenda. This section focuses on three of these issues: the question of the
nation; historical memory; and the vexed issue of African theory for African
practices.

In the process of becoming postcolonial, one of the most immediately necessary, and one of the most difficult, tasks is that of nation-building:

> If man is known by his actions, then we will say that the most urgent thing today for the intellectual is to build up his nation. If this building up is true, that is to say if it interprets the manifest will of the people and reveals the eager African peoples, then the building of a nation is of necessity accompanied by discovery and encouragement of universalising values. (Fanon 1967: 199)

Fanon's radical postcolonial approach to the question of the nation is frequently referenced, though not always fully understood. Writing in relation to African cinema, and particularly Hondo and Sembene, Frank Ukadike comments that 'Fanon's theory of ideology puts great emphasis on the importance of restructuring African society in order to create an emancipatory force formidable enough to take Africa back to its true national culture' (1994: 96). It is perhaps debatable whether Fanon did indeed have a theory of ideology; what is certain, however, is that he did not want to take Africa 'back' anywhere (the direction of his theorising, and his political vision, is entirely the opposite of that), still less did he believe that Africa had a (singular) 'true national culture' (his argument in the chapter 'On National Culture' in *The Wretched of the Earth* repeatedly rejects that kind of ungrounded generalisation). Although, as our chapter on Hondo argues, African filmmakers have generally not engaged in any sustained manner with Fanon's ideas, they have, nevertheless, been an influential part of the progressive politics of many of those directors.

For many African filmmakers from Chahine and Sembene onwards, cultural production has been inescapably tied up with the simultaneous production or reproduction of the nation. While they may approach it with differing political agendas, and widely divergent aesthetic visions, for them the nation (independent, committed to progressive values) remains the central – and as yet only partially realised – postcolonial project. For Chahine, the problem posed by the incompletely and inappropriately realised nature of the nation is the subject of even his most recent films, such as *Al-Akhar* (*The Other*) (1997). The fact that the nation, as increasing numbers of critics point out, is not only the subject of narration but also, and more importantly, actually constituted by narratives of various sorts,[7] gives the filmmaker, as someone working with what is *potentially* a medium of mass address (for, as we shall indicate below, the nature and size of African cinema's audience has been the subject of much critical debate), special opportunities, as well as responsibilities, in the deployment of their particular narratives.

In (re)constructing the postcolonial nation, the maintenance and recovery of historical memory is crucial, particularly as a method of combating the effects of colonial oppression:

> Perhaps we have not sufficiently demonstrated that colonialism is not simply content to impose its rule upon the present and the future of a dominated

country. Colonialism is not satisfied merely with hiding a people in its grip and
emptying the native's brain of all form and content. By a kind of perverted logic,
it turns to the past of the oppressed people, and distorts, disfigures and destroys
it. This work of devaluing pre-colonial history takes on a dialectical significance
today. (Fanon 1967: 169)

The felt need for the recovery of an appropriate, usable past is something
that postcolonial cultural producers worldwide have shared, and in the case
of Africa has been at the forefront of the cultural agenda at least since
Achebe's famous statement of 1965 regarding the pedagogic value of a
corrected historical memory: 'I would be quite satisfied if my novels (especially the ones I set in the past) did no more than teach my readers that their
past – with all its imperfections – was not one long night of savagery from
which the first Europeans acting on God's behalf delivered them' (1988: 30).
For Teshome Gabriel, the role of postcolonial guardians of memory is
perhaps best occupied by radical and politicised filmmakers (which would
again align the filmmaker with the traditional griot). As he writes in 'Third
Cinema as Guardian of Popular Memory': 'Between the popular memory of
the Third World and the wilful forgetting of the West, the gate-keepers of the
corridors of discourse cannot be but men and women of courage and conscience, committed to an urgent, activist cinema – in a word, Third Cinema'
(1989: 63). However, as has been mentioned above, and will be argued in
greater detail below, it would be misguided to cast all African filmmaking as
a form of activist Third Cinema.

   Historical memory acts as a vitally necessary addition to the non-specific
memories of the pre-colonial in films such as *Yeelen* and *Yaaba*. The important periods recalled include that of slavery, treated in such very different
ways in Haile Gerima's *Sankofa* (1993) and Med Hondo's *West Indies*
(1979); colonialism, from the time of the Scramble for Africa in the 1890s
in Hondo's *Sarraounia* (1986), via the Second World War in Sembene's
Emitaï (1971) and *Camp de Thiaroye* (1988), to its dying days in North
Africa in Moufida Tlatli's *Silences of the Palace* (1994); and the anticolonial
struggle, in its various forms and stages, in Chahine's *Jamila the Algerian*
(1958), Sarah Maldoror's *Sambizanga* (1972), Flora Gomes's *Mortu nega*
(1988) and Ingrid Sinclair's *Flame* (1996). The nature, status and effects of
remembering vary greatly in these films: for Sembene, it is a case of recording colonialism's atrocities – the events it wants everyone to forget – so it
can pretend they never happened; in *Sankofa*, loss of historical memory
brings on a kind of individual or collective cultural death, which is the starting point for the film's painful journey of recollection and healing; *Silences
of the Palace*, on the other hand, uses the process of individual remembering to bring to collective consciousness women's experiences, which were
arguably never part of general cultural memory in the first place, subject as
they were to the 'silencing' imposed by the structures of class, patriarchy and
colonialism in the context of the royal palace. For postcolonial cultural producers, as Edward Said points out, the dialectical process of coming to terms

with the past in order to move forward is both complex and potentially painful:

> The post-imperial writers of the Third World therefore bear their past within them – as scars of humiliating wounds, as instigation for different practices, as potentially revised visions of the past tending towards a postcolonial future, as urgently reinterpretable and redeployable experiences, in which the formerly silent native speaks and acts on territory reclaimed, as part of a general movement of resistance, from the colonist. (Said 1993: 256)

'Redeployable experiences', 'revised visions', and 'different practices' are very much part of the self-reflexive constitution of African cinema, to which we now turn.

As well as addressing questions of national and cultural identity, not least by the reconstitution of historical memory, cinema needs to look to its own identity, and one of the specific postcolonial tasks in relation to African film is the articulation of an appropriately African theory for the analysis of African cultural practices (although this task is viewed with greater urgency by some critics than others). The task is, of course, a more generally postcolonial one, applying to other regions of the world and other areas of cultural production, but it has a particular relevance to film. The long-running debate about the negative ideological implications for postcolonial writers of taking over a cultural form (the novel) developed in the West and at a particularly significant historical juncture (the rise of the middle class and the nation state, and the spread of colonialism), is replayed with increased vigour in relation to film. The fact that cinema emerges at the high point of colonialist expansion, as a technological system becomes tied ever more closely to the West, and, above all, involves a reliance on capitalist relations of production, means that, far more than any other postcolonial cultural medium, it exists in an ideological, political and economic nexus whose effect is potentially deleterious.

In a similar fashion, concerns regarding the implications of the 'Eurocentric' nature of theory (postcolonial, film, cultural) are strongly expressed by critics like Clyde Taylor and Keyan Tomaselli. However, while any pretensions on the part of European theory to provide a universally applicable mode of explanation, regardless of historical and cultural specificities, must be strongly resisted and critiqued, there is a concomitant danger of rejecting theory simply because of its European origin, rather than its unacceptable or irrelevant content, a move that would be both ahistorical and, indeed, untheoretical. So far, it has proved extremely difficult for critics to articulate a specific theory for a 'black aesthetic', which it is easier to indicate in different areas of cultural production than to analyse appropriately.

The question of the development of uniquely African practices and theories divides both practitioners and critics. Among the latter, Frank Ukadike states that: 'It is the contention of this writer that black African cinema, like any other filmmaking practice or national cinema, does not have to reinvent the conventions of cinema in order to remove it from the dominant film practice' (1994: 101). This is, however, directly contradicted by Djibril Diop Mambety:

> One has to choose between engaging in stylistic research or the mere recording of facts. I feel that a filmmaker must go beyond the recording of facts. Moreover, I believe that Africans, in particular, must reinvent cinema. It will be a difficult task because our viewing audience is used to a specific film language, but a choice has to be made: either one is very popular and talks to people in a simple and plain manner, or else one searches for an African film language that would exclude chattering and focus more on how to make use of visuals and sounds. (Pfaff 1988: 218)

There is always the possibility that the search for a theoretical perspective that is purely African is not the correct approach, and that African cinema and other postcolonial filmic practices might need to rethink their separate or conjoined nature in a fundamental manner together with theory: as the postcolonial filmmaker Trinh Minh-ha argues:

> There is a tendency in theorizing *about* film to see theorizing as one activity and filmmaking as another, which you can point to in theory . . . When one starts theorizing *about* film, one starts shutting down the field; it becomes a field of experts whose access is gained through authoritative knowledge of a demarcated body of 'classical' films and of legitimised ways of reading and speaking about films. That's the part I find most sterile in theory. It is necessary for me always to keep in mind that one cannot really theorize about film, but only *with* film. That is how the field can remain open. (Trinh Minh-ha 1992: 122)

Clearly, it is far easier for someone like Trinh, who herself already combines the areas of theory and filmmaking, to imagine such a possibility and begin to put it into practice, than it is for filmmakers in general. Nevertheless, one of the points she makes, the rejection of 'experts' in these fields, is more attainable. Gayatri Spivak, for example, has argued that work in postcolonial cultural studies 'must use specialisms, but also actively frame and resist the tyranny of the specialist' (1993: 74), and such an approach, informed and democratic at the same time, would be beneficial in the complex production of the theory-and-practice of African cinema. In addition, the importance of the openness to other currents of critical thought hardly needs to be stressed, and, in light of this, the final section of this introduction will chart some of the overlapping critical frameworks that need to be brought into dialogue within African film criticism.

Critical frameworks

The precarious existence of African cinema is in many ways mirrored by its liminal status within the university system. Film studies, African cultural studies and postcolonial studies all offer potential homes for the analysis of African cinema but, in general, it occupies a marginal position within each of these fields of research. As was mentioned above, within film studies, Asian film has largely displaced its African counterpart as the non-Western cinema of choice; African cinema has been of relatively little interest to scholars of popular African culture (until, that is, the emergence of 'popular' Nigerian and Ghanaian video films over the past decade or so); and, despite some important interventions on cinematic topics, postcolonial studies remains primarily concerned with literature (and literature in English, at that). As the previous sections have shown, this volume seeks to examine certain dominant trends within thinking about African cinema, and to explore ways in which a more active engagement with certain ideas from film studies, African cultural studies and, in particular, postcolonial studies might allow us to break out of a certain number of conceptual impasses.

As was mentioned briefly above, a particular tendency within African film criticism has, quite understandably, cultivated a form of exceptionalism, which views and classifies African cinema in very different terms from those we might find in film studies more generally. As African cinema was the last world cinema to emerge owing to Africa's traumatic colonial history, there has often been a strong desire on the part of filmmakers and critics alike to view African cinema as separate from other forms of cinematic expression. For instance, the classification of African films by the likes of Diawara, Ukadike and Boughedir is almost entirely thematic – social realist films, colonial confrontation films, return to the source films – and places particular emphasis on content over form. This is not to say that African film criticism has been uninterested in form but rather that this criticism has been wary of concepts such as style and aesthetics, which are often associated with Western notions of art and the artist.[8]

While acknowledging the circumstances that have led to this critical juncture, we would argue that it is now time to try and break down some of the barriers between African cinema and wider conceptions both of filmmaking and of postcolonial cultural expression. This does not entail a refusal to acknowledge the specificity of African filmmaking; on the contrary, our approach involves a systematic interrogation of both specific and general claims that have been made about African cinema, as will be illustrated in the remainder of this introduction, where we will briefly examine three representative issues from African film criticism. Firstly, there has been a strong emphasis, amongst critics, on the capacity for African audiences to 'identify' with an 'authentic' African cinema – whether 'authenticity' is referenced as an essentialist or a contingent concept – as opposed to one catering to Western tastes, which thus allows Africans to break free from the 'alienation' caused by systematic exposure to foreign films. Secondly, it is widely assumed that this authentic African cinema is a popular cinema in the sense that it deploys narrative techniques and motifs, and deals with subjects that are common within traditional or folk cultures, as well as contemporary African urban cultures, and it thus has the potential to attract a wide audience. Finally, there is often a great burden of 'representativity' placed on the

shoulders of the African filmmaker, who is charged not only with representing African realities on the screen but also with representing Africa as a sort
of spokesperson. The following pages will attempt to prise open each of these
three issues in turn through an engagement with a number of theories and
insights from film studies, African cultural studies and postcolonial studies.
In questioning these key ideas regarding African cinema, we are not suggesting that our approach in any way supersedes a somehow misguided, existing
critical model; in fact, most of the ideas we deal with have been discussed in
various guises in often disparate and unconnected locations. Consequently,
the primary value of our critical approach is that it draws together these
ideas, seeking to borrow from cognate areas, which are often overlooked
because of the artificial boundaries between academic disciplines.

Identification and alienation

The concepts of identification and alienation have been central to debates
about spectatorship in African cinema. The fact that African cinema screens
are dominated by foreign films has long led to calls for African films to be
shown more widely in African countries, in order to bring an end to this
process of cultural 'alienation'. The widespread distribution of African films
would thus give Africans the opportunity to see films featuring characters,
situations and stories with which they could 'identify'. These issues are often
enmeshed in debates about (Western) cultural imperialism, which can be
expressed in various ways, ranging from nativist to Marxist arguments
about the need to resist the 'imposition' of Western culture on African societies. While it is clearly necessary to formulate cultural theories that take
account of the economic and political imbalances between Africa and the
West, these ideas can often lead to a dead end in thinking about African
cinema, as assumptions are made about the ways in which audiences 'read'
films without actually taking into account the different modes of film spectatorship in Africa itself.

Consequently, we would argue that a potential route out of this impase
in thinking about African cinema might be to engage with recent critical
work on film spectatorship. Within film studies, questions of identification
and alienation have also been central: in various strands of film theory,
'identification' has widely been perceived as an illusion produced by the film
in the mind of the spectator, while 'alienation' (or 'distanciation') is something to be achieved rather than overcome, as it signals the creation of a
thoughtful, reflective cinema that allows the spectator to break free of the
illusion of 'identification'. One of the classical models of film spectatorship
posited the spectator as a 'dupe' of the process of cinematic 'illusion'. In
effect, agency was primarily accorded to the film, which was deemed to
'subject' the spectator to its cultural assumptions and vision of the world.
This model can take various forms; in a Marxist guise, as in Brecht's vision
of the naive spectator taken in by the cinematic illusion of the capitalist

world; or in a psychoanalytical guise, as in Lacan's notion of seeing as a process involving misrecognition and the loss of one's sense of self.[9]

In certain respects, these ideas would seem to reinforce the culturalist notion prevalent in African film criticism, which posits the spectator as the passive 'victim' of the film. However, theories of cinema as 'illusion' have come in for sustained interrogation over the past decade or so. Cognitive theorists such as Murray Smith return a sense of agency to the cinema spectator by underlining the importance of 'imagination' as a key concept that has largely been ignored or dismissed by previous strands of film criticism: for Smith, individual spectators, as agents, have the capacity – within certain limits – to imagine variations on, or changes to, the cultural 'schemata' present within films (1995: 46–52; see also Allen 1995). In turn, the work of the cognitive school has, in recent years, been critiqued by other film scholars for not taking into account either the spectator's cultural identity or the processes of reception at work in different social, cultural or geographical contexts (see Jancovich and Faire 2003).[10]

One of the major tasks facing African film criticism is thus to examine specific case studies of African cinema audiences' consumption of both African and 'foreign' films. Clearly, film theorists as well as scholars within the field of African cultural studies (who have direct experience of the type of fieldwork that would be required) will have much to contribute to these debates. In light of these ideas on film spectatorship, it is clearly necessary to re-examine certain assumptions that are made about the process of identification and alienation. Does exposure to Bollywood movies genuinely 'alienate' African audiences and, if it does, what exactly does such alienation entail? In fact, as will be shown below, such work that has been done on African audience responses to non-African films suggests that spectators actively reformulate these films within the terms of the 'default values' (to use Smith's term) of their own societies.

Essentially, we are arguing for a more sustained engagement with the ways in which African films work as narratives rather than simply focusing on what they are about. An example of how productive this approach might be is to be found in Ousmane Sembene's film *Xala* (1974). Many critics have argued that the symbolic, ritualistic nature of the film's opening sequence can be seen as a classic Brechtian distancing effect, highlighting the constructed nature of the narrative; equally, El Hadji is something of a classic Brechtian anti-hero, whose downfall permits the spectator to draw instructive lessons about how society really works. In this light, the film might be read as an example of avant-garde, modernist practice, which attempts to jolt the viewer out of received modes of viewing and consuming movies.

However, as many African critics in particular have pointed out, it is also possible to view *Xala* as an archetypal trickster narrative (Cham 1982). Within the West African oral tradition, the trickster – whether it be Leuk-the-Hare, Bouki-the-Hyena, or Aranze-the-Spider – is one of the most common characters; there are many different narrative variations on the trickster story but, in general, they might be said to follow one of two main patterns: the trickster deceives an unwitting victim or the trickster himself or herself is duped as a form of punishment for his or her 'crimes'. In *Xala*, El Hadji has previously duped the beggar out of his money and El Hadji is now duped in turn, and is forced into a series of ever more humiliating situations, many of them sexual. As with the oral trickster narratives, *Xala* has an instructive value that gives its tale of specific individuals a wider social resonance.

What we find here is a strange confluence between European, modernist practice and 'popular', African oral narrative devices, both of which might be seen to be based on the interplay of standard 'types' rather than inviting the audience to identify with 'sympathetic' characters, as in the classical Western film narrative. This raises important issues for critics of African cinema. Firstly, it points to the possible limitations of the gritty, neo-realist or social realist models that dominated the first two decades of postcolonial African filmmaking, and which were based on – but rarely limited to – individual character development or psychology, and on a sense of verisimilitude, both of which are largely absent from African performance traditions. Generally speaking, African performance arts are highly stylised and symbolic, and the type of character insight and development that are often central to Western plays and films can often leave an African audience cold. Pierre Haffner, author of perhaps the best account of film spectatorship in Africa, claims that, in his experience, African film audiences find the realism of certain early Sembene films (e.g., *Borom Sarret, Black Girl*) to be 'unpalatable' (1978: 138). Secondly, these questions force us to think more deeply about the 'popularity' of African cinema; for, in a curious way, what is 'popular' in an African context can sometimes meet up with the aesthetics of a Western avant-garde (as in Picasso's uses of African statues to create the 'high' art of primitivism). What then does it mean to speak of the popularity of African cinema?

African cinema: a popular art form?

It is, of course, one of the chief ironies of African cinema that, setting aside Nigerian and Ghanaian video-films, African movies are often better known on the international film circuit than in Africa itself. Without much in the way of empirical evidence to gauge the types of African film that African audiences find 'popular', the critical debate on the popularity of African films has thus generally been played out a very abstract level. The ambiguity of the term 'popular' has long been recognised by critics; it can by turns, depending on the context, be used to refer to a 'top-down' mass-produced, commercially popular culture or to a 'bottom-up' spontaneous, widely valued form of cultural expression; while in the African context, critics often oppose the notions of 'popular culture' – meaning a radical, consciousness-raising culture – and 'people's culture' – a spontaneous, but often fundamentally conservative culture.

Karin Barber argues, in her highly influential essay on 'Popular Arts in Africa', that the popular is often defined more in terms of what it is not, namely elite or folk culture, and she views popular African culture as a 'cultural brokerage between Western culture and folk culture' (1987: 12). It is interesting to note that Barber makes no mention of African cinema as a popular art form in her exhaustive study; conversely, she does list Western films under the heading of 'arts consumed but not produced by the people'. This is, arguably, a particularly important issue that has largely passed unnoticed in critical thinking on African cinema; for well over fifty years there has existed a vibrant cinema culture in Africa, which has shaped popular African expectations and understanding of how film narratives operate. As was mentioned above, critics have sought to trace the use of oral narrative elements in African films, seeing in this process an attempt to embed film narratives within a narrative tradition familiar to the audience. However, what significance if any should be accorded to the audience's familiarity with the narrative codes of Bollywood musicals or Kung Fu movies? Writing in the 1970s, Pierre Haffner called for a popular African cinema that would marry those film techniques that worked best with cinema audiences he observed in Mali with local performance-based arts such as the *koteba* (1978: 55–65). Haffner's comments seem unnervingly prescient when one considers the success of Nigerian and Ghanaian video films, which are often made by local theatre troupes, who forge a syncretic mix of local performance techniques and narratives with some of the more spectacular elements from foreign film styles that have enjoyed success in Africa.[11] However, when one looks further afield, this process seems less unusual; the non-Western countries that have managed to create genuine film *industries*, which have enjoyed success both at home and abroad, are Egypt, India, Japan, Taiwan and Hong Kong, all of which have worked to a very similar model, combining elements of local narrative tradition with melodrama and the visually spectacular.

In light of these issues, is it possible to think of African cinema outside of countries such as Nigeria and Ghana as a popular cinema at all? As many critics have observed, the work of Sembene, Djibril Diop Mambety, Souleymane Cissé and others might be described as a classic, *auteur* cinema. They place an individual authorial stamp on their films through their *mise-en-scène*, the construction of the screenplay, and they explicitly conceive of film as a form of art. (The commercially popular comic films made with government funding in Cameroon have often been derided by African film critics as mere escapism; see Chapter 9 on Jean-Pierre Bekolo.) The attempt to bridge the gap between 'radical' film theory and audience expectations has long occupied the minds of critics. In his analysis of the relationship between black film theory and black audiences in the United States, Tommy Lott writes of a 'top-down view that prescribes, more than it describes, the responses of black audiences' (1997: 297). Similarly, African cinema has often simply assumed that the continent's *auteurs* would be popular with

African audiences if only the problematic issues of production and distribution could be resolved. Once again, this is not to claim that African *auteur* films cannot be popular – for example, films as diverse as *Xala*, *Yaaba* and *Madame Brouette* have had major success in parts of Africa – rather it is a question of introducing to the debate on the popularity of African films the question of an audience's expectations based on the cinematic references that help to shape its understanding of film as a medium (as was argued in the previous section). African film criticism has had a lot to say about the role of the director but the spectator has largely been absent. As the French critic André Gardies has shown, African directors, in their desire to break with Western images of Africa, constructed an 'ideal spectator' to whom they would 'show' the 'true reality' of Africa, as opposed to the process of 'telling' them stories (1989: 14–16);[12] and this process requires much greater critical attention.

A striking example of the polarised debate about popularity is to be found in Med Hondo's extraordinary 1969 film *Soleil O* (for in-depth analysis of this film see Chapter 3). Some critics have described the film as unambiguously avant-garde, deploying Western modernist techniques, while others have stressed its continuity with the oral tradition. A classic example of this latter approach is to be found in a recent book by Melissa Thackway, which is by far the best account of the influence of the oral tradition on African cinema. Thackway situates elements of Hondo's work within an oral framework – circular narration, digression and so on – but the film's similarities to the experimental film-essays of Jean-Luc Godard, most notably *Weekend* (1968), are passed over in a single sentence denying any influence on the basis that Hondo made his film before Godard's (2003: 19). However, on many levels, the resemblances between the two films are striking: the use of direct address to camera to explore abstract ideas, the refusal of conventional narrative development, the constant shifts in register from drama to tragedy to comedy to farce. Hondo had been living in exile in Paris since the early 1960s so it is hardly surprising to find a certain convergence between his ideas on narrative and style and those of radical European directors, even if Hondo himself has always stressed the Africanness of his approach in the film. The point of highlighting these echoes of certain Western film styles in Hondo's work – and similar ideas could be explored in relation to Mambety's masterpiece *Touki Bouki* – is to suggest that, despite the Mauritanian director's recurring use of motifs and narrative devices from the oral tradition, *Soleil O* might also be situated within an experimental, cinematic narrative mode that would make it difficult to understand for many spectators not 'literate' in such forms. This is not to suggest that African audiences are 'incapable' of understanding such work; on the contrary, political filmmakers such as Hondo and Sembene have consistently shown their films to audiences of workers and peasants, organising debates to follow screenings, and both directors stress the acuity of these audiences' readings of their work. However, there is a fundamental difference between such occasions and what generally motivates a spectator to attend a film screening in Dakar, Bamako or Algiers; one must also consider the relatively trivial position occupied by cinema in the daily lives of the peasantry and the urban poor. Essentially, certain types of film narrative, or even film itself, are simply seen as alien to the tastes and expectations of audiences.[13] Critics thus need to beware of creating overly simplistic oppositions between what constitutes a Western and what constitutes an African film narrative (Western films can obviously engage in non-linear, digressive narratives too). What starts out as a seemingly objective description of the orality of an African film can often veer dangerously close to an essentialist reading, which posits an unchanging African culture captured in the film's narrative technique.

In the past decade, two important African films have explicitly addressed the relationship between African audiences and African directors: Jean-Pierre Bekolo's darkly comic *Aristotle's Plot* (1997) presents a conflict between a well-meaning film director and a cartoonishly thuggish band of hoodlums who are obsessed with Hollywood action movies (for in-depth analysis of this film see Chapter 9); while Mahamet Saleh-Haroun's *Bye Bye Africa* (1998) is a melancholic, self-reflexive meditation on the role of cinema in Africa, in which the character of the director (played by Haroun himself) attempts to come to terms with the indifference towards his work in his home country, Chad. In a case of life mirroring art, Haroun became embroiled in a row, at FESPACO 2005, with a Nigerian video film producer who claimed that the way forward for African cinema might be to adopt Nigerian production methods to which Haroun replied that he was an 'artist' not an 'entertainer'. With the continued success of the video-film, such confrontations between different conceptions of cinema promise to remain at the forefront of critical and artistic debates.

Before concluding this section, there is one further question, which is raised by the issue of popularity. As was argued at length above, the African filmmaker has long been associated with the griot, in an effort to embed African cinema firmly within the oral tradition. However, the true value of this invocation of the griot figure seems to be as a necessary symbol of cultural continuity, for the reality of cinema is that it is a commercial enterprise. The African spectator must pay to enter the cinema; it is not a 'traditional', communal gathering bringing together members of the same tribe or ethnic group. This should not be construed as a negative comment on the role of cinema, for, as Karin Barber has argued, popular art forms in Africa – such as cinema – have created brand new audiences:

> [Popular arts] can be said to attract a public rather than a community. Thus, though the prevalent use of popular implies, in one sense, limits, in another sense it points to the rise of a populace of a different range altogether from what was known in the traditional world. (1987: 15)

If, then, we are to view African filmmakers as 'screen griots', we should do so with a sense of both the continuity and the profound rupture constituted by the development of cinema on the continent.

Representing Africa?

Our third research question relates to the issue of representation. As Nicholas Harrison has recently demonstrated in relation to African literature, there has been a widespread critical perception of the postcolonial African author as 'representative' – whether it be of the 'nation' or of Africa, more generally. That is, the author is seen to be both a 'representative' type and to 'represent' his or her 'people', acting as a spokesperson (Harrison 2003: 92–111). In the aftermath of decolonisation, there is understandably a desire on the part of many artists to speak out on behalf of people within their society, but as Harrison rightly argues the 'representativity' of an author sometimes has far more to do with the context in which a literary text is received than with the nature of the text itself. As has been argued throughout this introduction, African films also find themselves caught in a complex web of representativity; we would argue that, unfortunately, African cinema criticism has not developed its problematisation of representation as readily as postcolonial literary theory. African films are regularly praised or condemned for failing to meet certain representational demands; for being too Western, too African, too political, too apolitical. There is insufficient space in this introduction to rehearse all of the different representational pressures placed upon African films, so the following pages will examine just a small number of key examples.

As was indicated above, from the 1970s onwards, it was received critical opinion to regard African cinema as Third Cinema, an oppositional cinema that deviated from the norms of Hollywood (Gabriel 1982). This categorisation is broadly applicable to filmmakers such as Sembene or Hondo but other directors were always less easily categorised in such a way. The political filmmaking of a Sembene may have become the dominant African film form of the 1970s and early 1980s but, when it emerged in the 1960s, it was just one strand amongst many.

The work of Djibril Diop Mambety offers perhaps the clearest example of an African director explicitly rejecting demands for his films to be 'representative'. The playful, ambiguous nature of his films is part of his refusal to become involved in the direct espousal of any political standpoint. For example, in *Touki Bouki*, Mambety uses the scene in which Mory is attacked by a band of student radicals to distance himself from the prevailing left-wing ideology of many within the African intellectual elite. In fact, the scene draws added attention to itself, as Mambety makes no attempt to integrate it into his narrative. After his public punishment at the hands of these radical students, we simply see Mory free once again and back on his motorbike as though the incident had never occurred. It does not take too great a leap of the imagination to suggest that Sembene himself might be one of those targeted by Mambety. In particular, the figure of the postman who wanders aimlessly through the film appears to be a sideswipe at the figure of the postman in Sembene's film, *Mandabi*, who is portrayed as someone who 'delivers' hope in the form of the film's political message of social solidarity.

Developing his own less explicitly political conception of the *griauteur*, Mambety would follow a different cinematic path to Sembene.

In the 1980s, a series of films were released that were set in rural African locations and avoided direct engagement with specific political issues: Gaston Kaboré's *Wend Kuuni* (1982), Souleymane Cissé's *Yeelen* (1987), Idrissa Ouédraogo's *Yaaba* (1989). Although varying greatly in style, these films were grouped together and depicted, both positively and negatively, as 'return to the source' movies. (See Chapter 6 on Flora Gomes for an extended discussion of the 'return to the source' in the context of Cabral's theories.) Supporters saw in such films the development of a genuinely African aesthetic that would replace the Western-inspired modernism of Sembene and his kind, while critics saw in them a shift away from the necessary radicalism of Third Cinema towards the essentialist aesthetics of a timeless Africa. This debate often involved a rather confusing and generally unsubstantiated set of assumptions about the audience being addressed by these directors. For instance, Ukadike praises *Yeelen*'s inventiveness in imitating the structures of orality but he is wary of its 'universalism', which is seen to be the result of the targeting of 'foreign' (i.e., Western) audiences; while Manthia Diawara claims that Ouédraogo's films are undeniably beautiful but sees them as imbued with a 'bourgeois humanism', that is, designed to attract a Western audience. However, neither critic attempts to account for the success of both directors at the box-office in Africa itself.[14] This situation strongly recalls Graham Huggan's recent work on the development of what he terms a 'postcolonial exotic'. As the postcolonial becomes a marketable commodity (which he terms 'postcoloniality'), what becomes of the oppositional discourse of 'postcolonialism'? (This point will be developed further in Chapter 5 in relation to Souleymane Cissé.) Equally, in charting the forces that might make an African film commercially popular in the West, we should not lose sight of the other meanings that a film might have in other contexts. African cinema exists in a Western-dominated global system and its politics of representation must be understood within the full complexity of this situation.

Conclusion

The question of representation takes us back to where we began our introduction. This volume is our attempt to present the reader with an overview of some of the most important directors and films of the past five decades of postcolonial African filmmaking. As we have made clear, we cannot make any grand claims to absolute representativity or to objectivity. However, in approaching a body of work from social, cultural and political contexts radically different to our own, and without wishing to privilege our position, we have kept in mind the words of the great Russian critic Mikhail Bakhtin:

> *Creative understanding* does not renounce itself, its own place in time, its own culture; and it forgets nothing. In order to understand, it is immensely

important for the person who understands to be *located* outside the object of his/her creative understanding – in time, in space, in culture. In the realm of culture, outsideness is a most powerful factor in understanding. . . . We raise new questions for a foreign culture, ones that it did not raise for itself; we seek answers to our own questions in it; and the foreign culture responds to us by revealing to us its new aspects and new semantic depths. Without *one's own* questions one cannot creatively understand anything other or foreign. (Bakhtin 1986: 6–7; emphasis in original)

We hope that the questions raised in this volume will lead to the 'creative understanding' of a neglected but hugely important body of cinematic work.

Notes

1 The latest book by Roy Armes (2006) appears to adopt a hybrid solution, offering both a historical overview of filmmaking across the continent and a small sample of case studies on individual directors. As Armes's text was published just as the present volume went to press, it is not possible to include extensive discussion of it.

2 Andrew (1995) explicitly situates African filmmaking (Souleymane Cissé, in particular) within an authorial, art house tradition. As will be shown at the end of this chapter in the section on the popularity of African cinema, this is a problematic argument for a variety of reasons.

3 Copies of the various FEPACI charters are reproduced in FEPACI (1995).

4 For a discussion of Western representations of Africa see Cameron (1994) and Sherzer (1996).

5 See Ruelle (2005) and *Cinquante ans de cinéma africain* (2005) for an assessment of the foundational role played by Vieyra's film in the development of sub-Saharan African cinema.

6 For a sense of some of the general arguments around postcolonial theory which are beyond the scope of this chapter to discuss see, for example, Childs and Williams (1996) and Moore-Gilbert (1997).

7 Following on from Benedict Anderson's enormously influential work on nationalism, *Imagined Communities* (1983), a whole sub-genre of studies of 'imagining' and 'narrating' the nation has emerged in a range of disciplines.

8 See, in particular, Taylor (1989), who calls for African film critics to abandon the whole field of aesthetics, which he views as fatally compromised by its Western (imperialist) connotations.

9 For a thorough and readable introduction to these questions see Lapsley and Westlake (1988).

10 For further reading on film spectatorship see Mayne (1993) and Campbell (2005).

11 Equally, recent West African *auteur* films such as *Madame Brouette* (2001) by Moussa Sène Absa and *Nha Fala* by Flora Gomes (2003) have embraced the musical as a genre liable to reach a popular African audience.

12 However, Gardies's Lacanian conception of cinema as a mirror, provoking 'identification', is not shared by the present authors.

13 See Karin Barber's (1987) ideas on university-based theatre troupes taking experimental plays to villages. These plays often work well with these communities but

Barber discovered that such forms disappear once students have departed. (Equally, one could not refer to Wole Soyinka as a popular author in any particularly meaningful sense solely on the basis of the fact that his works are deeply influenced by Yoruba folk culture.)

14 Gugler writes convincingly of the naive view of the country found in some African films (e.g., those of Kaboré and Ouédraogo), which he interprets as an urban view of a lost rural paradise, an exoticisation designed to appeal to Africans in the cities (Gugler 2003). We will return to these ideas in Chapters 5 and 7.

Chapter 1

Youssef Chahine

Introduction

E. M. Forster somewhere comments on Chahine's fellow Alexandrian (and fellow Greek), his late friend the poet C. P. Cavafy, as 'standing at a slight angle to reality'. The same might well be said of Chahine himself: never straightforward, never predictable, never one to toe the party line either in his political beliefs or in his approach to filmmaking, the difference constituted by his 'slight angle' to social taboos, political positions and cinematic norms alike is perhaps his most distinctive feature. The maker of more than thirty feature films and half a dozen shorts in over fifty years of film production, ranging across periods, styles and genres, Chahine defies easy definition or simple pigeonholing, while his refusal to adopt the required position – whatever it might be – has led to his being involved in a number of controversies, especially in connection with his 1994 film *Al-Muhajir* (*The Emigrant*), for which he was put on trial. Chahine's 'slight angle to reality' also includes his relation to his country: as a Lebanese Greek Christian in an Arab Muslim nation, Chahine's Egyptian identity is, on the face of it, not absolutely straightforward – though for Chahine himself it is quite simply not a problem.

Chahine was born in Alexandria in January 1926 of a Greek mother and a Lebanese father. To the latter, a principled but not particularly successful lawyer, Chahine feels he owes a love of literature, a love of life and an appreciation of the value of honesty. From a very early age, Chahine was interested in the cinema, and by the age of nine, as recounted in *Iskandaria . . . leh?* (*Alexandria . . . Why?*, 1978), the first part of his autobiographical film trilogy (very recently expanded to a quartet), he was the owner of a small ciné projector, which he used to show films to his friends. Attendance at a Chahine film show was apparently a serious matter, and therefore not necessarily a question of choice for the audience, as he explained in an interview in *Cahiers du Cinéma*: 'I used to gather the children of the neighbourhood to show them these films. Some of them didn't care for cinema and would come up with of all kinds of excuses not to attend. So I had no choice but to form a gang to beat up those who were late coming to the show' (Chahine 1996: 9).

Although his parents could not really afford it, they sent him to study at the English-run Victoria College, 'the up-market VC-Alex' as Edward Said termed it, whose alumni included the future King Hussein of Jordan. In his memoir *Out of Place*, Said paints a very unflattering picture of 'VC-Cairo', where he and Omar Sharif (in his earlier incarnation as Michel Shalhoub) were students, being decidedly unimpressed by the English as either teachers or moral examples (Said 1999). In *Alexandria . . . Why?*, Chahine in turn shows the staff as very happy to applaud his performance of speeches from *Hamlet*, but totally resistant to allowing him any sort of choice over a future staging of Shakespeare, even though, as Yahia (the Chahine character in the film) points out, it is a democratic decision and democracy is something which the College claims to teach its students. When he graduated, his father wanted him to train as an engineer, but Chahine had his heart set on a drama course, and, after a lengthy battle, persuaded his parents to send him – at very considerable expense – to the United States, where he studied at the Pasadena Playhouse in California. Apart from the quality of the courses on offer, the great attraction of the United States for Chahine was that it was the source of the films he most loved.

After his return from the States, however, rather than working in the theatre in line with his training, Chahine got a job with Twentieth-Century Fox, and, despite his lack of experience as a director, within two years had secured the funding to make his first film, *Baba Amin* (*Daddy Amin*, 1950). Shortly afterwards, following a whirlwind romance, Chahine married Colette Favaudon, whose long-suffering presence appears particularly in the Alexandria trilogy. Having made his unlikely and precocious start as a film-maker, Chahine proved unstoppable, and directed thirteen films in the 1950s alone. These, all in black and white, included some of the very best of his early work, such as *Bab al-Hadid* (*Cairo Station*, 1958) and *Jamila al-Jaza'iriyya* (*Jamila the Algerian*, 1958), both of which feature as examples of the trials and tribulations of filmmaking in the second part of his trilogy or quartet, *Hadutta Misria* (*An Egyptian Story*, 1982). Two of his films made in 1954 also introduced the renamed Omar Sharif to cinemagoing audiences for the first time.

The films of this first decade, including musicals, social problem films and anticolonial films, give an indication of Chahine's seemingly effortless ability to work across genres in different films, or to blend several in a single one. They also signal his willingness to break with tradition, defy taboos and court controversy. Even in his debut *Daddy Amin*, though it is a slight work by comparison with most of the films that followed, he is prepared to ignore the dominant plot forms of Egyptian cinema of the period in order to produce a film which combines entertainment (humour, three song sequences) and the discussion of serious topics of family life. It also inaugurates Chahine's use of autobiographical elements into his work (Amin is based on his own father), beginning a process which is probably unparalleled in its extent in world cinema. His second and sixth films *Ibn al-Nil* (*Nile Boy*, 1951) and *Sira fi-l-Wadi* (*Blazing Sun*, 1954) are the first examples of a long-running concern with the lives of the most ordinary Egyptians: here, the *fellah* (peasants), and four years later, and most memorably perhaps, the urban working class in *Cairo Station*.

The latter film, along with *Jamila the Algerian*, instantiates the controversies which have accompanied Chahine's career from its earliest years, marking his 'slight angle' to so many things in the film world and in Egyptian culture at large. Both films carry echoes of European styles and works: Italian neo-realism in the case of *Cairo Station*, Carl Dreyer's *The Passion of Joan of Arc* in the case of *Jamila the Algerian*, but in neither instance is that responsible for any of the negative reactions. In the former, Chahine's departure from cinematic norms was considered simultaneously excessive and insufficient, depending on the audience. For Egyptian spectators, the film was disconcerting and disturbing: too bleak in tone and depressing in its ending; over-reliant on image, rather than the dialogue which typified Egyptian films. For Western critics, however, it was flawed by its excessive use of the dominant Egyptian cinematic form, namely melodrama. It was, however, the reaction from ordinary Egyptians which affected Chahine (not least, perhaps, because he was spat on in the street), and made him determined not to lose touch with his audience in future – though that would not for him involve simply pandering to populist taste.

The problems in relation to *Jamila the Algerian* were very different, though they might also be seen as stemming from the film's failure to please a particular audience, namely the French government, who immediately banned any screening of it, especially – understandably – in Algeria, given the film's treatment of the real-life story of Jamila Bouhired, a leading militant in the bitterest phase of the Battle of Algiers, captured, tortured and sentenced to the guillotine by the French. Equally, however, it subsequently failed to please the new postcolonial Algerian government, who also banned it (the reasons for this ban may have included the fact that Jamila had married the French lawyer who defended her, and after independence returned to run the Algerian branch of Max Factor, neither of which was an appropriately revolutionary action). Finally, while not officially banned there, it was not screened in Egypt for a number of years. Despite this, the film was very successful in the countries of the Soviet bloc and in various postcolonial and non-aligned nations, and Chahine, as recounted in *An Egyptian Story*, was awarded the major prize at the 1959 Moscow Film Festival.

A much later, and altogether more serious example of Chahine being out of line with a particular tendency relates to his 1994 film *Al-Muhajir* (*The Emigrant*). Loosely based on the story of Joseph from the Bible, and set in the reign of the Pharaoh Akhenaten, it aroused the anger of Muslim fundamentalists who succeeded in having Chahine put on trial for blasphemy, notionally for having dared to represent one of Islam's prophets on the cinema screen. The trial eventually resulted in an acquittal for Chahine but, rather than being in any way intimidated by the experience, he proceeded to offer his response in the form of another film. *Al-Masir* (*Destiny*, 1997) is set in twelfth-century Muslim Andalusia, and tells the story of the philosopher Ibn Rushd (Averroes), best known for his detailed commentary on the works of Aristotle, and another intellectual at odds with authority because of the frequently unorthodox nature of his ideas, including reconciling Islamic and Greek thought via a theory of the 'univocality of being', denying the immortality of the individual soul, separating reason and revealed truth, and advocating a greater role in society for women. Despite the apparent distance in time and place created by the setting, it is a powerful, and contemporary, attack on irrationalism, religious intolerance and fundamentalism, and a similarly forthright defence of a broadly humanistic love of life, music, books, people and ideas. Against a background of the religiously inspired burning of Averroes' books, the film's final message is, 'Ideas have wings. No one can stop their flight.' This is far from being the only such articulation of Chahine's core beliefs, but it is clear and defiant – a politically necessary restatement of those things he feels forced to defend. His tenacious advocacy of a set of beliefs grounded in humanism, secularism, tolerance, rationality and an appreciation of culture in all its richness and variety also aligns him very closely with another intellectual under frequent attack, his friend Edward Said.

Despite so much time spent being out of step with authorities and audiences, in 1997 at the Cannes film festival Chahine became the latest of only a handful of directors to be given a Lifetime Achievement Award. This recognition has signally failed to produce a quieter or more conformist Chahine, however, as Mark Cousins noted: 'I've interviewed hundreds of film people but none – not Dennis Hopper or Roman Polanski – is more rebellious' (Cousins 2006).

Historical, social and cultural context

Given the length of Chahine's career, an appropriate contextualisation might seem to require something resembling a full history of Egypt in the second half of the twentieth century. Even that would not be quite sufficient, however, since the roots of the circumstances which produced Chahine go back as far as the early years of the nineteenth century. Given the constraints of these chapters, a very brief overview must suffice.

Although colonialism typically likes to present itself as bringing modernisation to a backward and unproductive non-Western world, in the case of Egypt the process was, with a particular historical irony, turned on its head. Under the rule of Muhammad Ali (like Chahine, another ethnic 'outsider'; in his case, Albanian-Macedonian) during the first half of the nineteenth century, Egypt had had the audacity to launch its own successful programme of social and, above all, economic modernisation without the benevolent intervention of the West; the West, for its part, then did all it could to restrain the development of an indigenously derived, modern industrialised infrastructure in Egypt. By the end of the nineteenth century, Egypt had been

incorporated into the British Empire, and its economic organisation was
therefore oriented to serve imperial needs, especially in the double role of a
market for British goods and the producer of raw materials from which some
of those goods might be made. Even this thwarted development, however,
meant that Egypt had a stronger social and economic base than other countries, either in Africa or in the Arab world, from which to develop cultural
forms such as theatre and cinema.

Although decolonisation notionally came early to Egypt, in the shape of
the Anglo-Egyptian Treaty of 1936, the British countered this by an early
form of neocolonialism, exercising influence at more of a distance, but also
retaining the right to station troops in the country, which they continued to
do throughout the Second World War and up until 1954. (The presence of
British troops in Egypt preparing for the Battle of El Alamein in 1942 leads
to one of the most interesting of the narrative strands of *Alexandria . . .
Why?*) After the war, the corrupt rule of King Farouk was brought to an end
by the 1952 revolt of the Free Officers Movement led by Muhammad
Naguib and Gamal Abdel Nasser. Nasser went on to take control of the
movement, and the country, and became one of the heroes of the early postcolonial period, particularly when he successfully resisted the combined
power of Britain, France and Israel in the battle for control of the Suez Canal
in 1956. In addition, he was one of the key figures in the Non-Aligned
Movement launched at the Bandung Conference in 1955, and became an
outspoken opponent of contemporary manifestations of imperialism. His
political philosophy – 'Nasserism' – combined socialist, pan-Arabist and
anticolonialist elements.

As was the case with other charismatic postcolonial leaders such as
Kwame Nkrumah in Ghana, the Nasser period began in a euphoric atmosphere, with an attempt at wide-ranging measures for social progress combined with high-profile projects; the former included his programme for
nationalisation, aimed at opposing the effects of neocolonialism and the
growth of capitalism in Egypt, while the latter was epitomised by the building of the Aswan High Dam with help from the Soviet Union. Unfortunately,
much of the progress achieved was overshadowed by the consequences of
Nasser's belief that he could win a war with Israel. The pre-emptive Israeli
strike in the Six Day War of 1967, resulting in the comprehensive defeat of
Egypt, Syria and Jordan, led Nasser to resign (even though nationwide
popular appeals pushed him to reverse his decision), and seemingly broke his
health, as he died two years later at the age of only fifty-one. (The popular
response to Egyptian defeat and surrender, the loss of prestige and the loss
of their beloved leader, in the final scenes of *Al-Asfour* (*The Sparrow*, 1972),
as the central character Bahiyya runs down the street screaming 'No! No!
We will fight!', is among the most famous images from Chahine's entire
career.)

Nasser was followed by a decade under Anwar Sadat, whose time as president is particularly remembered for the controversial 1977 signing of the

Camp David Accord, making peace with Israel, and for the fact that he was assassinated by Islamic fundamentalists from within his own army in 1981. The latter marked the latest stage in one of the enduring problems for post-colonial Egypt, namely the battle between militant Islamism and the modernising, tentatively liberalising, Egyptian state. It was also an act of revenge by the militant Islamists for the execution in 1965 of Sayyid Kutb, founder of the Muslim Brotherhood, following at least three assassination attempts on Nasser.

The 25-year rule of President Mubarak has also been marked by the struggle between Islamism and the state, characterised both by concessions to the former (such as the repeal in 1985 of legislation granting increased rights to women) and by the growing numbers of arrests of its members, particularly following events such as the massacre of foreign tourists in the Valley of the Kings. The same period has seen a general effort at liberalisation (one of the stated reasons for Islamist opposition), as well as a very rapid rise in population to a level where the economy can hardly cope (the Islamist movements are also opposed to all forms of population control). For Chahine, as we will see in more detail later, Islamic fundamentalism represents one of the greatest threats to a better future for Egypt.

Cinema reached Egypt very quickly: the first screenings of the Lumière brothers' films took place in Alexandria in 1896, less than a year after they were originally shown in Paris, and over the next decade a number of films were made in Egypt by crews working for the Lumières, typifying the dominant position of Europeans in the early years. Following the uprising of 1919, however, the development of a form of proto-nationalism was one of the factors leading to the making of films by Egyptians as part of a broader assertion of identity. Important early films included *Laila* (1927) directed by Istephane Rosti, and *Zeinab* (1930) by Mohamed Karim, but despite the fact that, as previously mentioned, Egypt possessed a better economic and social base than any other African or Arab country from which to develop filmmaking, films were fairly slow to emerge. As Roy Armes notes, 'Though Egyptian producers became interested in the possibilities of sound film making at the beginning of the 1930s, it was not until mid-decade that production passed double figures (13 films in 1934–35) to reach a peak of 25 in 1944–45, making a total of 170 features in all between 1927 and 1945' (Armes 1987: 198).

One of the factors bringing about a change in the nature of filmmaking in Egypt was the establishing of Egyptian studios – again thanks to the relatively developed status of capitalism in the country. A key figure here was the banker and industrialist Tal'at Harb, who in 1935 founded Studio Misr, the first in the country, or indeed the continent, with modern equipment and properly trained staff. Thereafter, there was a steady growth in output over the next decade, increasing quite dramatically in the postwar years owing to the availability of money from wartime profiteering (the type of amassing of fortunes at the expense of one's fellow citizens shown in the figure of the

Pasha in *Alexandria . . . Why?*). The prospect of ever greater returns for relatively modest outlay prompted numbers of businessmen to invest in filmmaking in this period: more film studios opened, the number of cinemas more than doubled, as did the number of films. In turn, this meant that Egyptian films were increasingly distributed throughout the Arab world, resulting in a long-lasting dominance of the foreign market.

Paradoxically, as Armes notes, this strength in the foreign market was matched by a vulnerability at home, where Egyptian films were often less highly regarded than the latest offerings from Hollywood by the audiences in Cairo and Alexandria who made up the bulk of the domestic viewing public. Another, and in many ways more unfortunate, paradoxical situation emerged in the Nasser period, where politically progressive state interest in, and support for, filmmaking (indicated, for example, by the creation of the government-run National Organisation for the Consolidation of the Cinema, the setting up of *ciné-clubs* like those which other North African countries had inherited from the French, and the introduction of film as an academic subject at Cairo University) was paralleled by the growth of competition both from television and from foreign imports. Under Sadat, the climate worsened: state support was withdrawn, and filmmakers like Chahine turned increasingly to foreign co-productions, or even left the country in order to make their films. Chahine also set up his own company, Misr International Films, which has produced, or co-produced, most of his films since the 1970s.

One obstacle which filmmakers in Egypt have faced at least since the 1940s has been censorship. While this may have been introduced in the form of restrictive legislation in the reign of King Farouk which made the representation of a range of topics from the lives of peasants to radical politics almost impossible, it nevertheless remained a problem, as the relevant sections of *An Egyptian Story* make clear, in the supposedly freer period of Nasser and Sadat. The irony here, however, is that it is Chahine's powerfully pro-Egyptian and pro-Nasser film *Al-Asfour* (*The Sparrow*, 1972) which is subject to the arbitrary decisions of the censors – in part, no doubt, because the political climate was already changing under Sadat. In the notionally more liberal atmosphere of President Mubarak's rule, however, the problem has only worsened. As Chahine commented in an interview: 'With the censors, nothing is ever clear or straightforward. They are bureaucrats, but who are they? Complete idiots. I know that, because the person in charge of censorship used to be one of my students' (Chahine 2001). The unfortunate consequence has been a climate of anxiety, if not fear, on the part of intellectuals in general and filmmakers in particular, resulting in self-censorship in order, it is hoped, to comply with the requirements of the state, 'Because people fantasise about what the regime might do. There are people who talk to you about torture. I don't really believe that they would torture a filmmaker, even if he was being political. They prefer to save that for their favourite prisoners' (Chahine 2001). Chahine attributes his ability to be outspoken with impunity to the fact that he is old, and that the authorities would not want to be seen mistreating someone of his age (who also just happens to be the best-known filmmaker in the country).

The counterpart to this has been a generalised depoliticisation of Egyptian society, especially as a result of two decades of the 'Emergency Act' which allows the police a very free hand in suppressing any sort of activity deemed subversive. Those elements – cultural producers, academics and students – who might otherwise have been expected to voice opinions, protest and demonstrate are the ones who currently seem to Chahine the most quiescent. In particular, he was angry at the lack of response to the near-fatal attack on his friend the eighty-year-old Nobel prize-winning novelist Naguib Mahfouz, who was stabbed in the neck by a Muslim fundamentalist: 'There should have been thousands of us intellectuals up in arms, but it was a real problem getting any of them to protest. A lot of them are held back by fear' (Chahine 1997). Chahine – typically – has responded to the mood of depoliticisation by suggesting that his next film will be an analysis of the problem represented by the Emergency Act. Asked in a recent interview, 'What do you think is the role of artists in the contemporary political situation?' Chahine replied, 'You must participate. You can't be an artist if you don't know the social, political, and the economic context. If you talk about the Egyptian people, you must know about their problems. Either you are with modernity or you don't know what the hell you are doing' (Chahine 2006). Although this indicates his desire not to abandon the fight, there is at the same time a growing sense that he now feels that for many the fight may well already have been lost: 'I see them [young people] in front of the German and French consulates: everybody wants to emigrate. I used to tell the young people: "Don't do it! If you have studied, we need you here." I was old-fashioned, thinking only of the beauty of my country. Now I tell them "leave!" They have no chance here, it's too corrupt. By staying here, you become corrupt' (Chahine 2006). This looks as if the analysis offered a number of years previously by the writer Yusuf Idris might be coming true, namely that eventually all writers and intellectuals would have to leave Egypt because their situation would be made intolerable. (Admittedly, the reason Idris gives for the intolerable situation is Chahine's other great adversary, Islamic fundamentalism, but there is clearly more than one way to drive out your intellectuals.) Despite that, Chahine's 1999 film *Al-Akhar* (*The Other*) is precisely about an educated young Egyptian-American who returns to Egypt and stays, eventually to fight the corruption rather than fleeing it.

The films

In his book-length study of Chahine, Ibrahim Fawal decides that he cannot usefully discuss more than fourteen films out of a total of more than twice that many; a section such as this can therefore only offer the briefest of gestures towards the richness and diversity of the *oeuvre*, highlighting a handful of themes.

A 'Description of Egypt'

Napoleon's invasion of Egypt in 1798 changed the nature of Orientalist knowledge through the enormous project of *La Description de l'Egypte*, which formed the textual counterpart – in twenty huge volumes – to the military conquest: 'The Institut, with its teams of chemists, historians, biologists, archaeologists, surgeons, and antiquarians, was the learned division of the army. Its job was no less aggressive' (Said 1978: 83–4). Two centuries later, the resisting and undoing of Orientalist forms of knowledge, some of which have not changed at all in the interim, remains an urgent political necessity: 'Perhaps the most important task of all would be to undertake studies in contemporary alternatives to Orientalism, to ask how one can study other cultures and peoples from libertarian, or a non-repressive and non-manipulative perspective. But then one would have to rethink the whole complex problem of knowledge and power' (ibid.: 24).

Modern Egyptian culture has nothing, apart, perhaps, from the novels of Naguib Mahfouz, to rival Chahine's panoramic survey of his country as a counter-Description of Egypt, as a fledgling anti-Orientalism, and as a potential basis for the kind of knowledge formation Said urgently desires. Although it lacks the systematicity of the original *Description*, Chahine's work also lacks the former's inherent will-to-domination; in fact, it could be seen as premised on a rejection of both of these in the name of freedom, artistic as well as national.

For fifty years, Chahine has offered images of, and insight into, the lives of his fellow Egyptians in a way which is both celebratory and critical where necessary, as well as 'non-repressive and non-manipulative' in the manner advocated by Said. His determination to put the concerns of ordinary Egyptians on the screen, and in a manner (his fondness for the fantastic notwithstanding) more psychologically and politically honest than any comparable filmmaker, makes it difficult to think of a rival for Chahine at this level in world cinema. From the difficult lives of peasant farmers in *The Earth* to those of the urban working class in *Cairo Station*; from the intimate issues of family life in *Dawn of a New Day* to the sprawling cross-section of the nation in *Alexandria . . . Why?*; from the simplicities of rural existence in *Nile Boy* to the hyper-sophistication of life under globalised capitalism in *The Other*, Chahine continues to articulate his very particular 'description of Egypt'.

History

Somewhat surprisingly, given the richness of the available material, historical films are not one of the principal genres in Egyptian film. Nor, it has to be said, are they Chahine's main genre, though, in spite of that, the historical films he has made do cover a wide chronological span, from the time of Akhenaten in the fourteenth century BCE to that of Napoleon Bonaparte in the nineteenth century. Among the elements they share is the use of the past not for its own sake but to provide commentary on, or insight into, the concerns of the present.

The first of Chahine's historical films, the epic *Al-Nasir Salah al-Din* (*Saladin*, 1963), is also the only one which is not strictly Egyptian, (though Saladin was also ruler of Egypt at the time of the conquest of Jerusalem which is the subject of the film). It is also the only example of Chahine inheriting a major project from another filmmaker, in this case the terminally ill Izzidine Zulfiqar. The narrative combines and contrasts the larger-scale political and military struggles with the more intimate difficulties of what has become something of a trademark in Chahine's films – a love affair which transgresses boundaries and proprieties, in this case, the love of Isa, one of Saladin's soldiers, for Louise, the 'enemy' European woman whom he has rescued. (Both struggles reach a successful conclusion.) The film is also trademark Chahine in another way: the flagrant disregarding of verisimilitude in the service of emotional truth or of cinematic effect. Here, examples range from the bizarre (the use of binoculars in the twelfth century) to the rather more comprehensible (the *muezzin*'s call to prayer and a Christian choir at midnight in Bethlehem on Christmas Eve providing religious, emotional and aural counterpoint – even though there is no midnight call to prayer in Islam). Verisimilitude notwithstanding, the contemporary resonances were impossible for audiences to ignore. In 1963, Nasser – evoked by the film's title – was a pan-Arabic hero, victor over the British in the Suez crisis, and leader in the Non-Aligned Movement, while Jerusalem was yet again occupied by usurpers, Jewish this time rather than Christian, and thus in need of liberation by a brave and victorious Arab leader. History, however, was not about to repeat itself.

Although set in the more distant past, Chahine's 1994 film *The Emigrant* proved to have even stronger resonances in the present, this being the film for which, as mentioned in the introduction, he was put on trial for blasphemy. Set in the reign of Akhenaten, and featuring a central character called Ram based on the Biblical and Qur'anic figure of Joseph, it highlights the shortcomings of institutionalised religion and the dangers of fundamentalist intolerance. The intolerant fundamentalist response to the film, including calls for it to be banned, merely proved Chahine's point, and, undeterred by having been put on trial, he made his next film, *Destiny* (1997), on a similar thematic subject, focusing on the twelfth century philosopher Averroes and his fight against censorship and repression. Among the points of contemporary relevance for Chahine was the fact that a young actor whom he knew had been, in his words, literally brainwashed by a fundamentalist group in the same way as one of the characters in the film.

A portrait of the artist

No postcolonial filmmaker, and probably no other director in cinematic history, has put himself into his films in the way Chahine has. For many critics, the autobiographical Alexandria trilogy (recently grown into a quartet with the addition of *Alexandria New York* in 2004) is the centre-piece of Chahine's career, but it is very far from constituting his only appear-ances – either as himself or someone else – in his films, and, even when he is not appearing personally, his life still does. The quartet follows Chahine under a variety of guises (Yahia al-Qadri, Yahia Shukri Murad, Yahia Iskandarani etc.) from adolescence to late adulthood. As cinematic self-revelation, however, it probably resembles the dance of the seven veils rather more than straightforward confessional or psychoanalytic soul-searching, as Chahine mixes reality and fantasy, elements which are incontestably part of his life (making films and winning prizes at film festivals), others which might be (homosexual relationships) and yet others which are unquestion-ably not (fatherhood) – though they are all presented as being so. As a result, although Fawal, for example, claims that the importance of *Alexandria Again and Forever* (1990) 'lies in the revelation of many key facets of Chahine's complex personality' (Fawal 2001: 142), the problem remains for the viewer of not knowing which facets – all? some? none? – might actu-ally be taken as revealing Chahine himself, as opposed to the on-screen persona.

The fourth instalment of Chahine's self-exploration, *Alexandria New York*, takes him more or less full circle as he returns to the United Sates, his desperately desired destination in *Alexandria . . . Why?*, and to Ginger, the woman with whom he had an intermittent relationship, and mother of the twenty-year-old son he never knew he had. The film examines those affec-tions and connections which endure (Yahia and Ginger; Yahia's love for American culture) and those which do not (Yahia's love for the US, destroyed by the country itself). The fact that, in the final words of the film, 'New York kills tenderness' is, in Chahine's eyes, unforgivable, while his criticism of the gulf between US self-representation as the land of freedom and the reality of its brutal foreign policy unsurprisingly elicited a quantity of hostile (US) commentary.

Song and dance

As Chahine comments, the typical image in the West of Arab films is of singing and dancing: 'The West still thinks that all our pictures are dancing pictures, bad musicals translated from the American or the French. That may have been the overall industry, but there was also a very strong movement for much better films, which now you discover coming out of countries you don't expect – from Lebanon, from Syria, Iraq, Tunisia' (Chahine, in Massad 1999: 90). His own work may be part of the 'movement for much better films', but it does typically include singing and dancing as well as the occa-sional full-blown musical. On one level, this connects Chahine most securely with mainstream Egyptian cinema, where musicals and action films are the staple. At the same time, Chahine's use of dance particularly is more cos-mopolitan and self-reflexive as it draws selectively on classic Hollywood scenes and styles in order to make its point. As well as this, the song and dance sequences illustrate the paradoxical operations of the real in Chahine's work. For most Western audiences, these sequences are likely to be the parts of the film which are simultaneously least realistic in themselves and most strongly work against the realism of the film as a whole. For Chahine, on the other hand, combinations of fantasy sequences and song and dance, in fact faithfully illustrate what life is like: 'So, there is an interplay between everything. That's why, in the same film, you might see a scene that is totally fantastic and two seconds later, they're dancing, and six seconds after that they're doing something else. This happens to me every day. This is life' (Chahine, in Massad 1999: 91). If life itself is constituted by radical generic discontinuities, non-sequential shifts and dispersed narrative structures, then Chahine's cinema makes perfect sense.

In addition, and unsurprisingly, dance is not simply dance in Chahine's films; it both adds to the specific range of meanings in a given film and is indicative of larger issues. *Al-Akhar* (*The Other*, 1997), for example, is dedicated to Julien Duvivier, whose film *The Great Waltz* captivated Chahine as an adolescent, and a dance scene from it figures as an example of the glamorous life Margaret feels her son Adam is throwing away by marrying Hanan, a young working-class woman. At the sumptuous wedding party held beside the Saqqara pyramid, the meaning of the proceedings in both class and national terms is transformed when the young Omar persuades ordinary Egyptian musicians to sing and play for the dancers. The intrusion of the ordinary, as we will see in a later discussion, is something Margaret will not tolerate. Beyond these specific meanings, however, dance stands for, among other things, a love of life and a readiness to open oneself to the Other which recalls Senghor's image of Africans: '"I think, therefore I am," wrote Descartes, the European *par excellence*. "I feel, I dance the Other," the Negro-African would say. He does not need to think, but to live the Other by dancing him' (Senghor in Irele 1981: 69). In an interview, Chahine recalls appearing on television and being allowed to invite a special guest and choosing the thinker Alain Touraine: 'At the end of the programme, I couldn't stop myself asking him, "Do you dance?" He wanted to know why I was asking him that question. "Because I can't imagine a philosopher who talks about happiness and doesn't dance . . . dancing creates happiness." With a very annoyed air, he replied, "Oh yes, yes, you are right"' (Chahine 2001). As Chahine might well have said (it was actually the early twentieth-century anarchist Emma Goldmann), 'If I can't dance, I won't join in your revolution.'

Openness to the Other

For some, Chahine, apart from the fact that he comes from a postcolonial nation, would not be the most obvious candidate for the category of postcolonial filmmaker. Indeed, some might argue that he does not fit the

category at all. This, we would suggest, is not the case, but before attempting to say where Chahine's (elusive) postcolonialism might lie, however, it is
worth indicating the kind of place where – appearances notwithstanding –
it does not lie. In their article 'What is Post(-)Colonialism?' Bob Hodge and
Vijay Mishra argue for two main forms of postcolonialism, the oppositional
and the complicit, the first comprising much of what is typically understood
as postcolonial, while the second, a more problematic but 'always available'
position, is represented by someone like V. S. Naipaul who is ideologically
close to the West and its cultural norms (Mishra and Hodge 1993). For
various unfriendly commentators, Chahine's lifelong love of American
culture, especially Hollywood and its musicals, would constitute just such a
condition of complicity, rendering suspect any apparently anticolonial or
anti-Western stance or statement. We could, however, understand this rather
differently, and more positively, as an example of Chahine embodying his
own best principles. Regarding his 1997 film *Destiny*, he said that the central
character Ibn Rushd (Averroes) embodied what he himself had always
advocated, namely 'openness towards the Other'. Chahine's fondness for
American culture could then be seen as just such an openness towards, rather
than an ideological complicity with, a culture which is in many ways very
much the Other to his own. Given postcolonial theory's investment in
analysing the construction of the Other, and more recently in the nature of
the ethical stance towards the Other, this is a profitable area in which to
examine Chahine's relationship to the postcolonial.

Should we then see Chahine as standing at a 'slight angle' to postcolonialism? This would be perfectly logical, given his 'slight angle' to so much
else. Also, a non-standard form of postcolonialism in his films would accord
with Chahine's view of the non-standard nature of Egypt's relation to colonialism: 'Egypt wasn't the victim of a colonisation in depth. It was nothing
like Algeria where the French eliminated an entire elite. Between the
Egyptians and their various colonisers it was a different relationship. You
could say that it was the Egyptians who colonised the colonisers bit by bit
with their indolence, with an easy life which made them see that the in the
end the Egyptians were right and you shouldn't rush things' (Chahine 2001).
Although Ibrahim Fawal in his book on Chahine does align Chahine and
Sembene as postcolonial filmmakers, it is perhaps not the most entirely convincing pairing, not least because they would seem to be at almost opposite
ends of the postcolonial spectrum in so many ways, and the argument is not
helped by extraordinary claims such as: 'After having shown that it is prefer-
able for a Senegalese woman to commit suicide than to be a servant for a
French family (*Black Girl*, 1966), and after having depicted the president of
independent Senegal as sexually and politically impotent (*Xala*, 1975)'
(Fawal 2001: 198).

One thing which Chahine and Sembene do share, but which Fawal does
not comment on, is their close attention to the question of the nation. For
Fanon, although the nation does not constitute a simple be-all and end-all in

the process of becoming postcolonial – and indeed must ultimately be transcended at some level – nevertheless the nation remains essential. Without the nation, and the struggle for the nation, there is no culture; together, they offer the possibility of something greater: 'If man is known by his actions, then we will say that the most urgent thing today for the intellectual is to build up his nation. If this building up is true, that is to say if it interprets the manifest will of the people and reveals the eager African peoples, then the building of a nation is of necessity accompanied by discovery and encouragement of universalising values' (Fanon 1967: 199). For Chahine, the commitment to 'building up' his nation and to the encouragement of universalising values has been a lifelong one, and stands at the core of the idiosyncratic form of postcolonialism which he represents.

As is well known, for Fredric Jameson, Third World texts necessarily, given the historical conditions of their production, constitute allegorical representations of the nation, and it is possible to see this relationship at work in Chahine's films. In Jameson's analysis, the national dimension properly takes precedence over the individual or personal, but, in another assertion of his 'slight angle', and without neglecting collective issues, Chahine's films forcefully insist on the centrality of the personal, and individual consciousness as the organising centre of the text. That is most apparent in his autobiographical Alexandrian trilogy/quartet, which, as mentioned, constitutes probably the most extensive self-revelation any filmmaker has ever attempted. That it comes from a cultural tradition not usually given to detailed self-examination makes it all the more remarkable.

The first of these films, *Alexandria . . . Why?* (1978), is the narrative of the adolescent Yahia (the central character, based on Chahine) and his family during the Second World War, leading up to his departure to study drama in America. Alongside this there are the three love stories, one central and two more peripheral, each illustrating different aspects of the openness to the Other. The central story concerns the great love of Yahia/Chahine's life, namely Art, in the shape of literature, drama and cinema, and, above all, as a practice of openness. For Yahia, art – whether it is performing Shakespeare soliloquies for anyone who will listen, organising disastrously over-ambitious drama productions or taking his first steps in filmmaking – is much more engrossing than anything that daily life currently has to offer, such as chasing girls or the picking up of prostitutes which his rich school friends indulge in. For Yahia/Chahine, art involves an openness to other cultures and cultural forms, other ways of thinking, seeing and representing, other lives, beliefs and sexualities, all of which the film explores, and all of which Chahine as filmmaker has remained faithful to over the last half-century.

The other two love stories, though they occupy less central positions within the film, are both important in terms of openness to the Other and the accompanying willingness to transgress. The first concerns Sarah and Ibrahim: she is Jewish and upper-class; he is Muslim and working-class; though they are least united by their membership of the communist group

which Sarah's wealthy father organises. Although their relationship transgresses borders of class, religion and ethnicity, the fact that it does not create
any marked antagonism is no doubt due both to the open, cosmopolitan
nature of Alexandrian society and to the secular, rational context provided
by communist beliefs. Even the fact that Sarah becomes pregnant does not
create any difficulty as far as her father is concerned, which has led one critic
at least to accuse Chahine of depicting Jews as alien: 'His cool reaction, as
well as her nonchalance at being pregnant out of wedlock, could not have
been more alien even to the most cosmopolitan Egyptians of the time'
(Massad 1999: 79). However, apart from the fact that the entire film refuses
to concern itself with questions of absolute verisimilitude, this could still be
seen as the product either of a pragmatic, rational perspective or, more ide-
alistically, of a radical openness to other ways of being.

The final affair, involving Adel, an upper-class Egyptian, and Tommy, a
British soldier in the army preparing to fight at El Alamein, is the most transgressive, and arguably the most significant. As an individual act of resistance
to colonial occupation, Adel 'buys' British soldiers, drunk or drugged, whom
he then kills. Having put in an order for an officer, he is sold Tommy, whom
he takes away to shoot; Tommy, however, comes round, and they end up
making love. This is the start of a relationship which negotiates, not without
difficulty, the Othering identities of race, class, colonialism and sexuality to
become one of true affection, as Tommy (ironically, perhaps, given his position as 'oppressor') teaches Adel the importance of caring, even for the radically Other. After the war, Adel goes in search of Tommy, only to find that,
despite his confident promises, he has not survived. Adel kneels, sobbing, in
front of Tommy's grave, as the scene shifts to other cemeteries, other nation-
alities – the massed, nameless and faceless Others also lost in the war.

According to Ibrahim Fawal, 'The title of Chahine's film on the subject of
globalisation – *The Other* – reveals his resentment of the pejorative label
imposed on his world' (Fawal 2001: 197–8). Arguably, however, something
rather more complex than a cinematic expression of postcolonial *ressenti-
ment* is happening here. In the lengthy credit sequence, two PhD students
from North Africa have a tutorial with Edward Said at Columbia University,
and although this cameo is Said's only appearance in the film, his presence
is in itself almost a guarantee of a more nuanced understanding of the Other.
The brief discussion with the two students, one of whom is Adam, the film's
central character, touches on identity, belonging, the universalism of culture
and the relationship to the Other. Said says, 'Don't think in terms of belonging! . . . With all my heart, I await the day when instead of saying "me" and
"you", we will say "us".' Here, the universalism of culture for which Said
has just been arguing is paralleled by a universal humanity. At the same
time, as anyone familiar with Said's work must know, humanity has hitherto
been all too ready, on the grounds of what Said in *Orientalism* calls 'imaginative geography', to subdivide itself into 'us' and 'them', with disastrous
consequences.

The creation of a category of 'them' – i.e. the Other – is, in *Orientalism*, the product of a relationship of domination, or at least one with an imbalance of power, and the Other which the powerful West creates, vilifies and oppresses in Said's study is the Muslim Orient to which Chahine belongs. At that level, *The Other* cannot avoid being aware that its world and its people are indeed the relentlessly stereotyped Other of the West, but that does not imply any necessary display of the resentment Fawal assumes, nor does it presuppose who or what will in fact constitute the Other within the particular terms of the film.

At one level, the Orientalist opposition of East and West survives in the film in the shape of the real – but also simultaneously stereotypically reductive – antagonism between, on the one hand, Western capitalism in its globalising phase and, on the other, militant Islam, fundamentalist and terrorist, with each seeing itself as the ideological antithesis of the other. This polarised relationship breaks down in a number of ways, as both sides are shown to have more in common than either would like to admit. For instance, the idea of the brutal 'law of the jungle', which Said denounces in the opening scene, characterises both the behaviour of the capitalists towards competitors or victims and the urban terrorism of the Islamist group. At the same time, although each declares itself the sworn enemy of the other, each is prepared to use the other, to do deals with and accept help from the other, in the furtherance of their own self-interested plans. Similarly, although each claims purity of motive, both are revealed to be corrupt, compromised, totally lacking in anything resembling purity of any sort.

As this classic Orientalist Self/Other opposition breaks down, both sides are shown to be Others to a different Self. Both are the real enemies of the 'good' national self: Egypt, the nation, the ordinary people; 'real' enemies rather than merely discursively constructed ones, because of their material effects: socially and religiously divisive and oppressive, murderous, destructive of national economic interests, etc. The film's key transformation in relation to this altered oppositional structure takes place in Adam. As he learns more about the kind of corrupt dealings in which his mother is involved, he increasingly dissociates himself from her and, to her horror, declares himself to be Egyptian, rather than American – to which he could also and equally lay claim, and which to her is clearly a far better identity to have. Worse than this in his mother's eyes, in both a literal and a symbolic way his gesture of identification is signed in blood: in the wake of a terrorist bomb attack he gives blood – 'to *them*!!' (i.e. ordinary Egyptians) as his outraged mother says.

Adam's powerful identification with Egypt and with the ordinary people is of central importance in terms of the film's politics; it is also interesting in the context of Said's opening remarks. What, for instance, are we to make of Adam's identificatory stance in relation to Said's injunction: 'Don't think in terms of belonging!'? Is it simply the case that Adam, and the film, have forgotten Said? Or could we perhaps see it, in Saidian terms, as an example

of affiliation rather than filiation, in other words, the conscious choice of a
'political' identity rather than the unthinking assumption of an inherited or
biologically derived one? That Adam's choice (of Egypt, with its millennia
of culture and tradition) does not necessarily look like the 'modern' act
which Said's model typically suggests nevertheless still makes sense in
Saidian terms: 'The second alternative is for the critic to recognise the difference between instinctual filiation and social affiliation, and to show how
affiliation sometimes reproduces filiation, sometimes makes its own forms'
(Said 1984: 24). In other words, even the modern choice, the conscious and
political act, carries the possibility of the reproduction of the traditional.

Alternatively, in the context of Said's comments, we could see in Adam's
gesture an attempt, by siding with the ordinary Egyptians, to transcend
the social divisions his mother instantiates, and exacerbates, and reach the
utopian space of an undivided 'us' evoked by Said. For Margaret, the
Egyptians are history's permanent losers, subject to one set of invaders and
one alien regime after another, and identifying with them makes you a potential loser too. Seen from the other side, however, taking a stand alongside
'the wretched of the Earth' is potentially revolutionary and the only ethically
justifiable course of action.

The question of the ethical is another aspect of the fundamental divisions
which the film addresses. Indeed, the refigured Self/Other opposition here
could be seen as a struggle between those who have, or embody, ethical principles and those who do not (whatever they may claim). In this respect, the
figure of Maher the architect is important: since he is the biggest loser in professional terms as a result of the non-existent building project used by
Margaret and her husband to fleece investors, his principled stance acts as a
focus for opposition to their predatory capitalist schemes. Also, his moment
of vision in the desert of the multi-faith centre which should have been the
outcome of the project is starkly contrasted with the tacky religiosity of
Margaret and the foreign investors thanking the Lord for the successful conclusion of their deal.

In a similar sort of opposition between real and false spirituality, good and
bad beliefs, Adam's young wife Hanan contrasts the true tenets of Islam with
the perverted and oppressive version espoused by her brother, the leader of
the terrorists. In Chahine's view, this distortion typifies the Islamists, and he
offers another controversial depiction of them as completely lacking any
redeeming features. This is clearly how he sees them, since the same type of
belief and behaviour occurs in several of his more recent films, but it is not
an image with which even some friendly critics are happy. Talking about
Chahine's previous film *Destiny*, Joseph Massad comments: 'Given
Chahine's depiction of the Islamists as a fantastic mix of Protestant puritans,
ruthless assassins, evil mafiosi, and obscurantist cultists – an image that does
not fit even the most extreme among them, much less the majority – it seems
hardly coincidental that this is the only film of Chahine's that has ever been
picked up by a US distributor' (Massad 1999: 82). While Massad is no doubt

correct that the film's ability to find a US distributor has much to do with the negative representation of the Islamists – 'a caricature' in Massad's terms – it is certainly debatable whether no Islamist is really as bad as Chahine depicts them. The behaviour of the Taliban in Afghanistan and the FIS in Algeria – to mention only these – would seem to go so far beyond Chahine's Islamists in terms of extent of repression and depth of cruelty as indeed to reduce the latter to a kind of caricature, though not in the sense in which Massad intends it. (A recent film which paints an even less flattering picture of the effects of Islamist extremism is *Rachida* (2002), the debut feature by the young Algerian Yamina Bachir-Chouikh.) Clearly, reinforcing Orientalist stereotypes through the negative representation of some element of Islamic culture is undesirable. Equally clearly, for someone like Chahine, failing to speak out against the unacceptable aspects of one's culture for fear of giving comfort to the enemy is even less acceptable when it seems that both the future of the postcolonial state and values deemed to be universal are at stake.

'Fundamentalism' also appears in Chahine's second most recent film, a contribution of eleven minutes, nine seconds and one frame to the collaborative project *11/09/01* – a response to the World Trade Center bombing, which brings together directors including Ken Loach, Samira Makhmalbaf, Claude Lelouch, and Idrissa Ouédraogo. On one level, this is, once again, a piece all about Youssef Chahine and his filmmaking, and, in a less self-absorbed way, about the responsibility of artists and intellectuals. On another, it is about violence – the violence of individuals, the violence of states – and those, particularly the ordinary people, who die as a result. As such, it combines yet again in Chahine's work the politics of the personal – what have we done?; what could we do?; how might we respond? in relation to events like these – and the politics of the interpersonal, in particular the ethical stance of openness towards the Other. Here, in a manner which recalls some of the poems of the Palestinian Mahmoud Darwish, the Other whom Chahine humanises is one of the 283 American marines killed in Beirut by a suicide bomber in 1982, and whose ghost he can see and talk to – unlike other people – 'because you're sensitive to things that happen – to my life, to my death'. Chahine, however, feels that his humanity and humanism extend beyond that, as he says, 'I think I'm sensitive about everyone's life.' Sensitivity may be far too little, however: Chahine's sympathy for the suffering and dying Other – 'I was thinking about you . . . all of you. I'm angry that we don't do enough for others' – elicits the stark response, 'You've done nothing to make yourself heard' from the marine.

The brevity of the pieces in this collaborative film sometimes requires the viewer to do a lot of the work of interpretation. Here, Chahine presents two large-scale attacks against Americans – Beirut 1982 and New York 2001 – implicitly inviting comparative analysis of their contexts and causes, and then contrasts these with the lonely death of one Palestinian, which in turn alters the analytical frame. Although there are areas of relatively clearly defined culpability (Chahine and the dead marine examine statistics for the victims of US aggression in the twentieth century; an old man narrates the daily Israeli violence in Palestine), there are also cycles of human stupidity and refusal to understand which perpetuate violence, and which complicate analysis. In the end, after the analysis and the position-taking, the final words, those of the dead Palestinian, are a plea for humanity and the memory of suffering: 'Remember my mother's eyes. If humanity means anything to you, never forget them.'

'Who can resuscitate the dead?' the film asks. The openness to those who are, and are not, humanity's ultimate Other – so unlike us, being dead; still so close to us in many ways – provides a kind of answer. 'Never forgetting' is the most human method – indeed the only one – of keeping the dead alive. As Chahine said in an interview, 'I think the idea of eternity doesn't lie in the building of pyramids, but in handing on [ideas]. That's why I've taught for forty years' (Chahine 2004). At the level of form or narrative, what Chahine's films hand on may not, apparently, be the most radical postcolonial critique. At the ethical level, however, they respond to the far-reaching challenge articulated by Said in a way which few postcolonial cultural products have been able to do, handing on, at the very least, a deeply humane perspective on humanity, one which is at the very heart of the postcolonial project articulated by thinkers and activists from Césaire and Senghor onwards.[1]

Note

1 On postcolonial thinkers and the project for a 'new humanism' or new humanity see Williams 2003.

Filmography

Baba Amin (Daddy Amin) (1950)
Ibn al-Nil (Nile Boy) (1951)
Al-Muharrij al-Kabir (The Great Clown) (1952)
Sayedat al-Qitar (The Woman on the Train) (1953)
Nissae bila Regal (Women Without Men) (1953)
Siraa fi-l-Wadi (Blazing Sun) (1954)
Shaytan al-Sahra (Devil in the Desert) (1954)
Siraa fi-l-Mina (Dark Waters) (1956)
Wadda'tu Hubbak (Farewell My Love) (1957)
Inta Habibi (My One and Only Love) (1957)
Jamila al-Jaza'iriyya (Jamila the Algerian) (1958)
Bab al-Hadid (Cairo Station) (1958)
Hubb lel-Abad (Forever Yours) (1959)
Bein Edeik (In Your Hands) (1960)
Rajul fi Hayati (A Man in My Life) (1961)
Nida al'ushshaq (Lovers' Complaint) (1961)

Al-Nasir Salah al-Din (Saladin) (1963)
Fajr Yom Jedid (Dawn of a New Day) (1964)
Biya al-Khawatim (The Ring Seller) (1965)
Id al-Mairun (Sacred Oil) (1967)
Al-Nass wal Nil (People of the Nile) (1968)
Al-Ard (The Earth) (1969)
Al-Ikhtiyar (The Choice) (1970)
Rimal min Dhahab (Golden Sands) (1971)
Salwa (Salwa, the Girl Who Talked to Crows) (1972)
Al-Asfour (The Sparrow) (1972)
Intilak (Forward We Go) (1974)
Awdat al-Ibn al-Dal (The Return of the Prodigal Son) (1976)
Iskandaria . . . leh? (Alexandria . . . Why?) (1978)
Hadutta Misria (An Egyptian Story) (1982)
Adieu Bonaparte (1985)
Al-Yawm al-Sadis (The Sixth Day) (1986)
Iskandaria, Kaman wa Kaman (Alexandria Again and Forever) (1990)
Al-Qahira munauwwara bi Ahlaha (Cairo as Told by Chahine) (1991)
Al-Muhajir (The Emigrant) (1994)
Lumière et compagnie (Lumière and Company) (1995)
Al-Masir (Destiny) (1997)
Al-Akhar (The Other) (1999)
Skoot Hansawwar (Silence . . . We're Rolling) (2001)
11/09/01 – September 11 (2002) (segment 'Egypt')
Alexandrie New York (Alexandria New York) (2004)

Chapter 2

Ousmane Sembene

Introduction

The Senegalese director and novelist Ousmane Sembene began his film career in the early 1960s, and is often hailed as 'the father of African cinema' for his role in the development of filmmaking on the continent. Born in 1923, in the provincial port of Ziguinchor, Sembene is credited with a series of landmarks 'firsts': the first film by a sub-Saharan African in Africa, *Borom Sarret* (1962); the first feature film by a sub-Saharan African, *La Noire de* (*Black Girl*, 1966), and the first black African film in an African language, *Mandabi* (*The Money Order*, 1968).[1] However, his pioneering role cannot simply be reduced to this impressive series of 'firsts', for his films, particularly those of the 1960s and 1970s, have been both politically radical and stylistically innovative. Sembene's work has attempted to chart an African film style that reflects African realities, while also remaining accessible and meaningful to an African audience. In a cinematic career spanning forty years, he has displayed an extraordinary aesthetic range, combining elements from the Senegalese oral tradition (the 'trickster'-inspired narratives of *Mandabi* and *Xala*) with Brechtian set pieces (the opening sequence of *Xala*), intimate domestic realism (*Guelwaar*, *Faat Kiné*), as well as symbolism (*Emitaï*, *Ceddo*) and social satire (*Mandabi*, *Xala*, *Moolaadé*). He has also shown a distinct talent for comedy, which has been a refreshing influence in the sometimes rather didactic and moralistic world of African filmmaking. By the time of his death in June 2007, he had twelve films to his credit, three short films and nine feature films, which constitutes a long and relatively prolific career within the troubled context of sub-Saharan African filmmaking.

By the time Sembene (the name is sometimes seen as 'Sembène', but he preferred the spelling without the accent) began his film career, he was already an established author, and his third novel, *God's Bits of Wood* (1960), has been acclaimed as one of the most important African novels of the twentieth century. For over forty years, he led a dual career as writer and film director, although his film output exceeds that of his fiction.[2] While the vast majority of Francophone African writers from this period were members of an educated elite, Sembene stands out as a largely self-educated man from a relatively unprivileged background. An often-related story about Sembene's early life claims that he was expelled from school for punching a teacher. Whatever the precise details of the incident, it is indicative of a stubborn streak in Sembene's nature. Indeed, the idea of resistance to authority is central to Sembene's worldview, and his films are imbued with a burning anger at all forms of injustice.

After his truncated education, he variously worked as mechanic, stone-mason and carpenter, before enlisting in the *tirailleurs sénégalais* (France's colonial African troops) in the Second World War, serving in Germany and North Africa. In 1946, Sembene returned to Senegal where he took part in the railway workers' strike of 1947–48 (later to become the subject of *God's Bits of Wood*) but he was back in France within two years and he remained there until 1960. His work as a docker in Marseilles led him to become a trade union official for the Communist Confédération Générale du Travail (CGT), and access to the union library inspired him to begin a crash course of reading that took in both Marxism and the key texts of the French literary canon, which soon inspired his own literary ambitions.

However, on his return to Senegal after its independence from France in 1960, he saw just how little impact the emergent African literature was having on the illiterate African masses. Throughout 1960, he travelled around West Africa and further south as far as the Congo, assessing for himself the reality of the process of decolonization. It was during this trip that he decided to turn to cinema, a decision he has often described in terms of a sort of epiphany: sitting in a boat on the Congo river, he had a vision of cinema's power both to represent and to communicate with the masses. Seeking to learn the cinematic techniques that would allow him to fulfil this vision, he applied to a number of countries for a grant to study filmmaking, and it was eventually the Soviet Union that invited him to study under the renowned director Mark Donskoi at the Gorki studios in Moscow.[3] Sembene first became interested in cinema when sent to live with relatives in Dakar as a teenager, avidly attending as many films as possible. At the same time, he was gaining exposure to local storytelling traditions as he and a group of friends regularly gathered to hear the folk tales and legends told by the story-teller Yahi Lalo at the Sandaga market in central Dakar. Twenty years later, Sembene would seek to combine these various influences when he began to make films.

Sembene's long film career might roughly be divided into three distinct 'periods'. In the first period, from 1962 to 1970, his work was highly influenced by Italian neo-realism and his films explored the artistic possibilities and limitations of this style within an African context. His first three films – *Borom Sarret*, *Niaye* and *Black Girl* – are often considered quite 'literary' in particular because of their use of voiceover. However, they also display a distinctive cinematic vision, and a striking sense of shot composition: in *Borom Sarret*, the low angle shot of the cart driver looking up at his tormentor, the policeman, standing over him with the high-rise homes of the bourgeoisie in the background; or, in *Black Girl*, the extremely poignant sequence at the end of the film in which the camera insistently cuts back and forth between the worried Frenchman hurrying back to his car, and the 'ghostly' mask worn by the young boy who follows him.

Sembene is conscious of the political limits of filmmaking, and, right from the start of his career, his work has shown a high degree of self-awareness. Mid-way through *Borom Sarret*, the cart driver (Borom Sarret, a 'wolofisation' of the French 'bonhomme charette') is accosted by a griot, who has overheard his surname, which is of noble origin. The griot promptly proceeds to sing the praises of the cart driver's family line, attracting an admiring crowd, in the hope that this flattery will make Borom Sarret part with his hard-earned cash, which it does. Sembene here depicts the ambiguity of the griot's traditional role in West African societies. Charged with preserving the myths and values of these societies, the griot is also in the service of specific noble families whose praises he or she sings (in modern Senegal, many griots have sought patronage from politicians and Islamic leaders). In Sembene's vision, the filmmaker may be the new griot, but he or she will not engage in the flattery employed by their predecessors, choosing instead to tell the stories of the weak and powerless in society. This is illustrated very subtly in a small incident within this scene. As we hear the griot's flattering homage, the camera turns its attention to a shoeshine boy who tries to drum up business from the crowd. A man in a sharp suit allows his shoes to be cleaned but departs without paying, the camera focusing on the newly shined shoe kicking away the shoeshine boy's box. For Sembene, this is the type of story the new griot will tell.

His first two feature films, *Black Girl* and *Mandabi*, give an indication of the artistic range of Sembene's work. *Black Girl* is a dark psychological portrait of Diouana, the Senegalese maid of a French family in Dakar, who follows her employers to Antibes, on the French Riviera. She dreams of wealth and happiness, and her arrival in France sees the film shift from black-and-white to colour as she enters the land of her dreams. However, the dream soon turns to a nightmare, and the film returns to black-and-white 'reality', eventually leading to her suicide. In contrast, *Mandabi* is a wonderfully observed black comedy, filmed in vibrant colour in the streets of Dakar and its suburbs. The central character, Ibrahima Dieng (played with superb comic timing by the diminutive and peerless actor Makhourédia Guèye),[4] is a poor, illiterate Muslim, who feels all at sea in the modern world of independent Senegal. This comic dimension of his work is often neglected in critical appraisals but in fact comedy is deployed in most of his films, and it would play a key role in *Xala*, his biggest commercial success in Africa.

The period from 1971 to 1976 is seen by many critics as the most creative period of Sembene's career. During this five-year period, he made a cycle of three highly innovative films, *Emitaï* (1971), *Xala* (1974) and *Ceddo* (1976), each of which pushed his exploration of cinematic form far beyond the label of 'social realist' that has clung to his work. These films are organised visually around a series of competing rituals that are engaged in a struggle to occupy the screen: *Emitaï*, set in a village in southern Casamance during the Second World War, contrasts the futile attempts of the Diola menfolk to summon their gods to intercede on their behalf against the French colonial army with the more active and practical resistance of the women; *Xala* opposes the excessive and extravagant rituals of the post-independence African bourgeoisie with the communal solidarity and the animist rituals of the urban poor; *Ceddo* contrasts the rituals of an 'indigenous' animist Africa (those of the eponymous 'ceddo') with the 'alien', 'colonising' forces of Islam and Christianity.

After this extraordinarily creative burst of cinematic energy, Sembene entered a long hiatus from filmmaking from which he did not emerge until 1988.[5] Since then, he has made only four films, which have, by and large, retreated from the experimentalism of his middle period. However, it would be wrong to view the waning in output and creativity in this late period as the terminal decline of a once great cinematic vision. Both his early and his late movies may not be as experimental as his middle period but they are all, to greater and lesser degrees, skilfully constructed and very effective 'classical' narratives. In *Camp de Thiaroye* (1988) and *Guelwaar* (1992), Sembene sets out to celebrate and to salvage instances of resistance that have been suppressed and silenced by the authorities (although both films suffer from occasional *longueurs*). *Camp de Thiaroye* is based on a historical incident from the end of the war, in which thirty-five *tirailleurs sénégalais* were killed and hundreds of others wounded in a brutal act of repression by the French army after an aborted revolt over pay and conditions.[6] The film paints a sympathetic and naturalistic portrait of the soldiers but sets it clearly within the symbolic context of the profound challenge to Empire that is produced by their experiences of the war; this is powerfully represented through the character of Pays, the traumatised, mute *tirailleur* and escapee from Buchenwald, who wears an SS helmet, reminding his white 'superiors' both of France's vulnerability and of the fact that the 'motherland' was partly liberated by its colonial 'subjects'. In *Guelwaar*, Sembene again mixes realism with powerful political symbolism in a narrative that recovers the suppressed story of a murdered political militant who had denounced African dependence on Western aid and the denial of political responsibility within the African political elite. The flashbacks of Guelwaar's life build to a hugely powerful climax at the aid rally where the political activist uses the words of Senegalese 'philosopher' Kocc Barma to castigate his audience for allowing themselves effectively to become beggars.

Sembene's final two films – which form part of an unfinished trilogy called 'The Heroism of Daily Life' – focused on issues facing women in contemporary Africa. *Faat Kiné* (2000) presents a fascinating picture of the evolution of women's roles in Senegalese society. Perhaps the most remarkable feature of the film is its ability to capture the boisterous and often scandalous behaviour and bawdy humour of Faat Kiné and her friends. Far from the virtuous virgins and wise old mothers of 'tradition', they are complex human beings with their own sexual and emotional needs, who are well capable of surviving without men. The second part of the trilogy, *Moolaadé* (2004), has been hailed by many critics as a 'late masterpiece'. It is ostensibly an 'issue' film, which focuses on the opposition of a woman in a village in Burkina Faso to the practice of excision (that is of the clitoris and labia; an act rightly labelled 'female genital mutilation' by campaigners who oppose it). However, in its extremely complex realist portrait of the hierarchies of village life, and its beautifully filmed exploration of the rituals of the 'Moolaadé' (the rite of asylum) and those of the 'Salindana' (the women who carry out the 'excisions'), the film manages to recapture the heights reached by his best work.

At the time of his death Sembene was preparing the third part of the trilogy, *The Brotherhood of Rats*, which was to focus on the issue of state corruption. At the same time, he was in talks with the African-American actor Danny Glover about the possibility of bringing his epic novel *God's Bits of Wood* to the screen. Despite being in his early eighties, Sembene was intent on pursuing his film career well into its fifth decade.

Social, cultural and political contexts

The strength of Sembene's political convictions has been a central factor in critical assessments of his work, and this section will focus on defining the precise nature of his political vision. Sembene entered into both politics and art via his involvement in the 1950s with the CGT, a trade union affiliated to the French Communist Party, and he has remained a staunch Marxist ever since. In terms of his filmmaking, he is not a dogmatic Marxist (his pronouncements in interviews are often another matter entirely) and his films do not, as certain critics have claimed, impose a 'simplistic' socialist framework on a complex reality (see Harrow 1995). Admittedly, his representations of the African bourgeoisie (*Mandabi*, *Xala*) or of white, colonial oppressors (*Emitaï*, *Camp de Thiaroye*) are often quite caricatured but his work also deftly observes the ambiguities of life for the urban and rural poor. Two of his earliest 'social' films, *Borom Sarret* and *Mandabi*, include scathing attacks on the emerging African bourgeoisie, but they offer no simplistic, revolutionary 'solutions'. It is Islam that frames and informs the lives of both the cart driver (the opening shot of *Borom Sarret* is of the Great Mosque in Dakar) and the hapless Ibrahima Dieng: they feel but do not understand the political and economic forces controlling their existence. Furthermore, poor communities themselves are prone to conflicts and tensions: both Dieng and the cart driver are at various points exploited by neighbours who are just as poor as they are. With the exception of *Xala*, Sembene's films make few direct references to government policies and ideology. They are in fact far more interested in politics 'from below', and this attention to the specific details of daily life in Africa nuances the ideological dimension of his work.

Sembene's Marxism must also be seen within the context of his profound pan-Africanism, a belief in the unity of purpose and destiny of the different peoples of his continent, which, as can be seen elsewhere in this volume, is common to many African filmmakers. However, in Sembene's case, this appears specifically to have been born of his experiences during the independence struggle, as is illustrated by his classic novel, *God's Bits of Wood*, which constitutes a dazzling attempt to imagine a socialist future for the entire continent. This vision proved chimeric, and Sembene clearly feels that the failure of socialism to take root in Africa is one of the reasons for its present economic and political predicament. His post-independence work has thus consistently examined the need for socialism in Africa, while recognising the difficulty of bringing it about (a paradox seen most clearly in *Xala*). Sembene's pan-Africanism is also expressed at times in the form of a cultural 'nationalism'. *Emitaï*, *Xala* and *Ceddo* are as much concerned with expressing the dignity and values of African cultural practices that have been denigrated by Europe or a colonised elite as they are with exploring social and political ills: *Ceddo*, in particular, is a vigorous defence of the society and culture of precolonial Senegal. Although his films are generally set in Senegal (the exception is *Moolaadé*, set in Burkina Faso), Sembene clearly conceives of his work as contributing to a wider pan-African culture: 'For me, Africa is the centre of the world' (Murphy 2000a: 228).

Sembene has enjoyed a freedom of expression that has often been denied to artists elsewhere on the continent, which has allowed him to be an outspoken critic of neocolonialism and the corruption of post-independence Africa. Under the rule of Léopold Sédar Senghor, the renowned poet, who was president from 1960 to 1980, Senegal enjoyed a (largely justified) reputation, which it has since maintained, as a relatively stable democracy and an isolated haven for artistic freedom of expression. However, the reality of relations between Sembene and the state are rather more complex than this somewhat idealistic picture allows. The best example of this is to be found in *Xala*, which was in part funded by the Senegalese authorities through the newly created Société Nationale de Cinéma (SNC). Sembene uses the film to deliver his most direct and most stinging critique of Senghor's regime, which is claimed to use the forces of law and order to maintain the privileges of a tiny elite. In response, the government censored the film, imposing ten cuts in all.[7]

A similarly ambiguous situation arose with Sembene's next film, *Ceddo*, which was also partly funded by the SNC. In one of the more bizarre incidents from Sembene's career, the film was banned by Senghor, not because of its controversial version of local history but because the word *ceddo* was spelt 'incorrectly'. This may seem an almost farcical point today but it was not trivial to Sembene who, in the early 1970s, had invested heavily in a Wolof-language newspaper, *Kaddu*, which promoted the use of Wolof as the national language. (Sembene makes direct reference to *Kaddu* in *Xala* through the young man who sells it in the street, and who is rounded up by

the police alongside the beggars and the peasant farmer.) The banning of
Ceddo appears to have brought the strained relationship between Sembene
and Senghor to a head. Although Senghor was lauded in the West for his
democratic and literary credentials, Sembene always viewed him as a sort of
pro-consul, ruling Senegal on behalf of its former colonial masters. Senegal
was France's oldest African colony, and the coastal areas had been permitted to elect a deputy to the French National Assembly since the late nineteenth century. Under Senghor, Senegal maintained close cultural, economic
and political ties with France, and French troops were stationed on
Senegalese soil. Equally, Sembene was deeply critical of the hypocrisy of
Senghor's espousal of 'African socialism' (satirised so effectively in *Xala*),
which the filmmaker saw as a mere smokescreen designed to obscure the
reality of neocolonial exploitation. There also existed a major cultural and
personal opposition between the two men. Senghor was chief theorist of
Negritude, which posited an essential black personality based on sensuality
and instinct, a concept that was anathema to the Marxist, rationalist mind
of Sembene. The largely self-educated Sembene viewed the intellectual
Senghor, graduate of elite French universities, as a man who had become
remote and alienated from his own people, and Senghor's often abstract,
occasionally academic, poetic style stands in stark contrast to Sembene's
committed political works. (Senghor for his part appears to have viewed
Sembene as a rabble-rousing populist of little artistic merit.) Although their
differences were primarily ideological, Sembene was not 'above' personal
attacks on Senghor. In *Xala*, the President of the Chamber of Commerce is
played magnificently by Makhourédia Guèye, a man similar in stature to the
diminutive Senghor. He is clearly associated with Senghor through his tone
of voice, the title 'Président', and also through his use of key words from
Senghor's political vocabulary: the scene in which the dapper and smooth-
talking Guèye invites El Hadji's tall and elegant second wife to dance clearly
mocks Senghor's alleged vanity and egotism.

In the mid-1960s, Senegal effectively became a one-party state, and,
during the decade that followed, when there often appeared to be a stifling
cultural and political consensus in the country, Sembene played a key role in
articulating an oppositional stance, becoming a hero to many young artists
and academics who would come to challenge Senghor's legacy in the 1980s.
Senghor's retirement in 1980 may have brought an end to the glaring
hypocrisies of Negritude and African socialism but the uninspiring manage-
rialism of his successor, Abdou Diouf, who served as President from 1981 to
2000, was not viewed any more favourably by Sembene. Unsurprisingly,
Sembene was not a fan of the new President, Abdoulaye Wade, an economic
liberal, who finally brought an end to forty years of one-party rule in March
2000.

Perhaps the most 'political' of Sembene's late films is *Guelwaar*, which is
a stirring polemic on African dependence on Western 'aid'. From another
angle, *Guelwaar* can also be seen as a key example of Sembene's regular

interventions on the question of 'memory'. We discover in the opening stages of the film that Pierre Henri Thioune, known as 'Guelwaar' (the noble one), is dead, and his body has gone missing from the morgue. The rest of the film is an attempt to recover Guelwaar both physically and symbolically, with the film's series of flashbacks culminating in his remarkable, electrifying speech to the gathered dignitaries at an aid rally in which he denounces the entire aid process and calls on his fellow Africans to find their own solutions to their problems.

A similar desire to counter 'official' versions of the past is present in *Emitaï* and *Camp de Thiaroye*, which both revisit 'forgotten' acts of colonial violence from the Second World War. They can also be read as further examples of Sembene's pan-Africanism. *Camp de Thiaroye* represents the awakening of an African consciousness amongst colonial soldiers from across the continent, while *Emitaï* is dedicated to 'all the militants of the African cause', and it was filmed on the Senegalese border with Guinea-Bissau at the height of the Portuguese colony's fight for independence. *Ceddo* is undoubtedly his most complex historical intervention. It is a film that seeks to uncover the violent social and political forces that produced a Senegalese Islam that was increasingly seen as a 'natural' presence in 1970s Senegal. As Philip Rosen argues, in his brilliant reading of the film: 'In *Ceddo*, the issue of the nation and its representation is located as a problem of history and its representation. Only in the constructions of its histories will a nation be defined' (1991: 148). *Ceddo* thus acts as a striking example of Sembene's belief in the power of cinema to intervene in the process of transmitting historical memory, opening a space in which the dominant historical narratives of the nation can be questioned.

In his final films, *Faat Kiné* and *Moolaadé*, Sembene appeared to have 'parked' his socialist concerns in order to concentrate on gender issues, which have, in fact, always been central to his work. In the past, the bourgeoisie were consistently seen by Sembene as enemies of progress, but Faat Kiné is presented as a successful businesswoman, and the film's narrative focuses on her attempts to overcome the obstacles placed in her way by self-obsessed men, while *Moolaadé* is an exploration of the fault lines of power and gender in an isolated village. Rather than acting as a 'departure' from Sembene's earlier socialist aspirations, these late films might allow us to revisit the earlier work in order to see the full range of Sembene's concerns, which were often obscured from view in the more ideologically polarised era of the 1960s and 1970s.

The films

This section will examine various aspects of Sembene's filmmaking practice, beginning with an assessment of aspects of his film style that have been relatively neglected. (Given the large body of work that he has created, it will be necessary to focus on just a few of his most important films.) One of the most important aspects of Sembene's work – and one that has received surprisingly little critical attention – is its use of humour. As well as the political irony and satire that one might expect of Sembene, there can be found in his films a series of comic techniques ranging from sophisticated verbal comedy to physical comedy and even the bawdy sexual comedy of *Xala* and *Faat Kiné*. A fan of Charlie Chaplin from his teenage years, Sembene appears to have learned the lessons not only of wrapping political 'messages' within a comic context but also of exploring the comic potential of situations in their own right. This sense of comic observation is evident even in his ostensibly 'serious' films: for example, the pregnant woman's head leaning on the cart driver's shoulder in *Borom Sarret*; the sharp comedy of the belligerent *tirailleur* in *Emitaï* (played with excellent comic timing by Sembene himself) commenting bemusedly on 'two-star' General de Gaulle replacing 'seven-star' Marshal Pétain;[8] or, in *Guelwaar*, the young Pierre Henri Thioune running naked from a hut pursued by the husband of his latest 'conquest'.

Sembene's most sustained comic film is undoubtedly *Mandabi*, and his greatest comic creation is its main protagonist Ibrahima Dieng. From the outset, Dieng is presented as a comic figure who seems at times like an innocent and helpless child. In the opening ten minutes, Sembene consistently cuts back and forth between a burping Dieng who has gorged himself on the copious meal prepared by his wives, Méty and Aram, and the baby attached to Aram's back. Later on, the image cuts between Dieng exaggeratedly rolling his eyes in pleasure as Méty washes his feet and one of the children sitting outside washing her (white) doll. He also loves finery, which is depicted by his magnificent, but comically over-sized, magenta-coloured *boubou* (a long flowing robe), which he is endlessly forced to adjust: when Dieng gets angry and shouts at his wives for revealing the 'secret' of the money order's existence, Sembene undercuts this patriarchal display of authority as the sleeves of his *boubou* keep slipping down over his hands, while the waist gathers around him like a tent.

As the film progresses, the humour becomes progressively darker. Gone is the over-sized *boubou* and in its place Dieng wears white robes, on to which his blood drips forlornly after he is beaten up by the photographer's assistant. Whereas earlier in the film, Sembene had gleaned wry comedy from the intricate proverbial 'jousts' surrounding the half-lies and duplicity involved in Dieng trying to fend off his friends' and neighbours' rapacious demands for money, the humour now becomes increasingly dark. Even the sharp comedy of his wives' inspired lie that he has been mugged and the money stolen is trumped by the reality of Dieng's cousin subsequently using a similar lie after he steals the money order (or so the viewer is invited to believe). Rather than offering a temporary escape from the harshness of reality, the comedy acts as a central component in the critique of society (a similar process is at work in *Xala*).

Equally little remarked upon has been Sembene's thoughtful use of music and the soundtrack. Although his films do not disrupt the connection between image and soundtrack in the often highly experimental manner of Med Hondo or Djibril Diop Mambety, he has consistently used the soundtrack in extremely interesting ways. In *Black Girl*, he makes a virtue of the constraint of having to work in French (as the film was funded by the French authorities). The maid, Diouana, can barely speak French but Sembene uses the voice of Toto Bissainthe, an actress from the French Caribbean, to deliver the interior monologues that accompany her melodramatic plunge into despair. This technique plays a similar role to the voiceovers in his first two films, giving the film a strangely poetic quality. She may be poor and uneducated, but Diouana's thoughts are complex and deeply human: she is shown to enjoy an interior life that her French employers simply cannot imagine.

Sembene also uses different musical styles in a contrapuntal fashion in order to emphasise underlying thematic oppositions in his work. In *Borom Sarret*, the sound of the *xalam* (a three-stringed guitar) accompanies the cart driver as he makes his way through the poorer districts of the city but this is replaced by the strains of Mozart as he makes his way to the middle-class *Plateau*, where carts such as his are banned. As his fear grows, the sound of Mozart is drowned out by the extra-diegetic pounding of tam-tams followed by the diegetic piercing shriek of the policeman's whistle. In *Xala*, the lilting sound of the Afro-Caribbean music played at the society wedding is pitted against the sparse sound of the *xalam*, played by one of the beggars who are constantly harassed by the police on behalf of their bourgeois masters. The *xalam* is accompanied by a harsh, guttural voice, singing a political allegory in Wolof, denouncing the bourgeoisie. In this musical duel, the traditional *xalam* is victorious, and is presented as the cultural expression of the masses while Afro-Cuban music is aligned with an urban, Westernised elite.[9]

The most fascinating use of music in Sembene's work is to be found in *Ceddo*. Most sequences in the film are accompanied by the Afro-jazz of Manu Dibango, while the slave sequences feature the gospel music of The Godspells. The wilfully ahistorical function of the music contributes to the elasticity both of the film's timeframe and also of its geographical location, through the evocation of the African diaspora. As Rosen argues, the spectator is constantly invited to link the present to the film's depiction of the past (1991: 159–62), and the music, which is both familiar and unsettlingly 'different', plays a key role in this exploration of historical and cultural (dis)connection. At one point, the phrasing of the main guitar line in Dibango's score picks up on the diegetic sound of a *xalam*, played by Fara Tine, the griot, who accompanies the *ceddo* warrior. As will be shown below in a more detailed discussion of *Ceddo*, this invites the spectator to make connections that span different eras and cultures, directly bringing the past into the present.

Another recurring feature of Sembene's films has been the exploration of the hidden meanings of specific objects (the money order in *Mandabi*, the briefcases in *Xala*, the Qur'an in *Ceddo*), often through focusing on a series of rituals whether these are 'traditional' (the Diolas' debates with their gods in *Emitaï*), 'modern' (the rituals of the Chamber of Commerce in *Xala*) or simply invented by Sembene himself (the spitting 'ceremony' at the end of *Xala*). This focus on ritual can be interpreted as a visual struggle between competing forces within society and, as such, they constitute yet another feature of Sembene's focus on the interaction of groups rather than individuals.[10] None the less, this focus on groups is not always undertaken at the expense of individual character development. Sembene remains conscious of the claims of individual psychology and desires (see, for example, the 'failings' – vanity, stubbornness – of Pierre Henri Thioune, the hero of *Guelwaar*). Sembene's heroic main characters 'make history' but only within the limits of their environment and their own personalities.

Above all, his films often act as a crucible in which new rituals of resistance are forged and previous orthodoxies are challenged. This process is perhaps seen most clearly in *Ceddo* (which is also, arguably, the most 'artistically' successful of his films). As was mentioned above, it is a historical film that deliberately telescopes events from the seventeenth to the nineteenth century in West African history into the life of an unspecified Wolof kingdom. The film presents the struggle for power between different social groups and it represents this struggle as a battle between opposing discourses and rituals. At the beginning of the film, it is the rites and ceremonies of the traditional monarchy that occupy centre stage, and many of the opening scenes are shot from the point of view of the *ceddo*, whom Sembene casts as the 'common people' (which is a rather dubious claim historically), standing before the king.[11] Within the shot, the king and his entourage occupy the centre of the screen, but the monarchy's dominant position is threatened on several fronts. Some of the *ceddo*, who have become wary of the steadily growing influence of Islam on the monarchy, have taken the king's daughter Princess Dior hostage. Marginalised and excluded by their adherence to their values and their religion, the *ceddo* see no alternative but to go into open revolt.

The main threat to the monarchy, however, comes from the representatives of Islam. The *imam*'s challenge to the monarchy is represented visually as he progressively moves closer to the source of power that is the monarch's throne, until eventually the king dies, off camera, and the *imam* takes his place at the centre of the screen. Launching a *jihad*, the *imam* forces the *ceddo* into submission, murdering those who refuse to convert to Islam. This *coup d'état* marks the end of the entire *ceddo* way of life: the *imam* has the 'pagan' fetishes destroyed and, in a long and beautifully crafted sequence, the *ceddo* are given Muslim names and have their heads shaved. Islam takes over the state, and the change in regime is marked even in the physical appearance of the people.

Another set of rituals exists outside the site of the village. Within this space, the values of the *ceddo* reign supreme, but they finally appear to have been overthrown when the *imam*'s soldiers kill the brave *ceddo* warrior. Despite this defeat, the values of the *ceddo* are not dead: as was shown earlier in the discussion of the soundtrack, the film's innovative use of music indicates that elements of *ceddo* culture have survived down the centuries. More importantly, the Princess rallies to their cause, won over by the pride and honour of her *ceddo* captor. The *ceddo*, who have increasingly been pushed to the margins of society, are shown in the film's final scene – in which the Princess shoots and kills the *imam* – to remain a force within Senegalese society, and their values will not be so easily excluded by Islam. For Serge Daney (1979), the power of Sembene's film is that he seeks to imagine that which was lost to Africa by the arrival of Islam and Europe and, in so doing, he gives voice to an oral culture often denied the very status of culture.

As has become clear from this analysis of the exploration of rituals in Sembene's work, his narratives are often concerned with the conflict between opposing social forces, and, as one might expect, his sympathies lie with those who resist the power of their oppressors. At times, resistance is embodied by an entire group, while at others it falls on specific individuals to carry out 'representative' acts of rebellion. As was argued above, the schematic opposition between individual and group is one that is difficult to maintain in Sembene's work, for his films always insist on the individual's position within the larger social group. In *Emitaï*, it is Djiméko, the chief, who leads the villagers' resistance but it is subsequently the women as a group who continue this revolt; in *Guelwaar*, Pierre Henri Thioune's speech at the aid rally is a heroic act of defiance on the part of an individual but his lead is taken up by young people in the Catholic community when they destroy the latest delivery of aid. Conversely, in *Ceddo*, it is the actions of the collective that inspire an individual act of revolt: the Princess's actions in killing the *imam*, far from being an isolated act, must be seen symbolically in light of the destitution of an entire people.

The issue of resistance is often closely intertwined with that of gender. In interviews, Sembene has often spoken about his belief that post-independence Africa has been failed by men, and that women must thus play a leading role in any transformation of African societies (although it is possible to critique Sembene's position as predicated on the need for women to compensate for the failures of men rather than claiming freedoms that should rightfully be theirs). Sembene's films abound with strong female characters – Rama (*Xala*), Princess Dior (*Ceddo*), Collé (*Moolaadé*) – and he has done more than most directors (male or female) both to imagine new social roles for his female characters and to challenge male dominance. For Philip Rosen, Sembene's films consistently underline the necessity of 'rethinking the sociocultural place of African women' (1991: 162). This is most evident in *Ceddo* where Sembene imagines an alternative version of the past in which the survival of indigenous, animist culture is predicated on the emancipation of women, embodied in the figure of the Princess. However, Sembene's portrayal of the power relations between the sexes does not shy away from the complexity of these issues. *Xala* and *Moolaadé* both provide fascinating explorations of the tensions and rivalries that exist between women themselves and particularly between co-wives in polygamous marriages, and they also illustrate the changing dynamics of male–female relationships. In *Moolaadé*, Colle's husband is at first coerced by the forces of village authority (both men and women) to discipline his wife, leading him to whip her in public: however, by the close of the film, he can openly admit that it is her very independence of mind that draws him to her.

Although the spectator is consistently aligned with those who engage in acts of heroism and resistance in Sembene's work, his films are very frank about the suffering undergone by those who resist. In *Emitaï* and *Camp de Thiaroye*, resistance is ultimately met with violent suppression; in *Xala*, the film concludes with the beggars carrying out their punishment of the corrupt El Hadji but the police are none the less waiting outside; in *Guelwaar*, we witness the family of Pierre Henri Thioune attempting to come to terms with his violent death at the hands of hidden forces of power. This is not simply a process of glorying in the 'martyrdom' of his heroes or heroines for there is also a noticeable and intriguing lack of narrative resolution about the films of this ideologically committed filmmaker: this is particularly evident in those films that end with a freeze frame (*Xala*, *Ceddo*) or even a blank screen (*Emitaï*). Equally, his film *Moolaadé*, which concludes with the women's triumph in the struggle to bring an end to female genital mutilation, leaves the spectator with far more questions than answers when it provocatively cuts from the ostrich egg atop the village mosque to a television aerial on a rooftop: what change will television and its 'modernity' really bring? Effectively, Sembene often uses the conclusion of his films not to provide a sense of narrative closure but rather to suggest that the film itself is only the beginning of a process of reflection that should continue long after the film has ended, and it is this process that will be examined in the final section of this chapter.

Resistance and representation

In the immediate post-independence period of the 1960s and 1970s, many African filmmakers, and Sembene in particular, were classified as exponents of 'Third Cinema'. Definitions as to its precise meaning often differed quite significantly from one critic to another but there was a general consensus that 'Third Cinema' was different in style and content both from the dominant Hollywood cinema and from (mainly European) *auteur* cinema. For the influential Ethiopian critic Teshome Gabriel, and for many others following after him, this meant that Third Cinema was an inherently (Fanonian) revolutionary artistic practice (1982; 1989; see Chapter 3 on Med Hondo for a discussion of the influence of Fanon's ideas on his work). By contrast Paul Willemen plays down the politically radical nature of Third Cinema, and instead emphasises its capacity to represent the complexity of postcolonial societies. He sees in this form of filmmaking a flexible and constantly evolving attempt 'to speak a socially pertinent discourse' of the type excluded from Hollywood and *auteur* cinema (1989: 10). For Willemen, Sembene is an emblematic Third Cinema practitioner because his films acknowledge the 'many-layeredness' of African culture, and 'exemplify a way of inhabiting [this] culture which is neither myopically nationalist nor evasively cosmopolitan' (1989: 4). Willemen's assertion that Sembene avoids both the 'simplistic' binary oppositions of nationalism and the 'evasive' detachment often associated with the postcolonial intellectual is pertinent for a number of reasons: firstly because Sembene is often accused by his critics of falling into the 'trap' of using binary oppositions; and, secondly, because the antagonism between nationalism and cosmopolitanism has been at the heart of debates about African cinema and postcolonial studies, more widely. In effect, Willemen's ideas highlight the complex relationship between 'resistance' and 'representation' in relation to postcolonial filmmaking.

In the Third Cinema 'heyday' of the 1970s, 'resistance' was undoubtedly the privileged term in this relationship, as politically committed critics sought to define the development of an oppositional discourse. However, after the 'post-structuralist turn' of the 1980s, many critics began to focus on the complex and ambiguous nature of 'representation' rather than the politics of the work of art. A similar process occurred in the domain of postcolonial studies, which, as Ella Shohat comments (1992), largely retreated from the political critiques that marked its beginnings in the earlier field of 'Third-World literature' (although postcolonial studies never abandoned them completely, and Robert Young's recent work (2001) has taken political stances from an eminently post-structuralist position). In its place, there has developed a more 'textualist', poststructuralist critique – associated most closely with the work of Homi K. Bhabha – that borrows from the work of Derrida and Lacan, and focuses on the fundamental slipperiness of language and the 'mediating' role it plays in literary representation. According to this argument, the postcolonial author (or filmmaker) can never genuinely speak on behalf of a community or a nation because of the impossibility of 'accurate' representation.

In this context, realist, political art has increasingly become associated for many postcolonial critics with the demands of the era of decolonisation when artists mobilised binary oppositions between coloniser and colonised. It is argued that, in the post-independence era, such binaries have come to appear ever more arbitrary, leading artists to explore non-realist forms in which the concept of political representation is highly problematic. Conversely, over the past few years, a growing number of critics have begun to criticise the development of what is seen as an unquestioning poststructuralist orthodoxy in postcolonial studies. In particular, they have highlighted the way in which key post-structuralist terms such as 'hybridity', 'in-between', 'ambivalence' have become central to the postcolonial studies debate: *The Empire Writes Back*, by Ashcroft, Griffths and Tiffin (1989), is often considered to have 'institutionalised' this approach. In casting postcolonial work with a nationalist or socialist agenda as an outmoded form whose time has passed, certain poststructuralist critics have effectively promoted the work of authors whose preoccupations match their own. For the Marxist critic Benita Parry, this constitutes a process of exclusion, deliberately omitting the work of politically committed authors, leading her to conclude that: 'These variations suggest that, instead of attempting to compile a canon of Postcolonial Literature, we need to think about postcolonial literatures as a web of different strands, not all of which are woven out of "postmodern" materials' (2002: 72). Even John McLeod, a critic far more sympathetic to post-structuralist approaches, regrets the tendency towards excessive generalisation in Bhabha's work. In particular, McLeod is critical of the 'totalising representations of the "post-colonial perspective" ' in certain of Bhabha's essays, which lead him to align postcolonial studies exclusively with a post-structuralist position (2000: 222; Bhabha 1994: 173). What space, McLeod goes on to argue, does this leave within the field of postcolonial studies for a nationalist writer such as the Kenyan author Ngugi wa Thiong'o? Or, for that matter, for a Marxist such as Sembene?

Graham Huggan views the co-existence of competing materialist/Marxist and post-structuralist versions of postcolonial studies 'less as a sign of methodological incoherence than as further evidence of the field's unresolved attempt to reconcile political activism and cultural critique' (2001: 261). Postcolonial studies as a field of research often groups texts together on the basis of a shared historical-political context but does this mean that the 'text' is deemed to give direct access to this historical-political reality? Recent interventions within postcolonial studies have attempted to bridge the seeming divide between these positions. In particular, Nicholas Harrison provides a finely balanced negotiation of the competing claims of 'text' and 'context'. For Harrison, some materialists give far too little weight to the 'lit-erariness' of a text in their rush to pass political 'judgement' on it, while some post-structuralist critics give far too little weight to the context in which a text is produced and received.

In light of these ideas, what space should the critic of African cinema give respectively to the political and artistic dimensions of Sembene's cinema? Left-wing critics have generally lauded Sembene's films for their political stance, while other critics (from a wide range of positions) have accused him of simplistic, Manichean arguments, of 'artistic Stalinism', of disrespect for indigenous African cultures. The charge of Manicheanism, of engaging in binary oppositions, is a charge consistently laid at the door of 'political' artists by many post-structuralist critics. However, by what criteria are binary oppositions inherently 'wrong'? As Timothy Brennan has remarked in relation to the writings of Amilcar Cabral, the independence leader of Guinea-Bissau:

> [T]he dialectic of colonizer and colonized was simply not supposed to represent either a sociological explanation or a nuanced cultural model [for Cabral]. It was itself a focus – that is, a careful exclusion. He was not lumping difference together, nor was he unaware of multiple communities with their disparate interests. He did not emphasize the disparate because it would not then, in that project, have led to more than the impossibility of doing. (1997: 3)

Similarly, if Sembene uses Manichean oppositions at times, it is not because he is unaware of other positions, it is because he is attempting to mobilise people behind his own vision of Africa's past, present and future. His representations of the French colonial powers (*Emitaï, Camp de Thiaroye*) are the most caricatured in his entire *oeuvre* but, even in these cases, he nevertheless presents the 'opposing' camp of the colonised in a comparatively complex fashion, highlighting internal conflicts based on gender (*Emitaï*) and loyalty to the colonial powers (*Camp de Thiaroye*). Sembene's work equally rejects any simplistic opposition between a 'repressive' tradition and a 'progressive' socialist modernity. Instead, he presents socialism as a response to the needs of African societies, a socialism that emerges from the customs and practices of communal African life. In so doing, he counters both 'traditionalist' visions of an unchanging rural Africa and certain 'modernist' visions of the continent, which speak of the need for change, but which in reality call for a passive acceptance of the demands of the global capitalist economy. Sembene's work thus constitutes a fascinating example of a cinema that engages in the strategic use of binaries, but which is none the less consistently aware of the limits of fixed notions of identity and culture.

Cinema is for Sembene a site of public debate, and he conceives of the filmmaker as the closest figure to the griot, the guardian of the oral tradition in most West African societies, in that his or her work combines music, gesture and storytelling, in a communal gathering. Sembene has argued that cinema permits him to reach a much wider audience than his literature, and also serves as a sort of 'evening school', dedicated to the cultural and political education of his people. Indeed, when Sembene began making films, he did not wait for the masses to come to him, but chose instead to tour his films around rural areas of Senegal (and also into other African countries), organising debates after the screenings. His films are in fact structurally designed to inspire debate: using a variety of techniques, both 'African' and 'Western', Sembene taps into the capacity for film to act as a space in which social, cultural and political issues can be addressed, in a similar fashion to the role of African popular theatre as described by Karin Barber (1997: vii–xix). Far from the passive cinema spectator imagined in certain strands of film theory, Sembene's ideal audience is one that reflects and (in the best case scenario acts) upon the questions aired by his work. As Rosen convincingly argues: 'Ultimately then, [in Sembene's films] the spectator is . . . conceived as a historical agent, an agent asked to reflect on options for comprehending the history of Africa from his or her own historicized temporality' (1991: 168). The following pages will consider the different means by which Sembene's work engages with the audience, focusing on *Xala* and *Moolaadé*, each of which might be deemed in its own particular way to contain a political 'message'.

Sembene has declared in relation to his filmmaking practice: 'It is a question of allowing the people to summon up their own history, to identify themselves with it. People must listen to what is in the film, and they must talk about it' (Downing 1987: 46). In *Xala*, the audience is invited to laugh at the arrogance and stupidity of the bourgeoisie, and is aligned with the collective of beggars, peasants and student radicals who constitute an opposing and dissenting force.[12] Although this alignment of the spectator is primarily carried out through the narrative drama and the use of specific audio and visual devices, there is also an undeniably 'proselytising' dimension to Sembene's cinematic work. Virtually all of his films feature at least one sequence in which the central themes are 'verbalised' by one of the main characters: in *Xala*, it is for the most part Rama, the radical young student, who voices the cultural and political critique of the bourgeoisie (although El Hadji himself echoes this critique in the sequence where he is removed from the Chamber of Commerce). Within a dominant Western aesthetic, this practice might be deemed an artistic 'failing' but the precise nature of such sequences appears very different if they are assessed within the framework of the artistic practices of West African popular culture. As was argued in the introduction to this volume, African cinema has not worked in a strictly naturalistic register, and dialogue often enjoys a performative and declarative dimension. Anyone who has attended a film screening in West Africa can testify that cinema is experienced as a very public phenomenon in which the characters' words are often subject to a lively and vociferous debate: for example, within the narrative structure of *Xala*, Rama's denunciation of the bourgeoisie is designed to raise cries of approval from a local audience, for the middle class are represented as selfish and wholly unsympathetic. Even more so than in *Xala*, Sembene's film *Moolaadé* deploys a number of overtly didactic sequences in order to reinforce the film's position on excision: early in the film, in a scene that might have been lifted straight from a public health film, Collé invites the young girls to explain their decision to refuse excision. More dramatic in its construction is the film's extremely powerful climax in which Collé confronts both the male elders and the 'Salindana': the joyous nature of her defiance (as she is lauded by the female griot) is again designed to bring shouts of approval from a local audience. Rather than acting as unwelcome intrusions, such sequences fire the narrative along, creating moments of dramatic tension and inviting the African spectator to learn a specific moral lesson (an approach that is a powerful legacy of the oral tradition). Despite their didacticism, these sequences are thus generally woven into the fabric of the narrative itself. In light of this analysis, the most pertinent critical issue would appear to be to gauge how well Sembene achieves his aim in such sequences – for he does not always pull off these sequences as well as he might wish – rather than decrying the 'intrusion' of direct political comment: effectively, the critic must examine how well the director weds this approach to the drama.

This link between the dramatic and the political is central to an understanding of Sembene's approach, for although his films are primarily structured around ideological or social conflicts, his film style cannot be reduced to any one technique or type of narrative structure. In *Xala*, one can find distilled all of the major stylistic approaches that have been central to Sembene's cinema, each of which might in its own different way be termed 'realist'. It begins with the eminently political Brechtian symbolism of the ten-minute opening sequence in which the African businessmen chase the French from the Chamber of Commerce: here we are shown the 'reality' of independence (as Sembene sees it), namely the passing of power from a white to a black elite with the former colonial powers retreating to the background. However, he also provides the primarily naturalistic portrait of the mother–daughter relationship between Adja Awa Astou and Rama, which he uses partly to build a sense of character development and of the dynamics of their relationship (as he does in the sequence between the first two wives at the wedding reception) but also to reflect the differences between different 'types' or generations of women. Alongside such character development Sembene also reverts to 'types' or to 'stock' characters from tradition at various points in the narrative: Oumi N'Doye is the 'pushy' wife; the farmer who has his money stolen is the archetypal peasant who uses exaggerated gestures and speaks in the very harsh guttural Wolof of the countryside; the bourgeois guests at the wedding reception are without exception caricatures of the new post-independence elite, and they are held up for ridicule before a knowing, urban audience. In this way, the film sets up an opposition between different groups, in particular the beggars (and their companions) and the bourgeoisie who are locked in a social struggle, which is represented in part through a visual struggle, with the beggars originally dismissed to the outskirts of the city but eventually returning and occupying 'centre stage' in El Hadji's own home (see Mulvey 1993).

As Mbye Cham argues (1982), Sembene also uses elements of the oral 'trickster' narrative in which the protagonist is set a range of tasks, which he or she sets out to achieve using deceit and lies. However, in this modern version, the 'trickster' El Hadji Abdou Kader Beye is himself the victim of a number of trickster characters: his second wife; the 'fake' *marabouts*; his business 'friends'. In fact, Sembene presents a topsy-turvy world in which deceit and lies usually triumph (as is the case in his other great 'trickster' narrative *Mandabi*), perhaps most comically when the pickpocket (who steals from the peasant) is transformed into the respectable businessman, Monsieur Thieli, and is elected to the Chamber of Commerce as El Hadji's replacement just because he has bought a dapper suit (and cowboy hat to match): never perhaps has the notion that property is theft been illustrated in such a comic and laconic fashion. This use of comedy to convey a classic Marxist 'message' about capitalism is emblematic of Sembene's approach in much of this darkly comic film. For example, the bawdy comedy of the *Badiène* (the matchmaker) discussing El Hadji's 'manhood', belittling him as 'neither fish nor fowl', is intricately woven into the film's political argument about the impotent bourgeoisie.

A similarly diverse but none the less slightly different approach can be witnessed in *Moolaadé*, a film that is primarily addressed to a rural audience:

many (but by no means all) urban dwellers in West Africa oppose the practice of female genital mutilation. Sembene's film thus aims to win over those in rural communities where this practice is most common. Towards this end, he ensures that the critique of excision emerges from within the community itself: the young girls' decision to seek refuge with Collé brings into play the tradition of 'Moolaadé' (the right of asylum), which must then be balanced against the tradition of the 'Salindana' (excision). *Moolaadé* sets in train competing rituals, which represent values or beliefs between which the audience must choose, those of the 'Moolaadé' or those of the 'Salindana'. The repeated shots of the simple red and yellow rope hung low across the doorway, which constitutes the Moolaadé, deploy a range of narrative techniques: some involve gentle, observational comedy (the toddlers struggling to step over it, the chickens passing freely back and forth) while on other occasions it takes on a hugely symbolic importance (as is witnessed in the confrontations between Collé and the women of the Salindana). Within the space protected by the Moolaadé, we are given a glimpse of an embryonic 'Women's Republic' in which women stand shoulder-to-shoulder and where there is a sense of joy and solidarity. This is particularly evident in the aftermath of the first confrontation with the 'Salindana' when the women break into song and dance around the courtyard. However, this celebration is interrupted by the arrival of the eldest son: men are thus associated with dominance and power from which women struggle to escape. Far from dealing solely in symbolic, binary oppositions (Men v. Women, Moolaadé v. Salindana), the film also investigates conflicts within groups. Indeed, one of the most remarkable features of the film is the complexity of its 'realistic' representation of the hierarchies at work within polygamous marriages. (Sembene chooses not to include a critique of polygamy within his film: as his target audience is largely polygamous, he opts for a pragmatic approach that will not alienate those whom he seeks to convince.) Sembene also mobilises narrative devices that are present in his earlier films: Collé's act of bravery in refusing to yield as she is publicly whipped by her husband is one of the most powerful scenes of resistance in Sembene's entire *oeuvre*; equally, he is not averse to the deft (populist) manipulation of his audience's emotions, as is witnessed by the death of the little girl and her mother's subsequent lament. However, far from playing solely on the pain and tragedy associated with his subject matter, Sembene once more deploys comedy as one of his most effective narrative devices: the comedy of Mercenaire's endless attempts to bed the local women; Collé's sharp and biting tongue, which cuts the menfolk down to size; and her husband's final (proverbial) shot in the direction of his domineering brother that 'It takes more than a pair of balls to make a man' (the original Bambara saying refers to 'a pair of trousers').

These examples from Sembene's work illustrate that political filmmaking (and criticism) is not necessarily the reductive process (either artistically or politically) described by certain critics. His work may at times involve the use of binary oppositions but this does not necessarily entail a simplistic or dismissive approach to social or cultural difference. Sembene's cinema seeks to promote political dialogue in the broadest sense of that term but he is well aware of the limits of cinema's power to intervene on such matters. For the vast majority of African film viewers, cinema is primarily a form of entertainment, and Sembene's consistent efforts to bring his films to different African communities is a recognition of the need to foster political debate through an activist approach to cinema. However, in the absence of a wider change in the role of cinema and in society more generally, such efforts might seem chimeric, and his advancing years understandably caused him to cut back on such trips late in his life. Cinema has a limited capacity to develop and foster political discourse, and the rapid decline in cinemagoing over recent years in many parts of Africa has merely served to reinforce this. Moreover, as will be seen in later chapters, many younger African directors, such as Jean-Pierre Bekolo (see Chapter 9) have retreated from such activism. Consequently, in analysing the 'success' of Sembene's films in creating a public dialogue, it is necessary to define carefully what we mean by this. Nicholas Harrison has convincingly argued that the desire on the part of critics to measure the 'political effectiveness' (2003: 57) of works of fiction has often led to abstract and rather excessive judgements regarding their political impact. In assessing the 'politics' of a film, it is necessary to focus on the relationship between the 'text', the political discourse with which it engages and the expectations of its audience, rather than somehow attempting to 'measure' its 'impact' on the wider world, or parsing the actions or pronouncements of artists for clues to their political standpoint. At the heart of this debate lies the relationship between film and audience: Sembene recognises the agency at work in the audience's reception of a film, and critics of African cinema and film theorists more generally would do well to pay more heed to this process. In so doing, there must come a realisation that the 'political' film should be assessed as a work of art in its own right and not simply as the artistic appendage to a given political struggle. Although an eminently 'political' director, Sembene has chosen to work within the artistic field. Consequently, identifying the 'politics' of his work, whether from a supportive or a negative critical stance, can only ever be the start – and not the end – of the critical process.

Notes

1 Perhaps owing to his pioneering status, Sembene has been the subject of far greater critical attention than other African directors (book-length studies of his work include: Pfaff 1984; Gadjigo 1993; Petty 1996, Niang 1996; Murphy 2000a).

2 See Murphy (2000a) for analysis of his cinematic and literary output. Sembene has made film adaptations of two of his texts (*Black Girl, Xala*) and has also transformed several of his films into novels or short stories (*Niaye, Taaw, Guelwaar*).

3 Sembene has stressed the technical nature of his training in Moscow, perhaps as a preventive strike against critics who would search for Donskoi's influence upon his work.

4 Guèye was 'discovered' by Sembene working as a tailor; he went on to have an illustrious acting career, playing a number of major roles: the President of the Chamber of Commerce in *Xala*, the King in *Ceddo*; as well as the role of the mayor in Mambety's *Hyenas*.

5 Much of the time between 1976 and 1988 appears to have been spent trying to find the finance to make his long-cherished project on the West African resistance leader Samory Touré who fought an 18-year war against both French and British colonial forces in West Africa in the late nineteenth century.

6 For the best account of the incidents at Thiaroye see Echenberg (1978).

7 Of particular offence were the scenes featuring the white chief of police, which were read as a transparent attack on then Minister for the Interior, Jean Collin, a Frenchman who had taken Senegalese citizenship after independence: all of the scenes featuring the Collin figure were cut.

8 Sembene also makes cameo appearances in a number of his other films: in *Black Girl*, he plays a teacher who frowns upon the Frenchman's intrusion on the family's grief; in *Mandabi*, he plays a comic role as a public scribe who rows with Ibrahima Dieng; and he plays one of the *ceddo* in *Ceddo*.

9 See Gugler (2003: 135) for a translation of the lyrics to this song. The problematic aspects of the opposition between these two musical styles are discussed in Murphy (2007).

10 See Rosen (1991) for a discussion of the editing techniques and narrative structures that reinforce this focus on social groups. For more in-depth analysis of the competing rituals in *Mandabi*, *Xala* and *Emitaï* see Murphy (2000a).

11 For a discussion of Sembene's interpretation of Senegalese history in the film see Buuba Babacar Diop (1984) and Murphy (2000a: 172–8).

12 See Gugler and Diop (1998) and Murphy (2000c) for detailed analyses of the differences between the film and the novel, which underline the diverse nature of his filmmaking practice.

Filmography

Borom Sarret (1962)
Niaye (1964)
La Noire de (*Black Girl*) (1966)
Mandabi (*The Money Order*) (1968)
Taaw (1970)
Emitaï (1971)
Xala (1974)
Ceddo (1976)
Camp de Thiaroye (1988)
Guelwaar (1992)
Faat Kiné (2000)
Moolaadé (2004)

Chapter 3

Med Hondo

Introduction

Although the Mauritanian director Med Hondo is acknowledged as one of the great postcolonial chroniclers of the lives of the unrecognised and unrepresented masses in the various waves of the African diaspora, his own life and its relevance for his filmmaking is less acknowledged. While an overemphasis on, or overinterpretation of, biographical aspects in relation to a filmmaker's output is not necessarily either desirable or useful, elements of Med Hondo's life resonate so strongly with very many of the issues raised in his films that it is worth examining them in a little detail. Abid Mohamed Medoun Hondo was born in 1936, in Ain Oul Beri Mathar, in the Atar region of Mauritania. Part of the French Empire at that time, Mauritania has nevertheless had a remarkably tenuous, almost nebulous, existence. Despite being colonised, it was only formally created as a territory in 1904, but then not fully accepted into the French West African Empire until 1933. As an unprofitable colony it was given independence in 1960, but many countries refused to recognise it as a sovereign nation, rendering its status uncertain; in particular, Morocco withheld recognition for a decade. Mauritania has borders with five other countries, but only the one formed by the Senegal river has any substance, the others being part of the geographical imagination of empire. A sense of the porousness of borders, or their irrelevance, was part of Hondo's formative experiences, as he commented, 'My grandmother always reminded me that we had family in Mali, in Morocco, in the Sahara, in Algeria, in Senegal . . . I had the strange feeling, thanks to my grandmother's stories, of being born in five or six different countries at the same time' (Signaté 1994: 10). In addition, Hondo said of his family, 'We were nomads in our souls' (Signaté 1994: 10) and the migrant, diasporic spirit – as well as the frequently painful realities of life in the diaspora – is repeatedly reflected in Hondo's films.

The uncertainty of territorial boundaries is also reflected ethnically within the country. The major ethnic groups are the indigenous black Africans (Peul, Wolof, Toucouleur) comprising approximately 25 per cent of the population, and the Moors, Arab-Berber people who make up the rest. While this division might appear reasonably solid, the Moorish majority are internally divided into 'white' or Bidan, and 'black' or Harattin, where the significant epidermal distinction implied by the nomenclature does not in fact exist. This seeming substantial corporeal division is in reality purely one of social class and hierarchy: unsurprisingly, the 'white' Moors constitute the superior group, while the 'black' Harattin, as freed slaves or the descendants of slaves, are regarded as their social inferiors.

Hondo was born into a Harattin family where slavery, rather than some relic of the past, continued to be a daily reality, as, indeed, it did in much of the country, Mauritania being peculiarly resistant to abolishing the practice, even at the end of the twentieth century. Hondo's maternal grandfather was a slave – calling into question the idea that the Harattin were freed slaves or their descendants, rather than actual ones – and he recalls how much it shocked and pained him to see his grandfather forced to prostrate himself before his (black) masters. At the same time, his father worked as a 'boy' for the French, but of these two conditions of subservience it was the situation of his grandfather that profoundly affected Hondo, and he swore to himself as a child that he would not allow himself to be reduced to a comparable state. Nevertheless, structural subservience did not always involve complete submission, and part of Hondo's upbringing consisted of family stories telling of rebellious slaves who killed their masters and escaped to Senegal. Similar rebelliousness against those who would claim superiority was clearly part of Hondo's character from an early age, as he recalls pelting the 'noble' Bidan children with stones despite being severely punished for an action which his grandfather considered sacrilegious.

Above all, the significant, revelatory discovery in Hondo's childhood experiences was of the existence of social inequality, injustice and oppression, as well as the possibility, even the necessity, of opposing them, something which every one of his films does so powerfully. In addition, there was the fact that social boundaries might be grounded in ideological distinctions of hierarchy rather than the more substantial 'black' and 'white' ones of race (which is, nevertheless, profoundly ideological). Interestingly, despite his being born into colonialism and moving to France at a relatively early age – having taken 'my first step as a migrant' by going to hotel school in Morocco – racism, as an expression of social inequality injustice and oppression, seems not to have been an immediate problem for Hondo. His comment on the situation at the end of the 1950s was, 'Racism grew as the numbers of Africans arriving in France grew' (Signaté 1994: 15) – which ironically risks echoing the racist argument that prejudice is caused by the African presence, even though that is clearly not what Hondo believes. This kind of perception may, however, be attributable to the fact that, as Hondo recognises, his political consciousness was not highly developed – or even developed at all – at this point in his life. Certainly, it was an analysis whose oversimplifications would not satisfy him for long.

Hondo's first foray into cultural production was in the theatre, rather than cinema, once he had reached his self-declared goal as migrant and moved from Marseilles to Paris. His involvement was the result of a particular combination of positive and negative motivations. The positive was simply his love of the theatre and his desire to use it as a means of exploring important ideas and communicating them to a sizeable audience. The negative was his growing awareness of a troubling absence – that of black people, whether as performers, as directors, as authors of works to be performed; or simply as people whose lives were worth representing on stage. As would-be performer, Hondo soon found that his ambitions to play roles other than those stereotypically allotted to black people simply made no sense to white casting directors. This encounter with the structural racism of the theatrical establishment was profoundly disillusioning. Nevertheless, he founded his own theatre company, the symbolically named Griot-Shango, and his first production as director was a play by the Congolese writer Guy Menga. In the end, however, the combination of the frustrations represented by work in the theatre, the lack of interest in plays by or about black people demonstrated by mainstream audiences, the effort required versus the lack of financial rewards, and what Hondo referred to as theatre's 'ephemeral . . . fugitive' nature pushed him towards 'an art form which does leave a mark' (Signaté 1994: 19–20) – the cinema.

Much more than in the theatre, however, where at least he could take drama classes, Hondo is self-taught as a director; indeed, he is one of the great autodidacts of world cinema. Having learnt his craft through observation and analysis while working on other people's films as an actor and director's assistant, rather than through formal study, has meant that Hondo's approach is more than usually distanced from prevailing norms of filmmaking, whether formal or ideological, than is the case even for other postcolonial directors. Despite the necessary differences involved in working in the two areas, however, Hondo retained aspects of theatrical practice in his filmmaking. These range from the relatively slight but nevertheless significant in *Soleil O* to the full-scale in *West Indies*. In the former, there are, for instance, the stagy discussions between the central black character and a white interlocutor, as well as the scenes with the dysfunctional white couple which could easily have come from a contemporary play by Ionesco. In the latter film, the stage, and the staging of history, is everything, as the multi-level narrative unrolls in the shape of, in Hondo's words, 'a musical tragi-comedy', with verisimilitude taking a back seat.

A crucial element in the switch to making films was the fact that, by his own estimation, Hondo's political consciousness had now matured. For some time, he had been reading important black writers – Cheikh Anta Diop from Senegal, Kateb Yacine from Algeria, Frantz Fanon and Aimé Césaire from Martinique – but at first these had given him only 'political ideas', rather than a fully developed political consciousness. Later came the effect of the 'pell-mell' reading of Marx and Lenin, Mao, Nasser and Nkrumah. Whether or not the long process of maturation is responsible, or factors such as his disillusionment with the claims of Western culture and his increasing exposure to that culture's racism, Hondo's first full-length film, *Soleil O* (discussed in detail later in this chapter) burst on to the scene in 1969, both politically and formally radical, lucid and angry, disturbing and challenging. To a greater extent than most other African directors, Hondo has been both outspokenly and consistently radical in his political views: the Hondo of the early years of the 21st century may be battered and bruised from his experiences of four decades as a filmmaker, and disillusioned with so-called left-wing regimes both inside and outside Africa, but he remains committed to a socialist vision of a better future for his continent and, like Fanon, for the wider world.

Building at least in part on the experiences of his formative years, Hondo's approach to the cinema combines a politics of liberation and a politics of representation. The former is grounded in his earlier rejection of oppressive social hierarchies, relationships which strip human beings of their dignity (as Hondo says, 'There is nothing worse for a man than humiliation', Signaté 1994: 72), and extends it to a historically nuanced understanding of the ways in which these systems operated at continental and global levels in the past, and continue to do so in the contemporary world in different forms. A politics of representation in its broadest sense was already, as we have seen, a fundamental aspect of Hondo's cultural practice. If the absence of black people, as well as images of their lived experience, was already a problem in the context of the theatre, it became an even more acute one in the world of filmmaking, precisely because of the nature of the globally dominant form, categorised by Hondo as 'Euro-American cinema'.

Although Africans are not present in any meaningful way in mainstream cinema, as in the rest of the media, they are of course present in the shape of negative stereotypes, sometimes centuries old. As Hondo comments:

> This is the most basic reason why I make films. Seeing the image, tainted with racism, that the media offer of Africa, I couldn't help reacting, in my own way and with the means at my disposal, to try to show something else that was closer to the truth.
>
> Open the papers today: as far as Africa is concerned it is nothing but permanent contempt. (Signaté 1994: 75)

The ability of this media-produced 'mépris permanent' to influence the way in which African people see themselves is one of the reasons why the cinema is so politically and culturally important for Hondo, why the forms and the contents, the modes and the machineries of representation matter so acutely:

> Cinema is the mechanism *par excellence* for penetrating the minds of our peoples, influencing their everyday social behaviour, directing them, diverting them from their historic national responsibilities . . . This alienation disseminated through the image is all the more dangerous for being insidious, uncontroversial, 'accepted', seemingly inoffensive and neutral. (Hondo 1977: 20)

Alienation is one of the many areas where the thinking and analysis of Hondo and Fanon, which form the later part of this chapter, echo one another. *Black Skin, White Masks*, for example, was famously conceived as an intervention towards 'the effective disalienation of the black man', while in *Studies in a Dying Colonialism* Fanon talks of the alienation which for centuries made the colonised 'the great absentee of history' (Fanon 1989): the same combination of alienation and historical absence which Hondo rails against.

The films

In terms of his approach to filmmaking, whether stylistic, generic, technical or thematic, Hondo is nothing if not a migrant, a man of the diaspora. Fanon's comment in *Black Skin, White Masks*, 'In this world through which I travel, I am endlessly recreating myself' (Fanon 1986: 229) could certainly apply at least as well to Hondo as to himself; and, if he is not re-creating himself, then he is unquestionably re-creating his cinematic product. Hondo's restless search for the appropriate filmic form for his chosen subject matter has meant that none of his films has been the same as the previous one: black-and-white short documentary (*Balade aux sources*, 1969), followed by black-and-white short fiction (*Roi de corde*, 1969), experimental non-narrative black-and-white feature film (*Soleil O*, 1969) followed by colour film with more continuist narrative (*Les Bicots-nègres, vos voisins*, 1973); radical political documentary (*Nous aurons toute la mort pour dormir*, 1977), followed by historical musical (*West Indies, ou les nègres marrons de la liberté*, 1979); African historical epic (*Sarraounia*, 1987), followed by thriller set in Europe (*Lumière noire*, 1994); racist politics of the far right in contemporary France (*Watani: un monde sans mal*, 1998), followed by unearthing the memories of the war of liberation in Algeria (*Fatima, l'Algérienne de Dakar*, 2004).

One of Hondo's guiding principles is the need to avoid 'mimétisme' or mimicry of the West. Completely lacking any of those subversive qualities which Homi Bhabha's postcolonial reading famously attributes to it (Bhabha 1994), mimicry theoretically, politically and artistically bedevils Africans in the contemporary world. This holds good for almost any area of life, but, given his comments about the powerful effects of cinema, is especially relevant to the world of film in general, and to his own practice of filmmaking in particular. Both the form and the content of mainstream films – Hollywood above all – may have nothing to offer, but more is required than simple dismissal:

> It would be dangerous (and impossible) to reject this cinema as simply alien – the damage is done. We must get to know it, the better to analyse it and to understand that this cinema has never really considered the African and Arab peoples. (Hondo 1977: 20)

Although in Hondo's eyes the avoidance of mimicry is a general concern for postcolonial filmmakers, it does have a particular personal significance, since many critics – understandably, predictably no doubt – wanted to read *Soleil O* as a straightforward example of work deeply indebted to European avant-garde and auteurist approaches, whereas for Hondo it was the African tradition of digressive and multi-layered narrative which was the formative influence.

If escaping from the stranglehold of formal, thematic or ideological mimicry of the West at the level of film production is difficult enough, the practical problems in all areas of production, distribution and exhibition constitute potentially insurmountable difficulties for directors such as Hondo. The fact that these difficulties are also frequently produced by the West is the mark of another kind of stranglehold.[1] This has been true throughout his career, with *Sarraounia* offering perhaps the clearest instance – though at the level of distribution and exhibition it is an example not from the notoriously impenetrable circuits within Africa but from the notionally more accessible ones of Europe. Based on the novel of the same name by Abdoulaye Mamani, the film recounts the struggle of Sarraounia, the warrior queen of the Aznar people of modern-day Niger, against the French military incursions, in this case the Voulet-Chanoine expedition, as part of the 'Scramble for Africa' in the closing years of the nineteenth century. It was due to be co-produced with money from the government of Niger, and when, with no warning, they withdrew their funding shortly before the start of filming, the stress this caused Hondo resulted in a heart attack. The project was rescued by Thomas Sankara, subsequently President of Burkina Faso, whose country then provided both funding and locations for the filming, which was eventually successfully concluded. Although Hondo had incurred considerable debts in making the film, he had nevertheless found a distributor apparently willing and able to have the film screened far more widely than he had expected. In the event, however, and with no explanation, the film opened in only a third of the promised cinemas and with virtually no publicity, and therefore with little in the way of audiences. Such response as there was from critics was largely hostile: the film was deemed too political, even propagandist. (Given that the film severely – but justly – criticises the brutality of the invading French, these attacks should probably have come as no surprise: Sembene had already suffered in the same way several times in the past, and would do so again soon with *Camp de Thiaroye*, another exposé of the all-too-easily forgotten murderous side of colonialism.) The resultant lack of income generated by the screenings meant that Hondo was left with his outstanding debts, went bankrupt, had to close down his production company Films Soleil O, and was forced into further debt to enable him to buy back his own films in order to prevent them being sold off at auction. Hondo's verdict on all of this was simply, 'The film was assassinated' (Signaté 1994: 46).

Although this was perhaps a more extreme example, Hondo had already experienced something similar with *Soleil O*, where he was robbed both financially (by the owner of the cinema screening the film who refused to pass on the takings) and in terms of prestige (opposition from various postcolonial African heads of government, unhappy at the way in which they were collectively portrayed in the film, prevented it from winning the main prize at the Carthage Film Festival). Other instances of the kind of obstacles encountered by Hondo include not being allowed to film *Lumière noire* in the Paris airports and their associated hotels because of the politically sensitive nature of the subject matter – declared 'une sale histoire' by one of the bureaucrats responsible for the ban on the filming. 'Dirty' it may be, but it is based on real events – the secret deportation of Africans – and once again, this time despite a more favourable critical reception, the film encountered enormous difficulties at the level of distribution. Hondo's more recent, and also politically sensitive, film *Watani* was forced to carry a warning about its (alleged) level of violence, which in conjunction with its adult rating meant that it would inevitably be seen by a much more restricted audience.

Another possible reason for the resistance to Hondo's films is that he so frequently insists on doing what other filmmakers do not, or will not – for whatever reason – do. Constantly working against the grain of dominant cultural practice – even if it is dominant only within the relatively restricted field of African or postcolonial filmmaking – is almost bound to make him a controversial figure. Thus, for example, making a historical epic in the shape of *Sarraounia* might not appear to be unusual or challenging, but, surprisingly, as Josef Gugler points out, 'The imposition of colonial rule and the colonial experience have elicited little response from African directors' (Gugler 2003: 7). Similarly, one might imagine that discussions of metropolitan racism, such as occur in *Lumière noire*, *Watani* and *Soleil O*, would be almost obligatory for diasporic and postcolonial filmmakers, yet, as Melissa Thackway notes:

> the majority of second wave films are striking for their relative lack of preoccupation with questions of racism and discrimination, even though these remain very real issues in France. Both Carrie Tarr and Christian Bosséno highlight parallel trends in the films made by North African and second-generation *beur* filmmakers in France in the same period, which also tend to explore multiculturalism and integration, rather than racism and exclusion. (Thackway 2003: 130)

The tendency for directors to gravitate towards 'softer' subjects is something which Hondo has also noted: in a recent interview he comments on 'so-called African cinema' which is currently 'drowning in the anecdotal' (Hondo 2002) in contrast to the challenging, and still vitally relevant, subjects tackled by someone like Sembene. There is also a self-perpetuating mechanism at work here: given that the 'softer' films are the ones which are better received in the West, they are also the kind which African directors would then be tempted to make. For Hondo, both the cause and the effects are entirely negative: 'You have to say that a certain European paternalism, ready to go into raptures over the work of black or Arab filmmakers whose films don't create any problems, has, with its rubbishy exoticism, encouraged stagnation and mediocrity' (Signaté 1994: 39).

Although a comment such as 'so-called African cinema' might appear arrogant or dismissive (and there are ways in which Hondo is indeed rejecting a certain contemporary filmic practice), the phrase is also – sadly – simply descriptive. In so far as film production by Africans remains a sporadic, unpredictable process, there still does not exist in Hondo's eyes a sufficiently substantial body of work to merit the title of African cinema: 'There are African filmmakers, but no African cinema. To be able to talk about cinema, you need structures, infrastructures, laboratories, producers, scriptwriters, cinemas, an organised marketplace . . . For the moment, we are at the artisan stage' (Signaté 1994: 27).

One of the challenging and still relevant subjects which have occupied Hondo throughout his filmmaking career is dispossession, in its manifold forms and various histories. The losses he chronicles include that of one's country (under the impact of colonialism); of one's liberty (especially during the period of slavery); of one's history (written out, ignored or denied by the West); of one's culture (ditto); and, in all of these as well as in the context of metropolitan racism, of one's basic dignity as a human being. Although Olivier Barlet has argued that the latest African films display a concern with the human rather than any particular forms of political militancy, for Hondo this latest trend is something to which he has been committed from the very beginning. Comparing *Watani*, then his most recent film, with *Soleil O*, he said, 'My preoccupation remains that of the human being – immigrant or not' (Hondo 2002). At the same time, for him it is emphatically not a question of either/or: concern for, and defence of, the human being requires a sustained and rigorous political commitment on the part of the filmmaker.

This commitment comes at a cost, however, particularly that, as we have seen, of incurring the displeasure of those in authority. Thus while Hondo displays a strong attachment to Mauritania, appropriate for a man of the diaspora, the feeling is not reciprocated – at least at the official level – as the government opposed his being honoured by Tunisian President Ben Ali in 1994, and described him as 'an anti-national element fomenting disunity' (Haroun 2004: 2). Such an attitude comes as no surprise to Hondo, however, for whom, like Fanon, the postcolonial black elite in power in Africa constitutes one of the continent's major, and continuing, problems.

Hondo and Fanon: the dialectics of liberation

Since his death over forty years ago, Frantz Fanon has been widely recognised as a perceptive theorist of culture. More recently, he has become for some, especially in postcolonial studies, an indispensable aid in the analysis of culture. It is much rarer, however, to see him as exercising any constitutive or determining function in the actual processes of cultural production. In that respect, Ngugi wa Thiong'o's comment that much of postcolonial African fiction could be regarded as a series of imaginative footnotes to

Fanon (Ngugi 1993: 66) is remarkable for the (hierarchical) relationship which it establishes between theorist and cultural producer. No one has yet offered a similar evaluation of African filmmaking, but the remainder of this chapter will examine Hondo's early classic *Soleil O*, where the relationship is both more substantial and more reciprocal than anything implied in Ngugi's image of footnotes.

Soleil O, Hondo's first feature-length film, was released at the end of the 'Fanonian' decade of the 1960s. Both the film and its maker are marked by the events of the times and by Fanon's penetrating analyses of them, their histories and their contexts. As Hondo has commented, his (textual) encounter with Fanon was 'a great revelation' (Hondo in Signaté 1994: 18) in a period when he was also reading Aimé Césaire, Cheikh Anta Diop and others, and *Soleil O* is arguably the most Fanonian of African films. This is fitting, given the similarities between these important diasporic intellectuals. Both in their particular ways are representers (in the strong Saidian sense) as well as representatives of the greater African diaspora. Fanon's trajectory was more complex than Hondo's: from the Caribbean to Europe and back; to Europe again; to North Africa; and, as a dying man, to the US. Hondo's was much more straightforward – and in some ways straightforwardly post-colonial – from Africa to France where he went in 1957, typical of so many of those whom he portrays in his films. Both were part of the dream of self betterment or communal betterment which fuels so much of the 'free' migration which characterises the imperially segregated and hierarchised spaces of the capitalist world system. Despite – or perhaps precisely because of – the fact that they spent all of their adult lives in diasporic or exilic circumstances, both Fanon and Hondo were acutely aware of the profoundly negative dimensions of that sort of life, though the aspects they highlight vary. For Hondo, it is the determining historical conditions themselves which are the most pressing problem: 'For, if exile remains as the worst thing, what is essential, in the heart of that worst, is to be conscious of what has to be struggled against. And what is vital for us, here and now, is surely to struggle against capitalism under its different aspects and its multiple powers' (Hondo 1987: 70).

For Fanon, it is, unsurprisingly, the psychological damage resulting from particular historical conditions which is paramount. As he says in *Toward the African Revolution*, 'Psychoanalytical science considers expatriation to be a morbid phenomenon. In which it is perfectly right' (Fanon 1970: 25). Even at his most apparently straightforwardly psychoanalytic in *Black Skin, White Masks*, however, he is aware that the constructed inferiority of black people is, in the first place, an economically driven process before it becomes an internalised or epidermalised one. Although Fanon's analysis was formulated in relation to the circumstances of colonial domination, it is no less applicable to the postcolonial period. Indeed, it could be seen as even more relevant: as the 'Black invasion' which Hondo chronicles progressively advances into the European heartland, it becomes ever more necessary to white culture that black people accept and acknowledge their inferiority; otherwise, the degree of threat which they (supposedly) constitute risks becoming overwhelming. For Hondo, metropolitan racism was a direct response to the arrival of postcolonial migrant workers in ever greater numbers. This is true up to a point, though it does rather suggest that the racism was not already there – not an assessment which Fanon would agree with.

As well as their anti-capitalism, Fanon and Hondo share a belief in a Marxism which needs to adapt to colonial or postcolonial conditions. As Fanon famously said, 'Marxist analysis should always be slightly stretched every time we have to do with the colonial problem' (Fanon 1967: 31). For Hondo, deploring what he sees as a certain African tendency to swallow theories whole, and unreflectingly, it is the fact that Marxism is not a set of rules or formulae to be mechanically applied, that it changes – and needs to change – with different historical conditions, which makes it important. The fact that 'It appeals to people's intelligence' (Signaté 1994: 89), that it asks you to think for yourself, and, critically, means that you cannot be a 'fetishist' of Marxism, taking it as a once and for all dogma. While Marxism gives, among other things, a recognition of the importance of historical conditions, it in no way involves any loss of interest in the present. As Fanon says in *Black Skin, White Masks*:

> I will not make myself the man of any past. I do not want to exalt the past at the expense of my present and future . . . In no fashion should I undertake to prepare the world that will come later. I belong irreducibly to my time. (Fanon 1986: 226, 15)

The present is similarly the focus for Hondo: 'In making these films, at the cost of enormous difficulties, I had an unshakeable desire to be a witness to my time' (Signaté 1994: 24). For both, however, it is not simply a case of being passive witnesses of the unfolding present; on the contrary, the witnessing is part of the process of engagement in observation, analysis and action, in a very obvious Marxist-style combination of theory and praxis.

In Hondo's case, theory and practice are focused on the politics of cinema, in an obviously specialised way which takes him far beyond Fanon, but the two are still connected via more general concerns regarding the politics of cultural production and representation. For Hondo, although there are important battles to be fought around the question of cinematic distribution and exhibition, Hollywood's dominance in the non-Western world is not only expressed economically; the power of Western ideologies and modes of representation is another site of struggle for him:

> Audiences around the world have come to accept this [Hollywood vision of the world] consciously or unconsciously because they have had no alternative. Africans have been made to accept values and tactics of their oppressors. In learning to re-codify (as film-makers) we are breaking down the emotive identification with particular codes (as audience). (Hondo 1978: 29)

In Hondo's view, Hollywood films often propagate their ideologies in an 'underground' way which makes them even more dangerous. Even when African filmmakers are able to produce images of Africa (no small achievement in itself, as Hondo is at pains to point out), the nature of those images is still a sensitive issue:

> We therefore have to be very careful when we use images of Africa, on account of the ideology of the systems which are still, today, destroying and disturbing the dynamics of our culture. We have not yet escaped from colonialism and imperialism. We are still oppressed. (Hondo 1988b: 8)

Although, as mentioned earlier, Fanon indicates the primacy of the economic in the creation of black inferiority, it is significant that his analysis remains at the level of the cultural-ideological-psychological nexus as a recognition of its fundamental importance, and *Black Skin, White Masks* is premised upon his attempt to free black people from its effects. The power of this nexus, particularly as articulated through film, is also the driving force behind Hondo's oppositional cinematic stance. Anticolonial and postcolonial theorists from Fanon to Edward Said and Stuart Hall have commented on the ideological power of film to make one identify with the 'wrong' side – in their case, Tarzan (versus the Africans); the British army (versus various swarthy enemies); the cowboys (versus the Indians) – and the ability of the Western media – especially in this instance Hollywood – to recycle negative representations of Africans is one of the prime motivations for Hondo to make the films he does.

Hondo's relation to ordinary people in the production of his films stands both as a way of tackling the issue of negative representations and also as a practical example of the combination of theory and praxis involved in 'trusting the people' or 'being inside the people' indicated above. Hondo's filmic practice instantiates a range of ideas which left-wing theorists have long advocated but rarely seen carried out. Walter Benjamin, for example, in his famous essay on 'The Work of Art in the Age of Mechanical Reproduction' (Benjamin 1982: 232–4), points to the radical potential of filmmaking which, like some post-revolutionary Russian work, uses ordinary people to portray themselves, since on the one hand it brings the film closer to actuality, and on the other it diminishes the hierarchical distance between expert and lay person. Hondo, for his part, in films such as *Les Bicots-nègres, vos voisins* and *Soleil O*, has used African migrant workers to portray themselves, though more as collective representatives than as highly delineated individuals. Also, the Brechtian principle of the dialectical and dialogical process of production of the theatrical performance via discussion with the cast and audience – so often praised, and so little practised – has been deemed inappropriate for the cinema, given the process of filmmaking and the apparently unalterable nature of the text once produced. Ousmane Sembene, however, has attempted a partial enactment of Brecht's approach by making the screening of his films in Africa the starting point for discussions of them both as texts and in terms of the issues they raise, aiming to incorporate insights gathered in future films. For his part, Hondo has occasionally tried something more thoroughgoing, and his involvement of migrant workers in his films has extended to discussing the rushes with them and introducing modifications on the basis of those discussions.

As mentioned earlier, *Soleil O* may well be the most Fanonian of African films, but it is also, according to one critic, 'perhaps the least understood of African films, and has been grossly misinterpreted by Western critics' (Ukadike 1994: 81). One aim of this section will therefore be, while avoiding further 'gross misintepretations', to examine the Fanonian elements in the film, and thereby to offer one 'meaning' or way of understanding this supposedly impenetrable text. The apparent incomprehensibility of *Soleil O* perhaps says more about Western assumptions or unexamined expectations regarding forms of non-Western cultural production than it does about the film itself. Certainly, the film makes a number of demands on the viewer as it moves from cartoon to tableau, to historical re-enactment, to satirical pantomime – and all that in the opening fifteen-minute sequence. Nevertheless, at the level of formal experimentation, it is hardly very different from the work of a number of European directors of the same period – so much so that Hondo is often assumed to be working in the same kind of avant-garde mode as someone like Godard, though this, according to Hondo, is emphatically not the case.

Soleil O is grounded in the contemporary situation of diaspora blacks in Europe, but the multi-layered opening sequence just referred to provides brief contextualisation for the precolonial and colonial periods. After the opening cartoon sequence which shows an African chief being embraced by two European colonial officers, and emerging from the embrace laughing and wearing one of their solar topees, a solemn tableau sequence has a voiceover listing the qualities and accomplishments of pre-colonial African cultures: 'We had our own civilisations; we had our songs and dances; we minted gold and silver coins; we had our own literature and legal terminology; we had our own system of education and science . . .' This iconic moment is followed by the process of the 'fall' from the precolonial state, as Africans are first of all converted to Christianity – losing their language as well as their religion in the process – and then turned into cannon fodder for the colonial armies. In the darkest of ironies, Africans are not only co-opted to serve the Europeans but also used to fight and kill other Africans – all for the benefit of their white masters. After this sweeping panorama, the narrative (as far as there is one) follows a paradigmatic diasporic African on a journey which corresponds very closely to Fanon's famous three-stage development of the colonised intellectual. The first of these stages is that of 'unqualified assimilation', and in the words of the voiceover which begins the 'narrative' section, 'One day, I started to study your culture . . . to spout Rousseau and Molière; to analyse your graphs . . . Sweet France, I've been whitened by your culture . . .' As Fanon had commented earlier: 'The native intellectual . . . will not be content to get to know Rabelais and Diderot, Shakespeare and Edgar Allan Poe: he will bind them to his intelligence as closely as possible' (Fanon 1967: 176). In an ideologically powerful example of what Edward Said called 'the Voyage In', the unnamed central character declares: 'Dear France, your first city is also my capital. I'm coming to you. I'm coming home . . .' Much of what then follows is a pitiless dissection of what 'home' has to offer its returning son.

The central character arrives in France as a visibly representative figure: his suitcase adorned with the flags of many African nations signals his status as representative of postcolonial Africa, or already part of its internal, intra-continental diasporic movements, or both. His thoughts in the voiceover articulate the beliefs and aspirations of so many colonised or post colonial intellectuals: 'Here or elsewhere, I'm at home . . . Aren't we equals, you and I? We had the same ancestors – all Gauls! I know there is no discrimination here . . . Aren't I in the land of liberty?' The fact that these are all part of the same ideological package means that the patent absurdity of asserted common ancestry – though 'nos ancêtres les Gaulois' was standard in school books even in Francophone Africa – announces the slightly less blatant absurdity or hypocrisy of the ideals of liberty, equality and fraternity, whose (practical) emptiness in everyday metropolitan life the film progressively demonstrates. The other side to this claim of racial primacy is the fact – unspeakable in this context – that the real common ancestor is of course African, since Africa is where humankind originated.

In relation to the heightened expectations of the *évolué* intellectuals in particular, Fanon comments: 'Quite literally, I can say without any risk of error that the Antillean who goes to France in order to convince himself that he is White will find his real face there' (Fanon 1986: 153). In one sense, Fanon is perfectly correct – the black man is forced to recognise that for Europeans his 'real face' is simply, immutably, *black*. In other ways – and this is some-thing which *Soleil O* demonstrates – the 'reality' of the black face is anything but simple or straightforward, since it is the result of centuries of represen-tations, stereotyping and ideological constructions in Western culture. Conversely, it could be argued that, if there is a 'real face' being uncovered here, it is the repulsive physiognomy of the West, the truth of its racism, its contempt for others, its vulgar hypocrisy beneath the mask of liberal, civilised or progressive culture. The contempt for non-white, non-Western Others constitutes for Hondo an unchanging reality, 'le mépris permanent' facing postcolonial black people.

If the revealed truth of the West is of a society which is inhospitable, discriminatory, and oppressive, that could scarcely be further from the self-representation of that society. In Fanon's view,

The Western bourgeoisie, though fundamentally racist, most often manages to mask its racism by a multiplicity of nuances which allow it to preserve intact its proclamation of mankind's outstanding dignity. (Fanon 1967: 131)

Here, the recurrent obsessive trope of the racist imagination over the last four hundred years at least – that of the embattled domestic culture under threat from a 'black invasion' – is repeatedly invoked as the ideological mystification for the (normally) unspeakable truth: that the West cannot do without black people to exploit, that it has to be continuously 'invaded' in order to survive. In a similar way, official discourse on the 'open' nature of Western society, its desire to welcome or include or gently assimilate, is demolished by the racism which marks everything from state practices to individual behaviour. Fanon's comment that for black people the choice is 'turn White or disappear' (Fanon 1986: 100) seems almost to have become a form of Hobson's choice now: the first option, the 'strong' version of assimilation, being unavailable (since no matter how educated or cultured – i.e. 'white' – Africans become, they will never be accepted as white), 'disappearing' is all that black people are permitted. Once again, however, the double standard is in operation, because what they are required to do is to make themselves invisible, and therefore not offend white sensibilities, rather than actually going away, which, as already mentioned, would be economically unacceptable.

The film operates with a dialectic of acceptance and rejection, and the fact that their occurrences are so often unpredictable (and irrational, especially at the level of rejection) makes the experiences all the more moving or anguishing. The offer of something to eat from a small blonde girl is, on the face of it, the antithesis of the famous Fanonian (primal) scene of 'Look Mama – a Negro!' in *Black Skin, White Masks*, but, like most or all of the other more encouraging events, it slides into a kind of superficiality, emptiness or meaninglessness, as the offer of food becomes a repetitive infantile chant, which raises the question of whether it was real or genuine in the first place. Whether they are grounded in class solidarity (the young garage mechanic), intellectual standing (the political or philosophical discussions), sexual attraction (the relationship with the white woman), basic hospitality (the white nuclear family) or a kind of willed race-blindness (the man in the bar), these 'positive' moments either end badly – especially with the nuclear family – or, like the discussions which establish the intellectual parity of black and white, are completely undermined and contradicted by the everyday events of the film. To that extent, it is significant that the discussions take place in an atmosphere even more unreal and dreamlike than the rest of the film. Although the relationship of acceptance and rejection was described above as dialectic, it might be more accurate to see it as a version of the tortures inflicted in Greek myths, with the desperately desired object or outcome always just out of reach, or snatched away at the moment of its achievement.

One hard-won prize which Fanon worried might indeed be snatched away at the moment of its achievement was the fruits of the national liberation struggle, and one of his clearest premonitions concerns the emergence of the wrong kind of leadership, both in that struggle and, even more so, as the ruling class of the postcolonial state. In class terms, the 'wrong' group is the newly emergent black bourgeoisie, and some of the fiercest criticism in *The Wretched of the Earth* is directed against that class: 'because, literally, it is good for nothing' (Fanon 1967: 141). In addition, it typically perverts leaders of the liberation struggle into becoming its figurehead.

Soleil O has relatively little to say about the indigenous postcolonial black bourgeoisie, but the figure of the 'president' appears on various occasions, grotesquely and inappropriately wielding the trappings of power in a foreign country, and squandering his nation's wealth in displays of excess and corruption. We also hear about the new nation of 'Tomorania' – the president's, or someone else's, it hardly matters – whose inhabitants live in poverty, but which has managed to acquire a great many embassies. In addition, the president's comment that 'We have done away with politicians' marks the final step in the process which Fanon particularly feared: the move to the one-party state as 'the modern form of the dictatorship of the bourgeoisie, unmasked, unpainted, unscrupulous and cynical' (Fanon 1967: 132).

Although the central character, as an educated individual, potentially belongs to the bourgeoisie, his experiences in France are resolutely proletarianising. The film shows him sliding down the socio-economic ladder, being refused all jobs, including those for which he is apparently overqualified, until he swaps his suitcase for a street sweeper's broom – the iconic fate of Africans in the metropolis. (It is noteworthy that one of the central characters in Hondo's last-but-one major film, *Watani: un monde sans mal*, is a street sweeper.) The role may be iconic, but not all Africans are in the same condition as the central character. At the same time, and perhaps as a result of his proletarianising experiences, he is one of those intellectuals for whom there is some hope in Fanon's eyes, one who is capable of following the stages towards politicised or revolutionary consciousness. We have already seen aspects of the assimilated stage, and it is no doubt a mark of power of the ideological formations involved that for so much of the film, and despite all that happens to him in terms of his brutal education in the truth of white society, the central character seemingly cannot get very far into, still less beyond, the second or 'worried' stage. One of the important elements of that education, one which contributes to the growth of his 'worried' consciousness, and one which is also central to Fanon's concerns in *Black Skin, White Masks*, is the question of black–white sexual relations, especially black men and white women. The central character in *Soleil O* apparently misses out on something which for other new arrivals in France was essential, as Fanon notes: 'Talking recently with several Antilleans, I found the dominant concern was to go to bed with a white woman . . . Once their rite of initiation into "authentic" manhood had been filled, they took the train for Paris' (Fanon 1986: 72). However, the fact that for Fanon the myth of the 'quest for white flesh' is 'perpetuated by alienated psyches' may be a hopeful sign as far as the central character is concerned. Nevertheless, being black he is fixed at the level of the sexual or the genital in the white imagination, and as such, constitutes a particular kind of threat:

> One thing must be mentioned in this connection: a white woman who has had a Negro lover finds it difficult to return to white men. Or so at least it is believed, particularly by white men: 'Who knows what "they" can give a woman?' Who indeed does know? Certainly 'they' do not. (Fanon 1986: 171)

As an example of the contradictions of bourgeois ideology mentioned earlier, we note *en passant* a character commenting that he is a great believer in the brotherhood of man, but absolutely cannot stand the thought of black men with white women – that perennial phobic obsession of the white imagination.

'Who knows what "they" can give a woman?' Some women, as Fanon comments, and as the film illustrates, are desperate to find out. We see two white women scandalised, even revolted, at the discovery that one of their friends has had a black baby. They nevertheless speculate about what it would be like to have sex with a black man, and one of them proceeds to do just that, picking up the central character and taking him to bed. There, in the manner outlined by Fanon, she experiences the gap between the man's ordinary human reality and the erotic racist fantasy, and is profoundly dissatisfied.

> The women among the Whites, by a genuine process of induction, invariably view the Negro as the keeper of the impalpable gate that opens into the realms of orgies, of bacchanals, of delirious sexual sensations . . . We have shown that reality destroys all these beliefs. But they all rest on the level of the imagined, in any case, that of a paralogism. (Fanon 1986: 177)

Fleetingly, this looks like the most optimistic of the 'positive' moments, as the couple stroll around, seemingly happy and oblivious to the stares of the white population (not to mention the animal noises on the soundtrack). The latent possibilities here – healing the hurt of racist insults suffered, overcoming the alienation of diaspora – founder in the face of the white woman's fantasy-driven desire. Fanon recounts the case of a white woman who had intensely arousing fantasies of what black men would do to her in bed, but found the actual experience little different from sleeping with a white man. The problem for black men is that, in demonstrating their simple, ordinary maleness, they cannot even manage to be the thing they are supposed to be, or required to be by the world of white erotic fantasy – the sexual beast, the Negro-as-penis.

The central character's transition to the third and final 'fighting' stage comes via a series of rejections or departures: he smashes up his room and leaves; he leaves the city; he is welcomed and then revolted by the 'liberal' French family; he flees from them into the forest amid frantic drumming, apocalyptic images and savage screams with which he eventually joins in. Calmed or exhausted by this cathartic version of what Césaire called 'le grand cri Noir', he ends up in a clearing surrounded by images of black or Third World leaders, heroes and martyrs – Che Guevara, Patrice Lumumba, Malcolm X – and the noise of fire and destruction. The final shot shows him smiling quietly, grimly, while the closing caption, rather than the usual 'La fin', is 'A suivre' (to be continued).

'A suivre', with its echoes of the revolutionary 'A luta continua', could hardly be more apposite in Fanonian terms. Although reaching stage three represents the conclusion of a long and arduous personal journey, in other ways it is only the beginning, since for Fanon it marks the possibility of a fuller or more relevant integration into the collective struggle for national liberation, which is the one that really matters. However, as the closing pages of the chapter 'On National Culture' make clear, even this is not enough, and another step – qualitatively larger, more difficult and more important – has to be taken, as the fight for the nation necessarily leads beyond the nation:

> Far from keeping aloof from other nations, therefore, it is national liberation which leads the nation to play its part on the stage of history. It is at the heart of national consciousness that international consciousness lives and grows. And this two-fold emerging is ultimately the source of all culture. (Fanon 1967: 199)

There is something of this in the trajectory of the central character: he has gone from a position of diaspora as individual economic migrancy, of assimilation in his personal homecoming to 'La douce France', and of alienation disavowed, to one of diaspora as generalised alienation recognised, of the inter- or trans-nationalism of revolution, and of the realisation that there is more to be done. In the words of the warrior queen Sarraounia in Hondo's 1987 film, 'To stay free, we must fight a relentless battle.'

What happens next? What does the intellectual do? In Fanon's final, luminous pages, the dying hope of a fervent revolutionary, 'next' is the fight for human dignity, a 'new humanism', a better way of being: 'For Europe, for ourselves and for humanity, comrades, we must turn over a new leaf, we must work out new concepts, and try to set afoot a new man' (Fanon 1967: 255). For Hondo, speaking thirty years later, 'next' was sadly not quite like that, and it is Fanon's pragmatic fears, rather than his visionary hopes, which have been realised. African intellectuals (i.e. African intellectuals in Africa), for example, have been unable to carry on the fight, and have been reduced to silence and inactivity by repressive or dictatorial regimes – the 'triumph' of the black bourgeoisie which Fanon foresaw destroying all that which the popular struggles had created.

The current situation is one in which African intellectuals seem unable to act or to analyse appropriately; as Hondo comments, 'I don't know of a single problem facing Africa which has called forth a properly African response from Africans. They are all listening to Paris, New York, London or Berlin' (Signaté 1994: 64–5). The idea that Africans, and other postcolonial peoples, need to develop their own analyses, and solutions, brings Fanon and Hondo together yet again: the Conclusion to *The Wretched of the Earth* is marked by the urgent need not to copy European ways of thinking, and, especially, of behaving, since these have visited so much suffering on non-Western peoples in the shape of slavery, colonialism, racism, imperialism and the like. However, this is a question not of simply rejecting European models but of improving on them. For Hondo, as we saw earlier, the problem represented by 'mimétisme' or mimicry of the West is a particularly acute one for Africans in the contemporary world. As far as Fanon is concerned, any attempt to copy Europe is an obstacle to the proper progress of Africa – and humankind – given that 'the European game has finally ended':

> When I search for Man in the technique and the style of Europe, I see only a succession of negations of man, and an avalanche of murders . . .
> Let us decide not to imitate Europe; let us combine our muscles and our brains in a new direction. Let us try to create the whole man, whom Europe has been incapable of bringing to triumphant birth . . .
> Humanity is waiting for something other from us than such an imitation, which would be almost an obscene caricature. (Fanon 1967: 252–4)

As mentioned in the introduction to the chapter, Hondo is often regarded as inspired by European avant-garde filmmaking styles, or even mimicking them, in *Soleil O*, mainly because of the narrative and stylistic discontinuities. As far as he is concerned, however, the film is derived from African modes of storytelling: digressive, cumulative, multi-mode, using recitation, song and dance as required. The correlative of this is that ordinary Africans can understand complex or 'difficult' narrative forms, such as *Soleil O* is deemed to be:

> There are different perceptions of an image. *Soleil O* is crystal clear and is neither intellectual nor sophisticated. It has often happened that those who understand it best are illiterate. This film was shown in Algeria. There, the proletarians explained the film to the intellectuals because the proletariat thoroughly identified with it. (Hondo in Pfaff 1986: 45)

Hondo's attitude is part of a long tradition of left-wing thinkers and cultural producers who have faith in the people's ability to analyse or understand. Among African filmmakers, Ousmane Sembene is the most famous example, while Fanon, unsurprisingly, is one of the thinkers who have faith:

> We must above all rid ourselves of the very Western, very bourgeois, and therefore contemptuous attitude that the masses are incapable of governing themselves. In fact, experience proves that the masses understand perfectly the most complicated problems . . . Everything can be explained to the people, on the single condition that you really want them to understand. (Fanon 1967: 151–2)

Trusting the people, as we saw earlier, is central to Hondo's approach to filmmaking. People 'really understanding' is, for Fanon and Hondo, the whole point: the politicised 'prise de conscience' is something they both experienced personally, and forms an essential desired outcome of their writing, filmmaking and activism. For Fanon, for example, the liberation struggle is possible precisely because of the cumulative growth of people's critical awareness of the situation they face, their own capabilities and how the latter can change the former. For Hondo, 'the [filmic] image is the weapon of choice for making people aware, for the long-term transformation of their understanding' (Hondo in Signaté 1994: 31), and in his view it is one of Africa's particular problems that, as a continent, it has yet fully to grasp this fact.

A keen sense of the dialectical processes of cultural production and political development aiming at profound social transformation unites Fanon and Hondo. We have already seen Fanon's view of the linked twofold emergence of national and international consciousness as 'the source of all culture'. For Hondo, this includes the limits and possibilities of film:

> What is more, a political film is not necessarily a 'revolutionary' film. What is a revolutionary film? A film unlike those already seen? A film calling for insurrection? Which incites revolution? I have never heard of people running to look for rifles at the cinema exit, to overthrow the government or to chase out the village mayor. Revolutionary cinema without revolution: I do not understand what that means. (Hondo 1987: 71–2)

The absence of rifles at the cinema exit does not mean that Hondo is denying the possibility of either revolution or revolutionary film, simply that there is a necessary relationship between them, that the latter requires the appropriate conditions which the arrival of the former will create, and that the arrival of the former is not produced by the emotional uprush generated by even the best of political films. It also makes very clear the limits of formal radicalism, and even of would-be incendiary content. At the same time, it is important to remember that these 'conditions' do not simply happen, that they are the creation of conscious human agency:

> Africa will not be free through the mechanical development of material forces, but it is the hand of the African and his brain that will set into motion and implement the dialectics of the liberation of the continent. (Fanon 1970: 183)

That was Fanon in 1960. Despite all that has happened since, the 'dialectics' are, for someone like Hondo, still available – if less immediately accessible. 'A suivre', somehow, no doubt.

Note

1 The fact that many of Hondo's films simply cannot be currently accessed is a clear indicator of their non-distributed, non-exhibited status. Further, none is available for purchase in any format.

Filmography

Balade aux sources (1969)
Partout ou peut-être nulle part (1969)

Roi de corde (1969)
Soleil O (1969)
Les Bicots-nègres, vos voisins (1973)
Nous aurons toute la mort pour dormir (1977)
Polisario, un peuple en armes (1979)
West Indies, ou les nègres marrons de la liberté (1979)
Sarraounia (1987)
Lumière noire (1994)
Watani: un monde sans mal (1998)
Fatima, l'Algérienne de Dakar (2004)

Chapter 4

Djibril Diop Mambety

Introduction

At the time of his premature death in 1998, at the relatively young age of fifty-three, there was a consensus amongst many commentators that the Senegalese director Djibril Diop Mambety was the most gifted of all African film directors. If we examine the work of the first generation of sub-Saharan African filmmakers as a whole, his films certainly stand out for their rejection of the dominant, 'prosaic' social realism of his colleagues, in favour of a more 'poetic', indirect and highly experimental style. Despite the critical acclaim for his work, Mambety's cinematic career is, in many ways, emblematic of the difficulties that have faced African film directors. In his 30-year career, which includes a 15-year hiatus in the 1970s and 1980s, during which he abandoned film (or it abandoned him) altogether, he made only two feature films – *Touki Bouki* (*The Hyena's Voyage*, 1973) and *Hyenas* (1992) – and five short or medium-length films. Born and raised in Dakar, the Senegalese capital – or to be more precise in the suburb of Colobane, which features so centrally in several of his films – Mambety is best known for his groundbreaking film *Touki Bouki*. Hailed by many critics as the first African avant-garde film, *Touki Bouki* is undoubtedly a striking and very challenging work. However, this vision of Mambety as an experimental, avant-garde director is one that has been challenged by many critics in recent years, and this debate will be explored in greater depth below.

Whereas his compatriot Sembene became interested in cinema (and literature) via his ideological concerns, Mambety seems to have experimented with artistic expression from early in his life. In Laurence Gavron's fascinating documentary, *Ninkinanka, le Prince de Colobane* (1991), Mambety's father describes how his son wrote compulsively as a child in an attempt 'to understand the world'. Mambety was a passionate film fan from his teenage years, and he was a member of a Dakar film club in which he gained a broad knowledge of world cinema. As his friend Nar Sène recalls in his memoir on Mambety, theirs was a group of young men interested in art and self-expression (Sène 2001). After a successful period of stage acting with the troupe of the Daniel Sorano National Theatre in Dakar, he turned his attention to cinema at the age of only twenty-one, borrowing a camera from the director of the French Cultural Centre, and, with some friends, filming a first

version of *Badou Boy*: the poor quality of the film stock and of his equipment meant that this early version was never released, but this experience
had at least given Mambety his breakthrough. This precocious talent was
confirmed with his short film *Contras' City*, a pseudo-documentary taking a
female tourist on a guided tour of Dakar on the back of a horse and cart.
The film takes a comic and affectionate look at the city, and its humorous
juxtaposition of the traditional and the modern, as well as its immersion in
the street life of the city, presages some of the themes that Mambety would
explore in a much darker vein in *Touki Bouki*.

In 1970, Mambety returned to the streets of Dakar to film a 'remake' of
Badou Boy with virtually the same team as several years previously. The end
result is an occasionally breathtaking fusion of Western counterculture,
'traditional' or ethnic values and motifs, and street life in Dakar, in which
the eponymous hero wanders the streets of the city in a series of comic, picaresque adventures. The circular and fragmented narrative structure that
would later mark *Touki Bouki* is already in place, as are some of the characters: the fat, endlessly perspiring policeman, the menacing mother figure,
and in particular the rebel-cum-dreamer Badou Boy. The self-conscious style
that had been evident in embryonic form in *Contras' City* – the ironic and
mischievous voiceover, the placing of the final credits on the back of the
cart – is here more fully developed: the film begins with tightly edited shots
of Mambety and his crew filming the central character in what we later
discover is the final sequence of the film. Mambety's playful, non-realist aesthetic is evident from the start of his career.

After *Badou Boy*, Mambety spent several months in Marseilles: it was his
first trip abroad and his experiences there shattered his long-held illusions
about the mythical world of the former colonial power. Returning to
Senegal, he filmed *Touki Bouki*, in which the lure of France plays a central
structuring role. The young lovers Mory and Anta plot a way to escape
the poverty and limited horizons of their lives in Dakar but, at the end of
the film, Mory is unable to leave. Such a neat plot summary does little to
convey the complexity of the film's narrative structure, however: the film
consistently veers away from narrative realism into a series of fantasy or
dreamlike sequences, and the fragmented narrative structure obliges the
spectator to question his or her understanding of events. The film's heady
mix of Western youth culture – rock music, motorbikes and sex – and 'traditional' Senegalese culture – the slaughter of animals, the evocation of a
spiritual, mystical dimension to African life – reveal the cultural ambiguities
and tensions that make Mambety's filmmaking so powerful.

The next 15 years of Mambety's life and career are something of a mystery:
for over a decade, it seemed as though the career of perhaps the most talented
filmmaker of his generation was over before it had really begun. In the end,
it was one of the next generation of filmmakers, Idrissa Ouédraogo, who
offered Mambety the chance to get back behind the camera, inviting him to
film a documentary about the making of Ouédraogo's feature film *Yaaba*.[1]

The resulting short film, *Let's Talk, Grandmother* (1988), charts the process through which Ouédraogo constructs his film, but, in so doing, Mambety constructs his own film in the typically impressionistic, circular manner of his early films. His camera dwells on the main protagonists of the film, the old woman and the two young children, and (in French New Wave fashion) he delights in capturing moments of 'reality' that take place 'off screen' in the filming of Ouédraogo's movie: the smiling face of the old woman, the moments of boredom and exuberance on set for the young lead actors.

Let's Talk, Grandmother put Mambety back on the map and led to his final burst of artistic creativity in the 1990s. His three final films display all of the stylistic and thematic features of his early works but he marries them to a more coherent, linear narrative framework. His final feature film, *Hyenas*, is loosely based on *The Visit of the Old Lady*, a play by the Swiss dramatist Friedrich Dürrenmatt. An old woman who is claimed to be 'richer than the World Bank' returns to her home village in Senegal and offers vast financial rewards to anyone who will kill the former lover who betrayed her many years before. The lure of money destroys the bonds of family and community while the progress and happiness promised by the old woman ultimately prove illusory.

Money is also central to the narrative in Mambety's two short films, *Le Franc* and *The Little Girl who Sold the Sun* (the first and second parts of an incomplete trilogy on the 'ordinary people' of Dakar: Mambety died before he could film the third part, *The Apprentice Thief*). Both films are more optimistic than *Hyenas*: in *Le Franc* (1994), the musician-hero's success in winning the lottery is viewed in almost dreamlike terms, promising a blissful (and musical) escape from hardship rather than the chance to accumulate possessions; while the heroine of *The Little Girl who Sold the Sun* is a young, disabled girl who becomes a newspaper-vendor in the streets of Dakar, overcoming all of the obstacles placed in her path, in particular the open hostility of the young male newspaper sellers.

One of the many tragedies of Mambety's early death in 1998 was that he had finally found the critical acclaim that had escaped his earlier films, which were often mired in ideological debates about the 'true' nature of African cinema.[2] By the early 1990s, the demand in certain quarters for African films to adhere to specific aesthetic and political agendas had weakened considerably, which provided a much more welcoming context for Mambety's politically and culturally ambiguous narratives.

Social, cultural and political contexts

The chapter on Ousmane Sembene has already dealt with the Senegalese context in considerable depth (readers requiring further background information should refer to Chapter 2). Consequently, this section will deal relatively briefly with the main social, cultural and political issues that inform Mambety's films. It was argued in Chapter 2 that Sembene's early work often deliberately cast itself in opposition to the regime of Léopold Sédar Senghor.

Conversely, Mambety's films do not espouse any readily identifiable political point of view, although that does not mean that they eschew politics altogether. On the contrary, it is possible to identify within much of Mambety's work a critique of the effects of capitalist modernity upon Senegalese society. For example, *Touki Bouki* and *Hyenas* are films that deal explicitly with the role of money in Senegal in the increasingly capitalist system of the post-independence era. However, they do so in a somewhat oblique fashion that emphasises the cultural and moral dimensions of this huge shift in Senegalese society rather than analysing the specific political and economic dimensions of neocolonialism. There is anger in Mambety's films at various forms of political injustice – the racism of the French people on the boat at the end of *Touki Bouki*, the (self-)destruction of Colobane by its desire to acquire material possessions – but they are not driven by the deep political resentment that one finds in Sembene's work: where Sembene seeks to diagnose the problems faced by his society and/or to offer potential solutions to them, Mambety uses his work primarily to explore the ambiguities of post-independence Senegalese society in a far more meditative fashion (which is perhaps, in its own way, as 'political' as Sembene). Essentially, Mambety might best be viewed as an alternative kind of contemporary cinematic 'griot' to Sembene, one who taps into a more mystical and indirect storytelling tradition. Like Sembene, his films are often grounded in the reality of the 'petites gens' of Dakar but their films are extremely different in style. The difference between the two directors is encapsulated in their contrasting representations of the postman in *Mandabi* and *Touki Bouki* respectively (a contrast already evoked in the Introduction): for Sembene, the postman is deployed symbolically as an ordinary working man who 'delivers' hope while Mambety's postman is fat and bumbling, and Mambety derives great comedy from his seemingly aimless peregrinations around the city. While Sembene's films are always guided by an ideological or narrative purpose propelling them forwards, Mambety's films wander into dead ends, taking the time to stop and discover hidden elements of city life.

It is equally difficult to situate Mambety's work in relation to Negritude, the dominant Senegalese cultural philosophy of the 1960s and 1970s. Whereas Sembene saw in Negritude a deliberate obfuscation of contemporary realities in favour of an essentialist vision turned towards the past, Mambety's work often seems more in tune with certain aspects of Negritude thought. For instance, his two feature films, *Touki Bouki* and *Hyenas*, might be seen in part as an exploration of the impact of Western culture on Africa, in which Mambety laments the demise of 'indigenous' values and customs. However, Mambety never engaged in the indiscriminate praise of African cultural traditions that marked certain simplistic forms of Negritude: in fact, Mambety's work has much more in common with the vision of Negritude presented by his compatriot Cheikh Hamidou Kane in his classic novel *Ambiguous Adventure* (1961). Kane's protagonist Samba Diallo is, like Mory in *Touki Bouki*, a young man torn between the African culture of his childhood and the Western culture he encounters in later life. Both characters suffer an extreme form of mental anguish and alienation at their predicament, torn between their attachment to two cultures. Eventually, Samba Diallo is murdered for refusing to 'return' to Islam by a former African colonial soldier driven insane by his own failure to reconcile his two cultures, while Mory is unable to board the ship to Paris with Anta, and he abandons her, running wildly through the streets of Dakar, intercut with the images of animal slaughter that punctuate the film.

A key difference between Samba Diallo and Mory is that the former is introduced into Western culture via formal education while the latter is obsessed with Western popular culture and, perhaps most significantly, with gaining the financial wealth that will allow him to obtain all the material trappings of a successful, Western lifestyle. (Nar Sène claims that Mambety was primarily an urban African who looked outwards towards the West in negotiating his cultural identity, rather than looking inwards towards a timeless, rural Africa for an 'authentic' cultural identity.) If Samba Diallo's dilemma is how to reconcile Western rationality and Islamic spirituality, then Mory's dilemma appears to be the difficulty of reconciling his former self with the person that he has become in this rapidly changing capitalist society. This duality is powerfully suggested in the opening sequence of the film in which the young boy on the cow (is it Mory, as some critics suggest?) is replaced by the young man on a powerful motorbike. This is the face of a changing Africa and a dilemma facing the continent as a whole.

This concern with how individuals and communities in Senegal have been transformed by the arrival of capitalism is central to Mambety's work. As was mentioned above, the oblique, non-realistic aesthetic of his films may give the impression that he is uninterested in socio-economic questions but it is significant that money in fact plays a central role in many of his films, often helping to structure the narrative itself: Badou Boy steals from his mother and is chased from the house, thus setting in motion the picaresque adventures related in the remainder of the film (*Badou Boy*); Mory and Anta continually search for ways to steal the money that will allow them to escape to France (*Touki Bouki*); Ramatou buys the 'souls' of the people of Colobane (*Hyenas*); Marigo, the musician, is mired in debt only to find salvation in a winning lottery ticket (*Le Franc*); and Sili Laam, the young newspaper-seller, wanders the street of Dakar, striving to make ends meet for her family (*The Little Girl who Sold the Sun*).

Mambety's films explore and reveal the injustices and harm caused by the capitalist system, but unlike Sembene's Marxist-inspired work they are not concerned with apportioning political blame or offering ideological solutions. As was argued above, his films focus instead on issues of cultural identity, morality and spirituality. This sense of morality is most obvious in *Hyenas* with its comic but none the less coruscating view of the moral weakness of an entire community who sell themselves for a handful of material goods. This contrast between the material and the spiritual might perhaps be viewed as an expression of a diffuse Wolof-Islamic cultural identity in

Mambety's work, which exists alongside his fascination with Western popular culture (particularly evident in his early films with their 'cool' American-English titles and references to late psychedelic pop culture). His hybrid cultural standpoint is also made clear in a comic but revealing scene from the documentary, *Ninkinanka*. Mambety takes a seat at a roadside 'bar' (or 'buvette'), beer in hand, just as the *muezzin* calls the faithful to prayer in the mosque across the street. Speaking to camera, Mambety declares himself a Muslim but one who expresses his faith in his own way.

It seems possible to locate elements of Mambety's highly inventive and symbolic worldview within a form of Sufi mysticism, typical of Islam in Senegal, which is extremely syncretic in form, with Muslim beliefs and rituals often welded on to pre-existing animist practices and beliefs. Senegalese Islam often finds expression in terms of dreams and visions that combine Sufi mysticism and the more 'fantastic' elements of the oral narrative tradition: for example, there are many 'fantastic' stories about Cheikh Amadou Bamba, founder of the Mourides, one of Senegal's largest Muslim brotherhoods, who is believed by followers to have escaped on a cloud from his French colonial jailors. The final sequence in *Ninkinanka* provides a striking example of such mysticism: Mambety's father recalls a strange dream he once had about his sons and a horse with its innards hanging out; after the dream, he prayed for his sons to enjoy an obstacle-free life. Not only does this vision contain strong echoes of the images of animal slaughter that punctuate *Touki Bouki* but it also acts as an illuminating insight into the way in which mysticism and dreams can inform the perception of daily reality in a country such as Senegal. Mambety's experimentalism might thus be seen as a central component of his attempt to capture the 'reality' of the world as perceived from within this mystical or spiritual worldview.

The quasi-mystical dimension to Mambety's work was never likely to enamour him to sections of the socialist-inspired Third Cinema community in the early 1970s. Nar Sène describes Mambety (in rather stark and perhaps exaggerated terms) as an outsider in a Senegalese film scene dominated by Marxist ideologues (2001: 127–9). The opaque, playful and experimental nature of films such as *Badou Boy* and *Touki Bouki* were often seen by critics as 'Western', modernist, avant-garde works that had little to say to African audiences. However, beyond a relatively limited circle of film buffs, his films were in fact often quite bewildering to Western audiences, and his fifteen-year career hiatus indicates that he was not exactly favoured by Western funding bodies over other directors. Mambety's renaissance in the late 1980s and early 1990s might thus be argued to be a result of the waning of Third Cinema's star and the rise to prominence of a less ideological African cinema.

The films

This section will focus on Mambety's two feature films, *Touki Bouki* and *Hyenas* (although examples will also be drawn from his short films), as these two works offer an illuminating contrast between the early and late periods of Mambety's career. *Touki Bouki* is quite simply a remarkable film. Its somewhat conventional story of a young Senegalese couple who long to escape to a better life in Paris is represented in a highly innovative and original fashion: the wilful disruption of narrative codes, the fragmented and circular nature of the narrative, the use of narrative digression, all mark the film down as the work of a highly imaginative young director, pushing film to its limits. On the other hand, *Hyenas* is a more conventional narrative but it tells the intriguing and inventive story of a 'wronged' woman who returns to her hometown as the richest women in the world, intent on taking revenge on the man who abandoned her. Although it retains many non-realistic elements (which will be discussed further below), it is a more immediately intelligible film than *Touki Bouki* with a stronger narrative drive, and it addresses social, cultural and moral questions in a more direct fashion. Although the restless experimentalism of the early films is toned down somewhat in the second half of Mambety's career to accommodate a much greater degree of narrative linearity and coherence, his work can never be termed as straightforwardly linear or realist. The jarring use of music in his films is a good example of this experimental approach: the swirling electronic beeping and whirring of *Touki Bouki*; or the raucous, and unexplained, extra-diegetic sound of bagpipes, as Sili Laam is pushed to the ground by the band of newspaper sellers in *The Little Girl who Sold the Sun*. These are illustrations of Mambety's consistent desire to engage in formal innovation.

It is important to begin with an assessment of Mambety's film style, as he is widely seen by both critics and admirers as the most distinctive 'stylist' in African cinema (a mantle perhaps taken over in the 1990s by Jean-Pierre Bekolo, a director who greatly admires Mambety: see Chapter 9). His filmmaking practice must be situated within the context of the often radical, modernist experimentation prevalent in the (predominantly Western) art house cinema of the late 1960s and early 1970s. However, it does not follow that this experimental approach constitutes an absolute break with the form of traditional oral narratives. Essentially, it is invidious to place him exclusively within either a 'modernist' or an 'oral' camp.

Mambety's films might perhaps be generically termed road movies (with the possible exception of *Hyenas*, which will be discussed below), in the tradition of *Easy Rider* or the films of Wim Wenders, in which the fragmented and episodic nature of the story is related in an equally fragmented and episodic style. Compared to the slow pace of many African films, Mambety's work is consistently punctuated by abrupt changes of pace due to the restless movement of the characters, although the journeys undertaken by them rarely lead far: Badou Boy wanders aimlessly around the city in a series of peripatetic adventures (*Badou Boy*); the journey to France that so entices Mory and Anta ends in failure (*Touki Bouki*); Marigo, the musician, undertakes an epic journey across a rubbish-strewn urban landscape, balancing precariously on his head the door to his one-room shack, with the winning lottery ticket glued on to it (*Le Franc*). These journeys are in fact used as the pretext for non-linear film narratives that allow Mambety to interrogate notions of place, time and identity. In *Touki Bouki*, the narrative progression of the story is repeatedly interrupted by distressing scenes of animal slaughter, accompanied by jarring music, both of which induce a deep sense of unease in the viewer: these scenes are obliquely linked by the narrative to Mory's disquiet at the thought of abandoning his culture. The film also repeats, in highly fragmented fashion, the montage sequence in which Mory and Anta make love on the cliffs overlooking the sea. The repetition of the sequence has the unsettling effect of questioning the 'reality' of the event, a process that is reinforced by the rapidly cut, vertiginous, low-angle shots of Anta descending the path to meet her lover. However, it also stresses the giddy passion of their love for each other, the burning desire that seems to drive them in their quest for a 'better life' in France. It is the expression of such ambiguities that lies at the heart of Mambety's work.

Even *Hyenas*, which is perhaps his most 'straightforward', linear narrative retains certain episodic elements of the road movie, as it follows Draman Drameh, the man sentenced to death by Ramatou, as he embarks on a journey through his hometown and discovers that he no longer recognises this place and the people who live there. The film also contains many extravagant and symbolic features that take it beyond the bounds of conventional realism: the elephants that cross the barren landscape in the opening and closing sequences; the superhuman qualities associated with Ramatou – her golden leg which has replaced a limb torn off in an aeroplane accident of which she is the sole survivor; the ritual nature of Draman Drameh's 'execution', with the townspeople donning wigs and chalking their faces; the sequence in the church in which Draman's plight is linked to starving orphans on a television screen; the extravagance of the fun fair paid for and brought to the town by Ramatou. Mambety filmed the latter scenes in 1987 at the Fête de l'Humanité in Paris. Equally, the scenes of cheering crowds supposedly hailing a triumphant Mory in *Touki Bouki* were filmed during the national celebrations of Senegalese independence. This gives an indication of Mambety's ability to perceive in the everyday the basis for his extraordinary cinematic vision (and, more prosaically, it signals the importance of keeping costs down by filming 'reality' as 'fiction' rather than attempting to 'stage' reality at great expense).

As was argued above, the non-realistic, experimental dimension of Mambety's work cannot be seen purely as an indication of his attachment to Western avant-garde film practice, for his films constantly reference Senegalese oral narrative codes. The evocation of Bouki-the-Hyena in the titles of his two feature films leads the Senegalese spectator to expect a narrative dealing with duplicity and deception, and the episodic, fragmented nature of his films replicates many of the features of folk tales featuring Bouki and his more likeable partner in trickery Leuk-the-Hare (the boy who befriends the young girl in *The Little Girl who Sold the Sun* is first seen 'reading' a copy of Léopold Senghor's Leuk-the-Hare). The films also contain many stock characters both from the oral tradition and from the emerging popular representations of Senegalese life on television and in popular theatre: the domineering matriarch (this figure will be explored in greater detail below), played by the majestic Aminata Fall, herself a griote, in *Badou Boy*, *Touki Bouki* and *Le Franc*; the corrupt and/or incompetent representative of the state (see the overweight postman in *Touki Bouki* and his equally rotund counterpart the policeman in *Badou Boy* and *Touki Bouki*). However, Mambety's films were never a box-office success in Senegal, and he always acknowledged the experimental dimension of his work: 'One has to choose between engaging in stylistic research or the mere recording of facts' (Pfaff 1988: 218). (It is worth noting that this quote not only justifies his own work but also takes a swipe at the more 'prosaic' work of many of his African colleagues.)

One of the most distinctive features of Mambety's work is his evocation of place. As André Gardies argues, much African cinema has been concerned with representing emblematic or symbolic spaces rather than specific places: the village, the city, the family compound (1989: 21–5). However, Mambety's work is far more interested in conveying to the spectator a specific sense of place, namely Dakar. Born and raised in the Dakar district of Colobane, Mambety is a resolutely urban and urbane figure, at home in the city, and this fact is illustrated throughout his work. His very first film, *Contras' City*, is a comic and loving portrait of his home city: it is, essentially, a film about the sights, sounds, colours, and people of Dakar, as the spectator is briefly introduced to a whole host of characters: two barbers at work by the roadside, women at a water pump carrying loads on their head, believers outside the cathedral accosted by street traders who linger on the steps long after the worshippers have gone inside. In many ways, *Contras' City* sets the template for his subsequent films. As was argued above, the incessant movement of his protagonists gives his films a dynamic sense of energy but, as a director, Mambety is always willing to take time out of his narrative to explore the details of daily life. This is particularly evident in *Touki Bouki* (see, for example, the fight between the two women and the man at the water pump, which Mambety films in loving and quite lengthy detail, despite the fact that it does not advance the narrative at all), and in *Let's Talk, Grandmother*, which, like *Contras' City*, largely eschews narrative in favour of the evocation of place and character.

The exploration of sexuality and gender is one of the most significant features of Mambety's work. *Touki Bouki* echoes the 'gender-bending' of late 1960s and early 1970s Western popular culture (for example, Cammell and Roeg's *Performance*) through the 'boyish' character of Anta. This ambiguity towards gender is cast within the film as yet another dimension of the confused but highly vibrant African youth culture of the early 1970s. *Touki Bouki* is also highly unusual in its relatively explicit representation of sexuality, although it is still quite prudish by comparison with certain Western films of the period. Whereas most other African directors of this period (and even today) are rather coy and self-censoring when it comes to sexuality, Mambety deliberately emphasises the eroticism of Mory and Anta's love-making on the cliffs. (Désiré Ecaré's *Concerto for an Exile* is one of the only other African films of this period in which sexuality is treated in a similarly direct fashion.) Although the spectator is refused a voyeuristic view of the young lovers having sex, Mambety heightens the sense of excitement and anticipation by following Anta as she descends the steep, spiralling steps to Mory waiting for her below. We then see Anta remove her military-style shirt, finally revealing the truth about her gender, before she lowers herself down to Mory off camera. In the remainder of this long sequence, we hear Anta's groans of pleasure, amplified by the clanging, 'metallic' extra-diegetic music on the soundtrack, and see a medium close-up of her hand grasp the Targui Cross (symbol of the nomadic Touaregs of the Sahara) on the back of Mory's motorbike. These shots are intercut with scenes of a small boat bobbing on the ocean (thus echoing the film's central theme of escape) and waves crashing on to the rocks below, Mambety archly referencing one of the key, pre-1960s Hollywood codes for the representation of sex on screen.

Touki Bouki is also untypical amongst African films of the period in its depiction of homosexuality.[3] In one of their increasingly desperate attempts to raise the money to escape to France, Mory and Anta visit the villa of Charlie, a middle-aged, wealthy and flamboyantly camp gay man. Their vague plan is simply for Mory to 'woo' Charlie with his 'masculine charms', but it is clear that Charlie's interest in the younger man extends beyond mere flirtation. While Charlie takes a shower, inviting Mory to join him, Mory is packing suitcases with Charlie's clothes and the young couple flee the house in the rich man's open-top car. When Charlie realises what has happened, he rings the police and speaks to a 'Sergeant Mambety' with whom he is extremely flirtatious, and with whom he seems to have enjoyed more than a merely professional relationship in the past.

This entire sequence is played out as a sort of slapstick, bedroom farce, the self-referentiality of the police officer's name indicating that the spectator is invited to see this as an enjoyable romp that should not be taken too seriously. However, the sequence is also indicative of a major strand within Mambety's work that is concerned with the exploration of masculinity. Many of his films are in large part comic-heroic representations of male 'losers' and 'dreamers' who are often cast as inept, disorganised and even slightly effeminate. Mory accepts to act as 'bait' for the homosexual, Charlie, and, although he tries to rebel, he is unable to leave home at the end of the film. Badou Boy is presented as something of a dandy with his flowery, paisley shirt, and he even distributes real flowers at one point in the film. His flight from his nemesis, the fat policeman, is cast in part as a flight from a sexual predator: in a series of slow-motion shots first shown at the beginning of the film, and which reappear at various points throughout, we see the policeman trap a slight figure resembling Badou Boy, whom he attacks in a sexually suggestive manner, persistently pressing the young man against a fence with his body. Marigo, the musician, in *Le Franc*, is also an ineffectual dreamer who seems the antithesis of the strong male lead.

Perhaps the most complex exploration of masculinity is to be found in *Hyenas*. Draman Drameh is, in certain respects, the 'hero' of the film, for his stand against the rampant form of capitalism and greed that grips Colobane. Conversely, Mambety consistently reminds us that it is Draman's 'original sin' of abandoning his pregnant partner, the teenage Ramatou, many years before, which brought this fate upon the town. Draman acknowledges that he wronged Ramatou out of fear and cowardice but the domesticity and loss of freedom that that he sought to escape as a young man catches up with him before Ramatou does, in the form of his unloving and nagging wife. Both Draman's wife and Ramatou Linguere are just two of the many domineering older women in the lives of his male protagonists: Badou Boy's mother, Anta's Aunt Oumi and Marigo's landlady (all played by the peerless Aminata Fall) are presented as fearsome characters who 'police' the lives of the male protagonists, and are often responsible for setting them off on their travels. Sène argues that women are the dynamic force in Mambety's films while men are portrayed as weak and impractical (2001: 79–83). However, Mambety's treatment of gender is rather more ambiguous than Sène's view allows. Badou Boy, Mory and Marigo are all dreamers and rebels who want to follow their own paths, and, significantly, Mory, the only one of the three who is in a relationship, ends the film alone and on the run. Mambety's men may often be weak and ineffectual but his films are, on the whole, sympathetic portraits of slightly dysfunctional or marginal characters, including his final film, *The Little Girl who Sold the Sun*, which presents a rebellious female figure. It is thus tempting to read a 'queer' aesthetic into Mambety's work, that is, the exploration and celebration of marginal, nonconformist identities (rather than of homosexuality *per se*). For, throughout his career, rebelliousness and marginality are both highly valued. Even the chillingly amoral Ramatou Linguère in *Hyenas* is, on the whole, viewed sympathetically as an outsider, someone who overcomes all the odds to succeed in life. In *Le Franc*, Mambety makes a visual reference to his own childhood hero, Yaadikoone, through the poster on Marigo's bedroom door. Yaadikoone was an anticolonial activist whom Mambety has described in interviews as a Senegalese Robin Hood. It is significant that Mambety is particularly grateful to Yaadikoone for his habit of bursting open the doors of local cinemas after the lights had gone down so that the local children could get into the movie theatre for free. For Mambety, cinema itself seems to be a transgressive space in which social and cultural norms can be questioned: it is the space in which the contemporary griot can amuse, inform and entrance his audience.

This vision of transgression and rebelliousness is primarily a comic one. Unlike Sembene's radical heroes, Mambety's rebels are not loaded with any specific moral or political message. Their rebellion is designed to puncture pomposity, arrogance and authority, more than to draw attention to the ills of society: the 'rebellion' of Badou Boy, Mory and Anta takes the form of a burlesque caper, complete with comic chases, pratfalls and cases of mistaken identity. In *Badou Boy*, Mambety visually 'references' Chaplin in the scene in which Mambety himself, dressed as a dandy in a bowler hat, takes a seat in the back of Badou Boy's *car rapide*. Marigo's decision to carry his door first to the lottery office and then to the sea to remove the glued-on ticket is a triumph of comic absurdity. The rebellion against social norms by the strong-minded Sili Laam is in part presented as the comic victory of a seemingly defenceless little girl over a bunch of malicious, conniving but fundamentally dim-witted group of boys. Even the tension of waiting for the tragic fate of Draman Drameh (*Hyenas*) is in part played out as a dark comic pastiche of the classic Western *High Noon*. Above all, the consistent use of humour in Mambety's films reflects his position as an outsider who is sometimes angered but, more often, bemused and amused by the world.

The modern, the postmodern and the postcolonial

The final section of this chapter will explore the notions of the modern, the postmodern and the postcolonial, and assess how they relate to Mambety's work. Each of these terms is highly contested but they have all, at some stage, been evoked by critics as a way of categorising the sense of playfulness, ambiguity, ambivalence and irony that one finds in Mambety's films. Is his experimental style that of a high modernist seeking to impose his artistic vision on an ever more fragmented world? Or is it precisely a postmodern rejection of any sense of an all-encompassing artistic vision in favour of simply presenting the viewer with the absolute fragmentation of art and reality? Or, finally, is it resolutely 'postcolonial', in that it seeks to develop a new African film language that expresses the complexity of post-independence Africa?

At the heart of these debates – which go far beyond critical wrangling over terminology – is an attempt to understand and define the nature of the anti-colonial or postcolonial project. For modernism does not simply denote an artistic style: it encompasses an often complex relationship to the entire philosophical project of Enlightenment modernity, which promised the banishment of tradition and superstition by the forces of light and reason. Conversely, postmodernist thought posits itself as a critique (and, in some cases, a rejection) of the Enlightenment project, and underlines the relationship between power and knowledge, which has led to a distrust of what have been termed 'grand narratives', that is, attempts at explaining the world in an all-embracing fashion: in particular, the notion of a rational Europe bringing light to the dark corners of the world is often held up as a damning indictment of modernity, which would seem clearly to align the postcolonial with the postmodern.

It is often argued that anticolonial African cultural production was inspired by a desire to create both an African modernity – emerging African nations creating the structures of the modern, rational, democratic and industrialised nation state – and an African artistic modernism – developing the artistic forms (from the realism of Sembene to the experimental style of Hondo) appropriate for the representation of this African modernity. Such artists were often explicitly motivated by the quintessentially modernist project of Marxist-inspired socialism, which sought to create rational, egalitarian nation states in Africa. When disillusionment set in at the failures of independence, and particularly at the inability of Marxism to produce the desired change, it is argued that many writers and filmmakers lost faith in modernity and the nation state, and consequently adapted more fragmented narrative forms, which reflected the ambiguities of the postcolonial context. So, to paraphrase the question famously posed by the Ghanaian philosopher Kwame Anthony Appiah, can we assume that the 'post' in 'postcolonial' is the same as the 'post' in 'postmodernism'? The answer for some critics is a resounding no, for the very concept of the 'postmodern' has been highly contested in relation to African texts and contexts. For example, Clyde Taylor views the search for the postmodern in Africa as 'the shoe-horning of African reality within the frames of Europe-centred history', which 'satisfies a need of the colonising mentality' (2000: 136). Conversely, leading postcolonial critics such as Homi K. Bhabha and Robert Young have positioned postmodernist thought (Derrida, Lacan, Foucault) as central to the whole project of postcolonialism.

In order to attempt an answer to Appiah's question, it is necessary to re-examine precisely what is meant by these three terms. From the standpoint of critics such as Bhabha and Young, modernity often appears as a monolithic discourse, and they consistently write of the need to 'go beyond' or to 'correct' it: Bhabha seeks to demonstrate the inextricable link between postmodernism's challenge to dominant modes of thought and what he sees as postcolonialism's assault on colonial modernity, a process that he terms a 'postcolonial contramodernity' (1994: 175); while Young argues that 'Postcolonial theory operates within the historical legacy of Marxist critique on which it continues to draw but which it simultaneously transforms' (2001: 6).

However, was modernism or modernity ever as monolithic as its critics make out? For both the project of Enlightenment modernity and the various forms of artistic modernism that emerged in the late nineteenth and early twentieth century, as a response to increasing urbanisation and industrialisation, had multiple strands, many of which were deeply sceptical about certain changes that were taking place. One of the most readily identifiable of these strands is the (Marxist) critique of the dehumanising nature of the capitalist system. In the essay cited above, Appiah argues that modernity brought about the reign of capitalism, not Reason: 'namely, the incorporation of all areas of even formerly "private" life into the money economy.

Modernity has turned every element of the world into a sign, and the sign reads "for sale"' (1992: 145). It is this aspect of modernity that both repulses and fascinates Mambety. Far from bringing the light of reason and democracy to Africa, colonialism is seen to have introduced a pervasive and confusing urban, capitalist culture. Mory and Anta in *Touki Bouki* embark on a quest to obtain the material trappings of capitalist modernity prior to their departure, precisely because they view their journey to France as their entry into the heart of the capitalist world order: Europe in this vision is best represented, as Appiah argues, by money, not reason. Equally, in *Hyenas*, Mambety presents us with an Africa that might be said to have already 'entered and left' modernity:[4] by the early 1990s, when the film was made, Mambety suggests that Africa has been largely bypassed by the capitalist system and left to exist on the margins of a global capitalist system in which the grand narratives of modernist emancipation have slowly been eroded, which simply leaves in its wake the values of the market, personified in the character of Ramatou who is able to buy the 'soul' of Colobane with the promise of consumer happiness.

Essentially, Mambety's work reflects both the utopian and the dystopian nature of modernity. Utopianism has been central to Western modernity, for its rationality offers a potential cure for all of society's ills, past, present and future. On the other hand, capitalist modernity in the West has also produced rapid change, uncertainty and a certain dystopian despondency at the breakdown of previous communal values. (Georg Simmel's landmark essay 'The Metropolis and Mental Life' famously charts the 'alienation' of urban life in the early twentieth century.) Modernity is a mass of contradictory social forces that produced variously complex responses from writers and artists long before the advent of a body of thought termed 'postmodernism'. Mambety can thus be seen as a modernist precisely because his work embraces the complexity of the postcolonial city in a multifaceted, experimental film style. He does not 'go beyond' modernity but rather seeks to carve out a space for Africa within the modernist project.

While African film directors have been keen to engage with modernity as a concept, few have adopted the experimental, narrative techniques seen as characteristic of high modernist artistic practice, and Mambety's work is thus something of an exception. The opening sequence of *Touki Bouki* provides some flavour of Mambety's fiercely modernist negotiations with modernity. The initial shot of a cattle drive, to the accompaniment of an African flute, seems like the quintessence of 'tradition', with overtones of peaceful, quasi-utopian rurality. This then cuts to lengthy and brutal scenes as the cattle are butchered in an abattoir, while the young boy who led the cattle drive rides away alone. The noise of a motorbike drowns out the sound of the flute, and we cut to an over-the-shoulder shot of Mory riding his bike (decorated with the huge skull and horns of the type of animal we have just seen being slaughtered) alongside a shantytown and then out on to the open road.

Formally, the sequence is typical of Mambety's modernism in its use of unsettling (often shocking) juxtapositions and a general absence of narrative continuity, explanation or, ultimately, closure. Part of the effect of that is that there are many ways of reading the sequence: for instance as the encapsulation of a linear history (the transition from the rural to the urbanised modern, bloodily embodied in the move from the examples of individual animal slaughter, which intersperse the narrative, to the larger-scale capitalist enterprise of the commercial abattoir). Equally, the sequence could be read as the coexistence of different ways of life, rather than the replacement of one by another – an overlap or simultaneity that complicates things, necessitating processes of negotiation, but also creating spaces for ways of 'entering and leaving modernity'. To remind us of this transition, or this coexistence, the cattle/motorbike link runs right through the film: from the opening sequence to the scene where Mory, surrounded by cattle, looks as if he is going to lasso one of them, but in fact lassoes and ties up his (previously out of shot) motorbike; and to the final crash, when the bike is left lying in the road, looking like a dead ox, its leaking oil and petrol echoing the blood in the abattoir.

Another way of reading the opening sequence might be that the old ways of life lead nowhere (or to the slaughterhouse), while the modern leads to the open road, the future, escape. That utopian sense of modernity's possibilities is what drives Mory and the narrative (such as it is). Mory and Anta plan to escape to the utopian space of Paris: 'Paris, the gateway to paradise' is how Mory describes it, and at this point we hear, for the first of many times, Mado Robin singing 'Paris, Paris, Paris – it's paradise on earth' while the camera pans across a rather desolate vista of dried-up trees. Again, there are different possible readings of this sequence: as emphasising, for example, the distance between the characters' harsh surroundings and Paris, the capital of modernity (to rephrase Walter Benjamin). Equally, it could be seen as highlighting precisely the *absence* of Paris, the non-existence of the utopian city that Mory (certainly) and Anta (possibly) will never reach, and whose most substantial embodiment remains the repetitive (and slightly irritating) song lyrics.

If at one level Mory and Anta's scheme looks like an ageless and universal romantic quest for a utopian future, it is nevertheless at another level firmly grounded in the very much more prosaic historical specificities of the economically driven population movements of late modernity, which for many have been much more of a dystopian experience (memorably represented in one of the other great African modernist films, Med Hondo's *Soleil O*, discussed in Chapter 3). In a similar kind of parallelism, alongside the utopian dream of Paris, there is an awareness, running through the film in muted fashion, of certain realities that risk rendering the dream pure illusion. In particular, Mory himself, riding off with the proceeds from another robbery and dreaming of the future, declares 'You city niggers, you street-sweeping niggers – I'm not one of you', revealing perhaps the clearest knowledge of the dystopian fate of those fellow Africans who have made the journey to the postcolonial metropolis. Whether it is this knowledge – and the fear (or even likelihood) that in fact he will be just another 'street-sweeping nigger' in Paris – that later prevents Mory boarding the ship for France is, typically, left unclarified.

What Edward Said calls the 'voyage in' to the metropolis is not the only possible direction to be taken, however, and Mory and Anta's trajectory has another ironic parallel or reversal. When they have robbed Charlie, Mory leaves in Charlie's commandeered car and Anta follows on the motorbike. Anta is 'ambushed' by a wild, ragged figure and runs off, leaving the bike that the 'wild man' takes, rides into town on, and eventually crashes. Significantly, a comment from a bystander reveals that the 'wild man' is 'that white boy who lives in the baobab' – presumably (for viewers are left to piece together the narrative as best they can) a dissatisfied inhabitant of modernity, dreaming of escape from it into the supposedly utopian space of a pre-modern culture and a life closer to nature, and as such an ironic inversion of the desires and direction of the central couple. The simultaneity or juxtaposition of these quests is another indication that we are not dealing with a simple 'tradition versus modernity' duality. Modernity can be progressive or reactionary, future-oriented or nostalgic, and the coexistence of these opposing strands typifies its complex, hybridised not dichotomised, nature, while at the same time that very complexity makes the attribution of value-laden terms (progressive or reactionary) an uncertain business. Their coexistence once again highlights the misrepresentation involved in postmodernism's attempt to posit a single, monolithic modernity.

If the present reality to be escaped from in *Touki Bouki* is merely unsatisfactory, in *Hyenas* it has become more properly dystopian, with the little town of Colobane slowly dying from a combination of drought and economic collapse. This does not immediately look like a film about modernity: on the contrary, it has more the appearance of an evocation (or pastiche) of a timeless Africa (with images of elephants crossing an open landscape). Moreover, it does not immediately appear to be operating within the same forms or strategies of modernism as *Touki Bouki*. Gradually it becomes clear that this is a community that, rather than anticipating entering modernity, is in danger of leaving it altogether after a brief acquaintance, but which is desperate for re-entry. To that extent, Colobane is symptomatic of the condition of much of the continent after 30 to 40 years of deepening postcolonial immiseration, endebtedness and infrastructural collapse. The film details the conditions, and the cost, of that longed-for re-entry.

Ramatou Linguere's return coincides with something like the death throes of Colobane as a town: the town hall has just been closed down, its contents carried off by creditors; Draman Drameh's shop still suggests some vestige of a money economy, but no one seems to have any money, and goods are repeatedly bought with promises of future payment, and Draman describes himself as 'a bankrupt grocer in a bankrupt town'. Ramatou brings the promise of an instant utopia – untold wealth, smart clothes, consumer goods and cars – to a community that, in the mayor's words, has 'fallen into the abyss'. However, this is a pastiche of the promised modernity: it is the surface appearance of material success with nothing to underpin it. Ramatou's largesse provides an instantaneous and effortless transformation of the town, and is thus properly utopian, but there is in fact a high price to be paid.

At this point the proffered utopia begins to turn into its antithesis. Though Colobane might be dead or dying as a modern town, basic human values (the remnants perhaps of a particularly African sense of community), best exemplified in the behaviour of Draman Drameh, appear to be alive. The inhabitants of Colobane display a sort of 'solidarity in adversity', but the arrival of Ramatou changes that, and, though Draman Drameh's regular 'customers' may pledge 'solidarity, dead or alive', their stripping of his best goods on 'credit' (meaning the assurance that he will be killed, and that they will not have to pay) marks precisely the absence of that solidarity.

Although Ramatou brings about the moral destruction of the community of Colobane, she is not destroying an innocent community free from sin (and certainly not as moral as it likes to think of itself). Even Draman Drameh, perhaps the best of Colobane's citizens, has behaved extremely badly in the past, while the mayor's claim that 'We have always lived according to the rule of law' may in some sense be true, but crucially ignores just how fallible the law has shown itself to be, especially with regard to a vulnerable, notionally 'fallen', woman. At the same time, this moral decline requires the town's inhabitants to be honest, to face the difficult, unpalatable truth about themselves for the first time. It is noticeable, however, that the communal self-deception as compensatory activity reasserts itself even more powerfully as they prepare to murder Draman, chanting: 'The proposal is accepted. Not for the money. For justice.'

The final sequence of the film is a series of rapid cuts between shots of the bulldozers (repeatedly), the hunter – who makes his silent, enigmatic way through the film – throwing away his gun, Draman's jacket, a distant view of a bleached, unreal cityscape, and the closing image of the earth scarred by caterpillar tracks converging on a baobab tree that looks small and vulnerable, rather than the mighty tree of life it is for so many African cultures. However, it is the shot of the 'unreal' city, the tower-block-filled city of modernity, absent but hovering on the horizon, that emphasises the future that Colobane has (unwittingly) wished upon itself, as its present is crushed and flattened. Once again, various readings of the sequence are possible. Is it another compressed mini-narrative of the (necessary) transition from 'savagery' (the brutal killing of Draman Drameh) to civilisation (urbanisation)? Or is it the (ironic) juxtaposition of the (supposed) barbarity of a collectively administered and individually accepted cleansing of the community, versus the (actual) barbarity of the mechanised obliteration of the community's homes, way of life, values?

It would be misguided to view Mambety's career in terms of a gradual but programmatic shift away from utopianism to a growing dystopianism, for the darkly comic vision of *Hyenas* must be balanced against the 'lighter' tone of his final, short works, *Le Franc* and *The Little Girl who Sold the Sun*, in which the harsh social conditions of life in 1990s Dakar are overcome, or at least kept at bay, by the bumbling good fortune of Marigo the musician, and the indomitable spirit of Sili Laam, the young, disabled girl. At the heart of Mambety's work lies a fundamental optimism and an almost naive faith in his characters' capacity to overcome all the odds stacked against them.

In order to conclude these brief reflections on the relationship between the modern, the postmodern and the postcolonial, it seems appropriate to return to Appiah's influential essay. Appiah charts the emergence of 'post-realist' (literary) narratives in the 1960s, which criticised the nationalist project and the realist narratives that supported it. For Appiah, post-realist narratives reject all forms of grand narrative whether it be 'scientific rationalism' or a nativism that posits an essentialist African or ethnic identity. Appiah's main example is Yambo Ouologuem's classic and highly controversial novel *Bound to Violence* (1968), which satirises both the pretences of Western rationality and the oppressive framework of ethnic thought. However, for Appiah, this is 'not postmodernism but postmodernization; not an aesthetics but a politics' (1992: 152). Ouologuem and other African artists do not reject the nation, progress or socialism in favour of an ethnic, racial relativism: they seek instead to promote a more general sense of African solidarity and humanity. Like their postmodernist counterparts, these postcolonial authors are writing against earlier legitimating narratives (realism, nativism, nationalism), but, for Appiah, their work 'challenges them in the name of the ethical universal; in the name of humanism' (1992: 155).

This espousal of an (African) humanism is also present in Mambety's films. As was argued above, for all their sense of play and ambiguity, his films consistently display a profound belief in a sense of his characters' common humanity: they all have their weaknesses but Mambety's films are never judgemental towards them. (*Hyenas* is his darkest film precisely because the townspeople abandon their sense of a common humanity.) This is not simply a case of postmodern relativism, and his characters are never seen as postmodern representational ciphers, echoes of other representations of similar 'types' in other works. From *Badou Boy* to *The Little Girl who Sold the Sun*, his work is committed to exploring the world of dreamers, drifters and rebels. This desire to express a basic, shared humanity can be seen in Mambety's delight at discovering that his screenplay for *Hyenas* had unknowingly imitated elements of Dürrenmatt's play, *The Visit of the Old Lady*: for Mambety, the fact that two artists from different continents and hugely different backgrounds could come up with the same narrative was unexpected but welcome proof of their common humanity (Wynchank 2003: 71–5).

The implication of Western liberal humanism in the inhumanity of both the slave trade and colonial conquest has led many critics to view any notion of humanism as inherently flawed. However, many of the pioneering anti-colonial authors – Césaire, Memmi, Fanon – were explicitly inspired by a desire to create a reformed humanism. In particular, Fanon famously concluded *The Wretched of the Earth* with a call for decolonisation to bring about the creation of a 'new man', in order to replace the discredited humanism of colonial Europe: 'For Europe, for ourselves and for humanity, comrades, we must turn over a new leaf, we must work out new concepts, and try to set afoot a new man' (1967: 255). In recent times, such an endeavour has been seen as fundamentally misguided, and, indeed, it appears chimerical at best to attempt clearly to define a postcolonial humanism. None the less, as the films of Djibril Diop Mambety illustrate, the cinematic exploration of what it means to be human in postcolonial Africa might just help us to break out of the endless terminological debates about the modern, the postmodern and the postcolonial, and act as a useful and necessary step in exploring a common sense of humanity and elaborating a new humanism for the twenty-first century.

Notes

1 Although Mambety's career stalled for fifteen years after *Touki Bouki*, he was still only forty-three years old when he made *Let's Talk, Grandmother*, which serves to illustrate the precociousness of his talent in the late 1960s and early 1970s. Ouédraogo was in fact just nine years younger than Mambety, which means that they were roughly of the same generation.
2 He had also found a very sympathetic producer in Sylvia Voser, who produced his final three films.
3 In the past decade, Nouri Bouzid's *Bezness* (1995), Mohamed Camara's *Dakan* (1997) and *Karmen Gei* (2001) by Joseph Rokhaya Geye have explored homosexuality in contemporary Africa, which still remains a largely taboo subject.
4 For a more in-depth analysis of this concept of 'entering and leaving modernity' see Williams (2001).

Filmography

Contras' City (1969)
Badou Boy (1970)
Touki Bouki (*The Hyena's Voyage*) (1973)
Let's Talk, Grandmother (1988)
Hyenas (1992)
Le Franc (1994)
The Little Girl who Sold the Sun (1998)

Chapter 5

Souleymane Cissé

Introduction

The Malian film director Souleymane Cissé is best known for his breathtaking film *Yeelen* (*The Light*), which won the Jury Prize at Cannes in 1987 (the first sub-Saharan African film to do so). *Yeelen* was heralded not only as a crucial breakthrough for African cinema on the international film stage but also as the embodiment of a new form of African filmmaking practice, which was embedded in the oral narratives traditions and spirituality of West Africa, and which departed from the social realist 'norms' of a previous generation (although, as has been argued at length in previous chapters, this characterisation of the first wave of African films as primarily social realist in form is itself largely the result of an excessive generalisation). *Yeelen* was Cissé's fourth feature film and it clearly marked the culmination of an artistic journey away from the naturalism of his earlier works such as *Den Muso* (*The Young Girl*, 1975) or *Baara* (*Work*, 1978), which often had an explicitly 'political' or 'social' agenda. However, as will be discussed in greater detail below, many of the 'new' stylistic elements in *Yeelen* that struck critics were in fact already present in his early works. Cissé himself argues in response to a rather blunt question from Frank Ukadike on the 'evolution' of his style: 'My style has not changed. It is the story that has changed because I deal with issues under different situations. In terms of aesthetic and poetic dimensions, the same manner of approaching the topic and narrative construction applies to all of my films' (Ukadike 2002: 21). Although this statement displays a certain defensiveness and reluctance to engage with analysis of his work, which is characteristic of Cissé's occasionally belligerent stance in interviews, it is none the less a timely and salutary reminder to critics who might rush to make hasty judgements about the style of a film based solely on its subject matter: the fact that *Yeelen* deals with the precolonial past does not make it more 'African' than his previous films; nor does the depiction of the urban proletariat in *Baara* make it more 'Western' or 'social realist'. The depiction of Cissé as a director who has made the 'transition' from social realism to a more symbolic, more mystical, and consequently more 'African' form of filmmaking thus constitutes an important case study for the critic, necessitating a reassessment not only of Cissé's trajectory as a filmmaker but also of our understanding of the so-called social realist filmmaking of the 1960s and 1970s as a whole (on this issue see also Chapter 2 on Sembene).

Born in the Malian capital, Bamako, in 1940, Cissé moved as a young boy to Dakar in Senegal, where his father, a market trader, had found work. He developed a love of cinema early in life, after his elder brothers first sneaked him into a cinema when he was six. The family returned to Bamako after Malian independence in 1960, and Cissé became involved in a local *ciné-club*. Independent Mali was, nominally at least, a socialist country with close ties to the Soviet Union, and Cissé made the most of these links when applying for a scholarship to receive film training in Moscow. A first, brief trip to train as a projectionist was followed by a six-year stay (1963–69) during which he trained as a film director at the VGIK studios in Moscow, under the supervision of the great Soviet director Mark Donskoi (under whom Sembene had studied several years earlier).

Cissé made his first (and rarely seen) short films at VGIK between 1965 and 1968, and they give a clear indication of the artistic and political concerns that would mark his later career. The (very) short documentary film *Sources d'inspiration* (8 minutes), ostensibly about the work of the Malian painter Momadou Somé Coulibaly, rejects narrative linearity in favour of an impressionistic jumble of images, music and words. These include still images of colonial violence and slavery, interspersed with quotations from Aimé Césaire and footage of black resistance heroes, Martin Luther King, Patrice Lumumba, and are clearly designed to provoke reflection on the artist's role in newly independent African countries. This process of mixing the artistic and the political in an almost spiritual quest for truth and justice has continued to mark Cissé's filmmaking and it finds its most sustained expression in *Yeelen* and *Waati* (see Thackway 2003: 84–6, for discussion of the quest motif in his work).

After his return to Mali in 1969, Cissé was hired to work as a film director by the Service Cinématographique du Ministère de l'Information du Mali (SCINFOMA), and over the next few years he produced newsreels and documentaries for this state body. Indeed, all of Cissé's early short films were documentaries, and it was not until 1972 that he made his first fiction film, *Five Days in a Life*, with money from the French Ministry for Co-operation. *Five Days in a Life* is a *moyen-métrage* (45 minutes), which relates the hardships of city life for a young boy in a Qur'anic school in Bamako. Its episodic structure, with the camera following the boy around the city as he begs for money to pay for his upkeep, is reminiscent of Sembene's *Borom Sarret* (1962). The film thus marked out Cissé as an important new talent but one who was working primarily within the existing stylistic parameters of African cinema as a whole, a critical judgement that has clung to his early films ever since.

Cissé's first feature film, *Den Muso*, is viewed primarily as a 'social' film that deals with issues of class – Cissé creates a visual opposition at the start between Ténin's wealthy but ailing father Malamine and the young, virile factory worker Sékou – and the status of women in Malian society: the second half of the film is devoted to the treatment of Ténin at the hands of her father after she falls pregnant with Sékou's child. Despite the early scenes, in black-and-white, of manual labour outside Ténin's home, and some later scenes, in colour, of men at work in Malamine's factory, the film quickly seems to lose interest in class as an issue. Sékou is presented at first as a potential 'class warrior' when he stands up to Malamine but in the remainder of the film he becomes a manipulative and uncaring philanderer; in fact, he does not treat Ténin any better than her malicious father does. Class thus seems far less important than gender, but even the treatment of gender is dealt with in a fashion that cannot be classified unreservedly as belonging to the 'social realist' aesthetic so closely associated with Cissé's early films. For Cissé appears far more concerned with exploring the experience of being young in modern-day Bamako than with making specific political or social points. In fact, *Den Muso* might best be seen as an attempt to represent the world through the eyes of its central character, Ténin, with whom the spectator is so clearly 'aligned': we often see the world as though through her eyes, and are given access to her experiences and feelings to a much greater extent than any of the other characters.

A clear visual link between *Den Muso* and Cissé's second feature film, *Baara*, is created by the use of images of fire. At the end of *Den Muso*, Ténin burns down the hut in which she finds Sékou with a lover, while *Baara* opens and closes with mythical images of male figures crossing a burning landscape. Although *Baara* is Cissé's most 'naturalistic' work, these two sequences provide a powerful symbolic framework within which to read the events of the film.[1] Overall, the film can be read as an exploration of the world of work in 1970s Mali. The narrative intertwines the stories of a wide range of characters, each of whom has money troubles: from the factory owner, who has a wide range of creditors, to Balla, the lowly porter. The world of work and of human relations more generally – in particular, the relationship between the factory owner and his wife – are marked by indifference and exploitation: in the second half of the film, when Balla, the engineer, attempts to treat the workers as equals, the factory owner immediately orders his murder. Community is destroyed by greed and oppression.

Baara won the Grand Prix at FESPACO in 1979, as did Cissé's next film, *Finyé*, in 1983. In *Finyé*, the tension between the realist and symbolic impulses in the director's work finds its most creative expression. Although loosely based on the wave of student protests that hit Mali in the early 1980s, it is perhaps more useful to think of the film as a symbolic meditation on the nature of power and authority in Africa. Bâ and Batrou are teenage lovers from different ends of the social spectrum: he is from a once noble family line but is now a poor orphan, raised by his grandparents, while she is the well-to-do daughter of the local military governor. Their involvement in radical student politics conveys on them both a nobility that is expressed in 'traditional' terms and conveyed through the repeated 'dream' sequences in which Bâ and Batrou, both dressed in white, receive a bowl of water from a young boy. Effectively, *Finyé* reinforced the sense that Cissé's work was increasingly turning towards the African past in a quest to find models of behaviour and thought that might point a way out of the greed and corruption of the contemporary, post-independence reality.

Yeelen (1987) is generally considered by critics to be Cissé's masterpiece. A beautifully shot film, it abandons any trace of realism or naturalism in favour of a mythical and symbolic narrative that pits a rebellious son against his tyrannical father. Set at an unspecified moment in precolonial, rural Mali, it is a profoundly moving and dramatic tale of knowledge, power and generational conflict. However, although critics are generally in agreement on its outstanding cinematic achievement, there is little agreement on the precise nature of this achievement. For some critics, the film marked a retreat from the committed cinema of the 1970s in favour of a more 'aesthetic' cinema, which would appeal to a Western audience (its victory at Cannes was used as evidence by hostile critics that the film had been made with a non-African audience in mind); while, for others, it constituted the expression of an 'authentic' African cinematic aesthetic.[2] As will be argued in the final section of this chapter, these judgements are, in fact, much more revealing about the nature of certain debates within African film criticism than they are about the nature of Cissé's work. For *Yeelen* is, in many ways, not a radical departure from previous African filmmaking practice but rather the most accomplished product of a certain strand of African filmmaking practice that had hitherto gone relatively unnoticed.

After the critical plaudits heaped on his first four feature films, the negative critical and public response to *Waati* must have been a major blow to Cissé, especially as the film had gone through such a complicated and traumatic gestation period that at one stage production had closed down altogether owing to lack of finance.[3] A sprawling and ambitious narrative, set in both South Africa and Ivory Coast, *Waati* is ostensibly the story of Nandi, a young girl forced to flee apartheid South Africa after her father and brother are murdered by the police, and she kills a policeman in revenge. The first hour of the film, set in South Africa, makes for compelling viewing but most critics agree that the films loses its way in the West African section (at almost two and a half hours in length, the film suffers from more than the occasional *longueur*), as it depicts the main character's spiritual quest to develop her African 'identity': despite sequences of great beauty, the second half of the film can at times seem slightly portentous in its desire to stress the symbolic nature of Nandi's quest.

Cissé has not made a film since *Waati*, nor does a new film appear imminent. It is a sad reflection upon the precarious existence of African cinema that a filmmaker as celebrated as Cissé should find it so difficult to obtain funding for his work. That one of Africa's finest filmmakers should have made just five feature films in over thirty years is a crying shame but it is, sadly, the common fate of many African directors. The chief irony of this situation, as will be explored in the next section, is that Cissé's most creative period coincided with an extremely repressive political and social climate in Mali: Cissé might thus paradoxically be argued to have produced his best work when working within the constraints placed upon him by the military regime.

Social, cultural and political contexts

Mali gained its independence from France in 1960 as part of the short-lived Mali Federation, a political union with Senegal. Within a couple of months, the Federation had collapsed, with Mali and Senegal going their separate ways as independent nations. For the next eight years, Mali was ruled by President Modibo Keïta, who sought to establish a planned socialist economy. Allying Mali with the Soviet Union in the Cold War politics of the period, Keïta distanced the country from its former colonial rulers: he closed French military bases and withdrew Mali from the French-sponsored CFA to create its own currency the *Franc Malien*. Unfortunately, the President's brand of 'African Socialism' led to a soaring inflation rate and a marked devaluation of the national currency, which brought about increasing popular unrest.

Keïta was eventually overthrown in 1968 in a bloodless *coup d'état* staged by a group of young military officers. Led by a 32-year-old lieutenant, Moussa Touré, the hastily formed Comité Militaire de Libération Nationale (CMLN) imprisoned Keïta and other senior members of the government. The new regime, with Touré at its head, continued along the socialist path traced by its predecessor, and sought further support from both the Soviet Union and the communist authorities in China. Touré remained in power from 1968 to 1991, and, although the regime made half-hearted attempts to open itself to democratic reform, Mali was effectively under military rule for this entire period. The regime finally fell in 1991 after a sustained period of mass demonstrations, led by student protestors. Since 1992, Mali has been a relatively stable multi-party democracy but it is still one of the poorest countries in the world: a huge, barren and land-locked nation, its economic prospects remain rather bleak.

It is a major ambiguity of Cissé's career that he was a civil servant, and thus, in effect, working for the government, throughout the period of military rule. This raises important issues about the complex relationship between the African state and the filmmaker. Many calls have been made for African governments to allow their filmmakers greater freedom of expression (see Diawara 1992: 81), but few African regimes have been willing to do so: until recently, the primary source of funding for African films was either the national government or the French authorities, and it is perhaps unsurprising that they have rarely sought to sponsor politically sensitive work. Even where governments have allowed dissenting voices to be heard, it is important not to rush into hasty judgements as to the 'liberal' credentials of the regime.

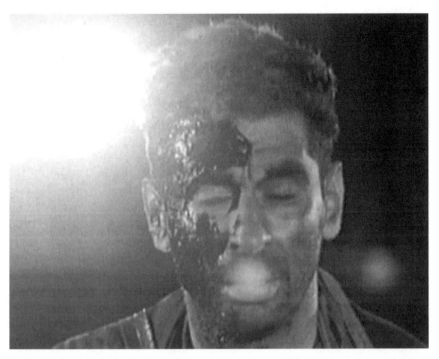

1 *Cairo Station*, directed by Youssef Chahine, 1958

2 *Black Girl*, directed by Ousmane Sembene, 1966

3 *Soleil O*, directed by Med Hondo, 1969

4 *Badou Boy*, directed by Djibril Diop Mambety, 1970

5 *Le Franc*, directed by Djibril Diop Mambety, 1994

6 *Nha fala*, directed by Flora Gomes, 2002

7 *Tilaï*, directed by Idrissa Ouédraogo, 1990

8 *The Silences of the Palace*, directed by Moufida Tlatli, 1994

Commenting on the unlikely support that *Finyé* received from the Malian military authorites, Ukadike (rather naively) suggests that: 'Tolerance and maturity prevailing, the government demonstrated that it is capable of listening to constructive criticism' (1994: 196). However, one might just as easily read into such a move a desire on the part of the military to buy itself some good publicity as an increasingly open and liberal regime, a phenomenon acknowledged by Ousmane Sembene who spoke of his work serving, in the 1970s, as an 'alibi' for the Senegalese authorities who could claim that the absence of censorship was proof of their belief in the freedom of expression (see Murphy 2000a: 225–6). For many other African directors, often living under more oppressive conditions and working within the constraints of harsh censorship laws, direct criticism of the government – if not of 'general' social ills – has simply not been possible: the experience of the radical director Med Hondo who has lived in exile from his homeland of Mauritania for several decades is typical of the fate that often awaits those who engage in direct criticism of the state. In this context, it is hardly surprising that Cissé's films have developed as indirect, and at times oblique, critiques of the problems he sees within his society:

> As my own experiences have shown, what you narrate may also put you into trouble. Sometimes, in order to survive a hostile environment one is forced, not necessarily to disarm, but to construct a narrative that is not too political nor devoid of pungent criticism of the system. (Ukadike 2002: 21)

Cissé does not appear to have experienced direct censorship;[4] indeed, somewhat remarkably, *Finyé*, the film that touches most directly on the political situation in Mali, received financial and technical support from the military authorities. Rather, it would seem that the political context within which he was working throughout the 1970s and 1980s placed limits upon what he felt he could or could not say when dealing with political or social issues. He makes this point explicitly in an interview shortly after the release of *Yeelen*: 'There was also tension building around me because of my previous films, and it was clear that if I wanted to stay in my country and enjoy a degree of freedom of expression, I had to lighten things a bit or make a different type of cinema' (Diawara 1988: 13). Essentially, Cissé argues that it is better to make a less direct political comment on current events, which will permit his film to be shown in Mali (and permit him to continue working there) rather than making a scathing political attack on the military regime that might garner him plaudits from an international audience but would undoubtedly be censored in his own country.

Thus, whether by political necessity or by artistic temperament – and, most likely, a mixture of both – Cissé has never really sought to denounce specific figures or regimes in his films (unlike Sembene, for example in *Xala*). His cinema works in a much less direct register in which spiritual matters, the clash of generations, gender conflict, are given far more importance than specific 'issues'. Even in *Finyé*, the film in which he refers most explicitly to specific political events, the precise demands of the student protestors are never clearly articulated; rather it is the symbolic significance of their stance that counts. As will be argued at length in the final section of this chapter, this allows his films to be read as 'human' stories (rather than say social or political films), which has had a profound effect on the critical reception of his work.

Generational conflict – or perhaps more accurately, conflict between young people and the forces of authority – might well be argued to be the motor of Cissé's work. All of his fictional films – *Five Days in a Life, Den Muso, Baara, Finyé, Yeelen, Waati* – focus on young protagonists who come into conflict with the restrictive practices and beliefs of their elders. In *Yeelen*, Nianankoro has stolen from his father the secrets of the *komo*, a powerful figure within this secret society. However, what appears to be a 'magical' or 'supernatural' tale can also be read in symbolic fashion as an allegory on the nature of power and knowledge in Africa, and Cissé himself has often cited the film as his most 'political' because of this fundamental questioning of the control and use of knowledge. Nianankoro and his father assure each other's destruction in their final showdown but the possibility of change lives on in his young son on whom the film closes. This was clearly a powerful political conclusion in the context of late 1980s Mali (and in Africa as a whole).[5]

Like many of his contemporaries (Sembene, Hondo) who were imbued with the 'modernising' principles of socialism and reason, Cissé is keen to address the role of women within his society. The most assertive female character in Cissé's work is Nandi (*Waati*), who is shown to have inherited much of her inner strength from her grandmother. At the end of the film, Nandi repeats to her adopted daughter the story that her grandmother had told her at the start: the assertive role enjoyed by women within African societies is presented as a time-honoured practice rather than as a new, Western-inspired departure from the past. Nandi murders the policeman responsible for her father's murder and builds a new life for herself in another country, before returning home to confront the past in post-apartheid South Africa. Nandi has a male partner but he is not an important presence in the film and they part in the desert before her return to South Africa. Batrou in *Finyé* is an equally strong and forceful character; she is prepared to stand up to her tyrannical father and berates those students who bow before the coercion of the military. However, her actions might easily be read as those of a lover who follows in the wake of the 'heroic' male, which would cast her role as much more passive than one might originally imagine. Equally, in *Den Muso, Baara* and *Yeelen*, there is sympathy for the plight of women but they are, by and large, victims of men with little possibility of altering the conditions in which they live. Except for Nandi, Cissé does not envisage new models of behaviour that might allow them to break free from the constraints within which they live.

Overall, then, Cissé's work might be said to investigate the underlying power structures and hierarchies of West African society rather than the specific social and political contexts of the post-independence period. In cultural terms, his films engage with the modernist or modernising discourse of the 1960s and 1970s but they are also clearly marked by a desire to explore the specificity of African experiences of the world, including the realms of spirituality and mysticism. In *Baara*, change is associated with the modernising presence of Balla, the engineer; however, in subsequent films, the source of change is located within forms of local knowledge: the 'traditional', spiritual knowledge of Kansaye, the grandfather in *Finyé*; the supernatural power of the *komo* in *Yeelen*; the exploration of the African past in *Waati* (as well as uncovering her African roots in the Ivory Coast, Nandi writes a doctoral thesis on the use of masks). The belief in secular rationalism never completely disappears from Cissé's work – see, for example, the almost hushed reverence for the words of the university lecturer in *Waati* – but it is increasingly bound to an approach that seeks to define arguments and find creative answers within the culture of Mali.

The films

As was discussed above, Cissé's work is often praised or criticised by critics for having abandoned his early social realism in favour of a more symbolic and less direct narrative form. However, Cissé's early feature films – *Den Muso, Baara, Finyé* – involve a complex mix of stylistic registers, which veer from naturalism to, at times, quite abstruse symbolic sequences. As with Sembene's films, these early works seem to be testing the limits of the neo-realist model that dominated the early period of African filmmaking. For example, *Den Muso* largely conforms to a social realist aesthetic, but there are also repeated breaks in narrative continuity in sequences where the director forces the spectator to make his or her own connections. This is particularly evident in the rape sequence. Sékou and Ténin have been thrown into the river by their friends in a youthful prank, and Sékou helps the flailing Ténin out of the water. The image cuts back and forth between the friends now back at their picnic fooling around, and Sékou, who helps a prostrate Ténin out of her wet clothes. However, these 'innocent' actions soon reveal a sinister intention as Sékou, without warning, tries to rape his companion. The sequence is filmed without music and the tension is heightened by ever more rapid cuts back to the friends, laughing and joking and slicing a watermelon, the pink flesh of the fruit perhaps working as a sinister echo of the sexual attack unfolding nearby. As Sékou overpowers the struggling young girl, the camera zooms in on their writhing limbs, forcing the spectator into the very midst of this brutal and seemingly unmotivated act. The oppressive silence of the sequence mirrors the silence imposed upon a mute Ténin, who cannot cry out for help.

A similar process is at work in the very next sequence of the film when we are given further evidence of Sékou's slide into depravity. A handheld camera pans round the crowded marketplace, then moves through the bustling

crowd as a series of faces brush past. Sékou and a male companion are occasionally visible in the crowd. Then, suddenly, we are thrown into the immediate aftermath of a mugging; a woman shrieks as Sékou's companion
appears to run off with her bag. Sékou backs away feigning not to have been
involved. A crowd gathers round and Sékou is captured; next time we see
him he is writhing on the ground in pain. These deliberate narrative 'jumps'
are reminiscent of the wilful anti-realism of the *nouvelle vague* – and 'art
house' filmmaking, more generally – and indicate a clear desire on Cissé's
part to develop a style of filmmaking that encourages the spectator to play
an active role in creating the narrative.[6]

Cissé sets out his artistic credo in Rithy Panh's beautiful documentary,
Souleymane Cissé (1991). In the opening sequence, Cissé describes the inspiration for his films as an almost dreamlike, visionary process, but one that
is firmly based in reality. He later speaks of his desire to create films that will
stay in the audience's memory, and will 'speak to' spectators in a dramatic
and symbolic visual language. This approach is illustrated in the conclusion
to *Den Muso*. In a breathless tracking shot, accompanied by the urgent
sound of extra-diegetic, chanting female voices, Ténin rushes through the
streets to confront Sékou whom she finds in bed with another woman. In her
anger and disappointment, she sets fire to the house, before returning home
to commit suicide. This final sequence is shot in an intriguing, non-linear
fashion: using jump cuts and rapid zooms in to Ténin's face and body as she
crumples to the floor, Cissé gives a vivid sense of this young girl slowly losing
her grip on life. These are the type of 'strong images' that he wishes to embed
in the mind of the spectator.

Baara is framed by opening and closing sections that clearly take the film
beyond the limits of a realist or naturalist aesthetic. The opening dreamlike
sequence of the two Ballas, the porter and the engineer, walking together
through a fiery landscape, sets the film within an almost mythical context.
After a series of medium close-ups of the naked torso of a male figure (whom
we later discover is Balla, the porter), filmed against a black backdrop, the
image cuts to a hazy, medium distance shot of a flaming rural landscape
across which two men advance towards the camera, their faces obscured by
the smoke. In the past, they would have been slave and master (as the engineer comments jokingly when they first meet) but now they are on the same
side of a struggle against the forces of authority and corruption within their
society. *Baara* thus sets out a template for exploring important social, political and cultural issues within a symbolic, mythical framework, which Cissé
has followed in all of his subsequent films. The one-word titles – *Baara*,
Finyé, *Yeelen*, *Waati* – emphasise Cissé's desire to engage with basic, often
elemental aspects of human existence – work, wind, light, time – and the
three most recent of these films all open with shots of majestic empty landscapes, as if to emphasise the timeless, epic quality of the narrative: swoop-
ing aerial shots over the primeval forest in *Finyé*; a static shot of the rising
sun over a barren landscape in *Yeelen*; and an aerial tracking shot over the

desert in *Waati*. The student protests of *Finyé* are situated within a wider reflection on how change emerges within society. As the Bambara ideograms in the credits proclaim: 'The wind stirs up men's thoughts.' This process is carried even further in *Yeelen* in which the epic confrontation between father and son is given an allegorical function as a commentary on the transfer of knowledge and power to the younger generation in contemporary Africa. In *Waati*, the violence and oppression of apartheid is cast as a scar on the history of Africa but one that will heal with time: the film is framed by images of the timeless beauty of the landscape, and the passing of cultural heritage from grandmother to Nandi (at the start), and from Nandi to her adopted daughter Aïcha (at the end).

This use of symbolism can readily be situated within an oral narrative tradition in which realism is not a major concern, and in which the 'disruption' of narrative development by the need to investigate the hidden meaning of symbols is a central component of narrative convention. Fire and water are the two most important recurring visual motifs in Cissé's work: both elements seem to represent a source of cleansing and purity that is often as painful as it is necessary. As was mentioned above, *Baara* opens and closes with images of the two central characters walking through a fiery landscape. In the opening sequence, their identities are blurred by the smoke, lending the images an element of mystery, and suggesting an almost epic context for the struggles that the film describes in largely realist fashion. In the final sequence of the film, as the credits roll, their identities are revealed, as we see the two Ballas advance side by side through this desolate landscape: although Balla, the engineer, has been murdered, leaving his poorer namesake disconsolate, the film's conclusion places this contemporary story within a wider, mythical framework, a timeless struggle against corruption and the abuse of power.

In *Finyé*, it is water that plays the main symbolic role. Bâ's recurring dreams of a pure, innocent union with Batrou take place by a river; the couple are dressed in white robes, and a young boy hands them a calabash of water from the river, from which they both drink; the young lovers then look coyly into each others' eyes. However, the calabash is thrown back into the river and the camera lingers on it as it floats away. What exactly is the meaning of the symbolism within this sequence? The white robes confer upon the young people a nobility and a purity that contrasts both with Bâ's current lowly social status and also with the depredations that they must face in this era of corruption and misrule. Significantly, Bâ's dream begins as he drifts off into a drug-induced stupor with his friends, as he tries to drown out the disappointment of failing to achieve the necessary grades to go to university: is this dream the new world that the students wish to bring about or is it merely a drug-induced, temporary escape from reality? The sequence is accompanied on the soundtrack by swirling electronic noises that evoke the sound of the wind. Is this the wind of change mentioned in the epigraph at the start of the film? The ritual drinking of water from a calabash is usually a sign of welcome and hospitality; is this dream a 'return' to a former way of life that predates the current military regime? However, the calabash drifting away down the river might suggest the precarious nature of any such dream. Water is thus a positive symbol but its meaning is ambiguous: the audience must debate its significance on the basis of the context of the story (as has been indicated elsewhere in this volume, in the West African context, this would often mean discussing there and then in the cinema the possible meanings of different symbols).

Yeelen is a film laden with symbols, with fire and water playing key roles (the final section of this chapter will focus more closely on the interpretation of this complex symbolic landscape). Fire is presented as an extremely powerful but destructive force: in the opening section, we see a chicken impaled on a stick burst into flames. This startling image is 'explained' several minutes later when we see Soma sacrifice a chicken to the gods; the bird is impaled on the 'magic' pestle and is then immolated in a sudden burst of flames, a second blaze taking hold of the sacred tree. Later we see Soma offer to the gods a red dog and an albino whom he will also immolate. Throughout the film, all use of the *komo*'s supernatural powers is accompanied by images of fire: Nianankoro repels the attack on the Peul (Fulani) village by stirring a swarm of bees against the invaders and by surrounding them in flames; in the film's final climactic confrontation between father and son, both characters disappear in a blinding flash of light that leaves behind a scorched and smouldering landscape.

Perhaps unsurprisingly the element invoked to counteract the fiery power of the *komo* is the purifying force of water. In one of the film's most memorable sequences, Nianankoro's elderly mother stands naked in a river full of reeds and, in ritual fashion, one after the other, pours four bowls of milk over her head, invoking the spirit of the goddess of water to save her son from his avenging father. Water is thus posited as a maternal source of life as opposed to the destructive, male fire of the *komo*. This association of water with purity and harmony is reinforced later in the film when Nianankoro asks to bathe in the source of the river when he arrives at the holy site of Bandiagara, the symbolic heart of the territory traditionally occupied by the Dogon people of Mali: before the final showdown with his father, he must be cleansed.

In *Waati*, it is the sea and the desert that play the most important symbolic roles. It is against the backdrop of the crashing sea that Nandi murders the policeman; the timeless freedom and majesty of the sea is harnessed visually by Cissé as a weapon against the time-bound injustices of the apartheid regime. In the opening shots of the film, the camera pans over a desert landscape with the film's 'epigraph' from the *komo* ringing in the head of the spectator: 'the world is an unknowable mystery'; while, later in the film, Nandi and her boyfriend discover an abandoned child in the desert. This child, whom they name Aïcha, is given a symbolic charge that works on several levels: adopting her is further evidence of Nandi's desire to be part of a shared African heritage or culture, and the child also seems to be associated with unspecified hopes for the future of a liberated South Africa as an integral part of the continent.

These symbols form an fundamental component of the film's exploration of the nature of time: from Nandi's desire to explore her African 'roots' to the ability of time to heal the scars of apartheid. Unfortunately, the use of symbolism in *Waati* seems less effective than in Cissé's other films. Whereas the symbolic dimension of *Baara*, *Finyé* and *Yeelen* is used to reinforce or give extra depth to elements within their narratives, in the second half of *Waati* symbolism begins to render the narrative increasingly opaque. For example, what is the spectator to make of the Rastafarian (played by Niamanto Sanogo, the avenging father from *Yeelen*) who leads a ceremony in praise of the lion – with a real lion perched on a pedestal beside him – and then preaches to an audience of students and Rastafarians about the dangers of taking drugs? It is visually stunning but both in narrative and symbolic terms it is difficult to decipher and it seems remote from the 'real' events of South Africa, depicted so powerfully in the first half.

The final aspect of the mythical/symbolic dimension of Cissé's films is his representation of the conflict between fathers and sons, in which he invariably takes the side of the son. Although the oral tradition accords great respect to the knowledge and wisdom of the elders, there has always been a narrative space within this tradition in which the abuse of power by elders can be criticised. This 'archetypal' aspect of oppressive paternal behaviour is underlined by the fact that the brutal fathers in *Den Muso*, *Baara* and *Finyé* are all played by Balla Moussa Keïta whose angular face and wiry physique are used to great effect to suggest a devious and callous ruling male elite. (Keïta finally plays more sympathetic roles as the Peul king in *Yeelen* and the university lecturer in *Waati*.) However, not all older male characters are unsympathetic: the factory worker in *Baara*, and Bâ's grandfather, Kansaye, in *Finyé* (both played by Ismaïla Sarr) are imbued with the dignity and wisdom traditionally associated in Africa with age. In particular, Kansaye constitutes a direct link to the values of the past: he dons his 'traditional' robes and consults with the spirits in the sacred forest before confronting the corrupt military governor who has no respect for the past and believes solely in the power of naked military strength. Equally, in *Yeelen*, the spiteful Soma is counter-balanced by his peaceful but estranged twin brother Djigui. There are also two important female models of traditional wisdom in Cissé's work: in *Yeelen*, Nianankoro's mother, in her prayer to the water goddess, displays a knowledge used in the name of peace, as opposed to the vengefulness of her husband; in *Waati*, Nandi's grandmother forms a link back to a pre-apartheid culture and knowledge, which is passed on through the female line of the family.

Despite his desire to cast his narratives within a mythical or timeless framework, it would be misleading to think of Cissé as a mystic detached from the 'real' world. On the contrary, his work often displays a keen sense of the physical realities of African life: for example, *Den Muso* and *Baara* between them contain more scenes of the urban proletariat at work than perhaps Sembene's entire *oeuvre*. Indeed, Cissé's films are often very insightful where the hierarchies and power structures at work in society are concerned. The situation of the factory workers in *Baara* is just one element of a much wider reflection within the film both on the nature of work and the nature of human relationships within the post-independence social order. The opening images, in which we see Balla's glistening body, immediately announce the issue of human labour. The film describes the exploitation of the workers by their corrupt bosses who care only for their own position in society. However, the narrative proper begins with a wife who has been thrown out of her home by her husband: in this largely capitalist social order, women such as this are forced to survive by becoming market traders or, in the case of the factory owner's wife, through the financial security of marriage to a wealthy man who transpires to be a petty tyrant and eventually murders her. There is neither love nor respect in this latter marriage and the wife seeks emotional and sexual gratification elsewhere through a series of lovers. This situation is not limited to the wives of tyrants, for Balla's wife seems equally unhappy with her lot. Although Balla is presented as an idealist with a real sense of social justice, his wife feels like a second-class citizen and there is a persistent tension between them: they fight over her 'lack of education' and his willingness to go out drinking with his friends. Significantly, Cissé cuts from the murder of Balla, towards the end of the film, to shots of his bored wife at home reading a magazine: Balla may be a hero to the workers but his marriage is far from ideal.

Although Cissé's films are almost always structured around a process of generational conflict, which is given a highly symbolic function within the narrative, his work does not cast the young leads as symbolic ciphers. On the contrary, they seek to explore the lived experience of young people in modern, urban Africa in an understanding and sympathetic fashion that is perhaps matched amongst other directors of the first generation solely by the work of Djibril Diop Mambety (see Chapter 3). Cissé allows his teenage characters the narrative space to act foolishly and just have fun: in *Den Muso*, a long sequence is devoted to a childish game between Fanta and Ténin in the garden, as they try to soak each other with water; in *Finyé*, Bâ and his schoolfriends get high and spend endless hours hanging around (as do Sékou and his friends in *Den Muso*); in *Yeelen*, Nianankoro is prone to hasty, selfish and childish behaviour, as he mocks the Peul king and takes advantage of his wife.

Perhaps the best example of this desire to capture the playfulness of youth is to be found in *Finyé*, in a teasing and sexually charged sequence in which Bâ and Batrou bathe together: Bâ suggests that Batrou bathe after her tennis match ostensibly so that he can see her naked; however, Batrou insists that they bathe together and she enjoys his discomfort as he hesitates over undressing in front of her; she then obliges him to undress by splashing him with water and the two continue to splash each other playfully (in a visual echo of the sequence from *Den Muso* discussed above); the camera prudishly captures them individually from the shoulders up in a series of tightly edited close-ups; finally, the camera draws them together in the same shot as it pans down to follow a drop of water gathering on Batrou's nipple; immediately, they wrap their fingers round each other as the sexual tension mounts; however, Batrou cuts this sexual exploration short as she abruptly announces that she is going home.

As is shown by the repeated 'dream' sequences in which Bâ imagines himself and Batrou dressed in white in a romantic, rural idyll, the film elevates their love for each other above the 'base' pleasures of sexual pleasure but, none the less, Cissé makes it clear that such carnal desires are present and entirely natural at their age. Equally, Cissé may see the use of drugs by Bâ and his friends as the result of despair and hopelessness at a corrupt and authoritarian society but the narrative is not judgemental about their behaviour. The film presents a society in which the children of the chosen few climb the social ladder, while the rest are forced into a despair from which escape is either through drugs or active revolt against the system.

In the early part of his career, Cissé was very much an 'urban' director, whose films charted the experiences of life in post-independence Bamako. The narratives of these early feature films were all located in the city and were informed, at least in part, by an appeal to modernity in the evolution of post-independence Malian society. However, increasingly, his work has turned towards rural communities and the values inherited from precolonial Africa. In this context, it is intriguing to note that in two separate cases, Cissé invokes a desire for rural, romantic idylls on the part of his male, urban protagonists: in *Baara*, Balla, the porter, daydreams about being welcomed upon arrival in a village by a beautiful young woman who carries water to him in the traditional mode of greeting for visitors; while in *Finyé*, Bâ dreams of an idyllic life in the country with Batrou. Some critics have posited this aspect of Cissé's work as an integral part of his call for a 'return to the source' (whether this is cast in positive or negative terms), a process of turning towards the rural past as a means of coming to terms with a troubled present and an uncertain future.[7] This process reached its fullest expression in *Yeelen*, and the concluding, theoretical section of this chapter will explore not only the artistic and ideological impulses at work in such a move but also the critical strategies at work in the reception of the film.

Postcolonialism and postcoloniality: marketing the margins?

In the preface to his book *The Postcolonial Exotic*, Graham Huggan calls for 'an examination of the sociological dimensions of postcolonial studies', that is of the material conditions in which postcolonial writing is produced, distributed and consumed:

> When creative writers like Salman Rushdie are seen, despite their cosmopolitan background, as representatives of Third World countries, when literary works

like *Things Fall Apart* (1958) are gleaned, despite their fictional status, for the anthropological information they provide; when academic concepts like post-colonialism are turned, despite their historicist pretensions, into watchwords for the fashionable study of otherness – all of these are instances of the *postcolonial exotic*, of the global commodification of cultural difference that provides the subject for this book. (2001: vii; emphasis in original)

Huggan's book thus seeks to investigate the coexistence of postcolonial studies' seeming commitment to radical, anticolonial politics and the growth in a commercial market for 'exotic', postcolonial material. Huggan employs the terms 'postcolonialism' and 'postcoloniality' as a way of explaining this dichotomy; 'postcolonialism' is defined as a discourse of anti-colonial resistance, whereas 'postcoloniality' is defined as 'a value-regulating mechanism within the global, late-capitalist system of commodity exchange' (2001: 6). Essentially, for Huggan, the former is the desire to promote or explore anti-colonial politics, while the latter is the commercialisation of what is perceived as an 'exotic' postcolonial otherness. However, Huggan argues that it is not possible to view these concepts in simple opposition to one another: 'the point that needs to be stressed here is that postcolonialism *is bound up with* postcoloniality' (2001: 6; emphasis in original); within the commodity culture of the late twentieth and early twenty-first centuries, postcolonialism's rhetoric of anticolonial resistance has itself become a commodity.

If we transfer these ideas to the context of African cinema, *Yeelen* provides an intriguing case study for the exploration of Huggan's ideas on postcolonialism and postcoloniality. As was outlined earlier in this chapter, Cissé's film has been lauded in certain quarters as constituting an important assertion of an 'authentic' postcolonial African form of filmmaking, but it has also been the subject of scathing critique for allegedly pandering to Western exoticist notions about Africa. Might the notions of postcolonialism and postcoloniality offer the critic a way of exploring both sides of this critical equation without having to reject one or the other out of hand? Might *Yeelen* best be understood as a film that belongs both to the anticolonial rhetoric of postcolonialism and to the exoticising discourse of postcoloniality?

Much of the ambiguity surrounding the critical reception of *Yeelen* is inextricably bound up with interpretations of the significance of the film's subject matter. Is a film about the quest to possess the supernatural powers of a magic pestle and a wing of *koré* an 'authentically' African film speaking to African cultural sensibilities, or is such a film inherently 'exotic', appealing to Western preconceptions of Africa as a pre-rational continent? Certainly in Western countries, the film was marketed and interpreted by many critics as an expression of the ineffable 'mystery' of Africa, although Cissé attempts to pre-empt exoticist readings of the film by claiming that it explicitly addresses an 'initiated' Malian audience:

For the first time a film decodes the secret ritual described by the song that [Malians] usually hear on the radio . . . My film positions the spectator in the midst of these secrets and keeps him/her busy looking, interpreting, exploring. It is this level of the film that is incredibly exciting for the Malian spectator. For the spectator who is not initiated, I mean the American, French or British, I am sure that the film is perceived literally. I mean that this spectator hears the ritualistic song, reads its translation; but, this direct translation is not what is expressed in the film. The sentences are translated and refer to other objects which obey the rules of a specific knowledge. The rules of this knowledge can only be decoded by initiates of the 'Komo'. (Diawara 1988: 15)

Philip Gentile provides an illuminating analysis of the ambiguity that marks Cissé's opposition between an 'initiated' Malian audience and an 'unitiated' Western audience. Malians may have greater knowledge of the *komo* and have more understanding of the film's symbolic landscape but we should not forget that the *komo* is a 'secret' sect whose practices are necessarily hidden from a wide audience even in Mali itself:

A potential level of meaning inaccessible to even the Malian spectator offers the possibility of a space within which 'initiate' and 'non-initiate' may keep 'looking, interpreting, discovering' with separate, conflicting and perhaps over-lapping spectatorial needs, interests, intentions, but in a way that does not nec-essarily affirm a textual unity based on simple codic-literal oppositions. (Gentile 1995: 127)

If the *komo* is inherently designed to be only partially 'legible' to the 'non-initiate', then the Western and the African viewer are on more of a level interpretative playing field than one might imagine: equally, Cissé's charac-terisation of Westerners as 'non-initiated' – in his very general sense of not knowing anything at all about the *komo* – might just as easily be widened to include Africans from outside Mali. Gentile goes on to question Cissé's contention that he had simply set out to record in almost 'documentary' fashion the rituals of the *komo*, in particular the ten-minute sequence in which the members of the sect gather in the sacred grove. Whereas Cissé has spoken of the respectful distance that he kept from the members of the *komo* during the filming of this sequence, Gentile provides a revealing and in-depth analysis of the wide range of long shots, close-ups, medium close-ups and different angles actually used by Cissé (128–31). The main benefit of Gentile's argument is that it replaces the question of the film's 'legibility' within the sphere of cinematic narrative codes rather than leaving it solely within the realm of the spectator's cultural knowledge where it had previ-ously existed in critical debates.[8] Cissé himself has argued that: 'When one makes a film, it is for people who are used to going to see films and who understand them' (Ukadike 2002: 21). Consequently, the spectator who watches *Yeelen* reads the film not only as an initiate or non-initiate of the *komo* but also as someone with a greater of lesser degree of film 'literacy'. As Gentile warns us, this does not mean that all 'literate' film viewers will read the film in the same way: however, to reassert the role of the film as narrative, rather than solely as ethnography, is to begin to engage fully with the complexity of Cissé's aesthetic approach to his subject.

Although Gentile's arguments provide the basis for a more nuanced interpretation of *Yeelen*, a further problematisation of the film's depiction of the
komo is necessary. For Gentile's analysis of Cissé's filming of the *komo* never
challenges the idea that what the viewer sees is a 'relatively untampered
ritual' (1995: 131). In fact, evidence exists to suggest that the rituals performed in the film by the members of *komo* are most definitely not the
'authentic' rituals of the sect. In his fascinating and beautifully filmed documentary on the shooting of *Yeelen*, Etienne Carton de Grammont (a cine-
matographer and long-time collaborator with Cissé, who shot *Baara* and
Finyé) captures both the mystical impulse at work in Cissé's artistic vision,
and also the very serious, practical difficulties that he faced in filming the
rituals of the *komo*. In the opening images of the film, we see Cissé in the
shade of a tree apparently directing a scene off-screen; the impression is
created of an artist transported by his work, as he appears almost to be
dancing to the music on the soundtrack, 'conducting' the actions of the
unseen actors. Later in the film, the sense that the film represents Cissé's personal (African) artistic vision is reinforced when he comments to Niamanto
Sanogo, one of the elders of the *komo* and the man who plays Soma, that
the white technicians on the film are working for him. However, elsewhere
in the documentary, the reality of shooting the film appears somewhat different. At one stage, a major row erupts as the elders complain that too many
'taboos' have been broken in filming at their sacred sites: Cissé is obliged to
promise that he will obey their wishes about what can and cannot be filmed,
and he also promises that they will be recompensed for the 'sacrifices' they
have made in allowing the crew to film there. Later in the documentary,
Sanogo reveals that he has chosen to take part in the film because he believes
that making it will allow Bambara traditions to survive. However, he makes
it clear that the film will not reveal all of the secrets of the *komo*; the rituals
that they are performing for Cissé's crew are merely a 'version' of the real
thing, which 'resembles' the *komo*.

These facts reveal a paradox at the heart of Cissé's film: what is often
posited as an 'authentic' representation of a specific group within Malian
society in fact transpires to be an aestheticised representation of that group,
one that has undergone a complex process of negotiation with the members
of the group itself. The largely glowing analysis of *Yeelen* by critics such as
Diawara and Ukadike specifically contrasts the 'authenticity' of Cissé's representation with the 'inauthentic' or 'biased' representations of the Western
ethnographic filmmaker.[9] However, the film might best be viewed as an
example of 'staged authenticity' (MacCannell 1976): Cissé's version of
the *komo* is the result of a negotiated compromise that seeks to present a
representation that will appeal to both his audience(s) and those being
represented.

Effectively, *Yeelen* appears to be weighed down with an enormous burden
of representativity, whether it is interpreted positively or negatively: it is
either lauded as an 'authentically African' representation of the *komo* or

seen as a betrayal of that representative imperative, which has chosen instead to speak to a Western audience. De Grammont's film forces us to reassess the critical gesture that posits Cissé as a 'cultural insider' whose 'direct' access to Malian culture allows him either to create an 'authentic' representation of the *komo* or to betray that insider knowledge in favour of pleasing a Western audience (depending on the critic's point of view). However, a film is an artistic representation, which cannot give direct, unmediated access to the 'real world'. Moreover, Cissé's representative status appears far less certain when one addresses the facts more closely: first of all, as de Grammont's film reveals so clearly, Cissé is not a member of the *komo* and does not have direct access to its secrets; in fact, he is not even a member of the Bambara ethnic group (he is a Sarakollé); perhaps most importantly, Cissé is an urban African whose engagement with rural, Malian society has developed as part of an almost spiritual quest for meaning in his own life. (This aspect of Cissé's character is clearly displayed in Rithy Panh's documentary in which the filmmaker speaks of the large amount of time he spends in the 'bush' in search of calm and inspiration.) In fact, as will be argued in greater detail in Chapter 7 on the work of Idrissa Ouédraogo, there is a compelling argument that the so-called 'return to the source' genre is in great part the product of recently urbanised film directors making slightly idealised films about rural communities for a recently urbanised audience ('staging authenticity' for them). None of these arguments makes Cissé's work 'inauthentic'. However, it does help us to qualify the judgements that are made about the nature of his work. For *Yeelen* cannot be read unproblematically as an 'authentic' representation of a social group filmed from the inside and intelligible only to fellow insiders.

To interpret Cissé's film as 'authentic' or 'inauthentic' is in effect to read it primarily for the cultural or anthropological information that it provides, rather than interpreting it as a film that has emerged from a specific social, cultural and political context: to do so is, to use Huggan's terms, yet another instance of the 'postcolonial exotic'. However, this does not mean that we cannot also view the film as an expression of 'postcolonialism': for the film's exploration of knowledge and power in the precolonial African past has a powerful political resonance. In effect, Huggan's argument is that the postcolonial critic must explore the ways in which a film such as *Yeelen* is transformed into an 'exotic' product for consumption within Western capitalist societies: 'the postcolonial exotic is both a form of commodity fetishism and a revelation of the process by which "exotic" commodities are produced, exchanged, consumed' (2001: 264). Cissé's film – like all 'postcolonial products' – is open to very different interpretations in different contexts. Neil Lazarus reminds us (in an argument echoed by Huggan) that acknowledging the exoticising role of capitalism in the circulation of cultural commodities from Africa does not mean that other potential meanings are foreclosed. Although Lazarus's arguments are made in relation to 'world music', they seem equally pertinent to the field of 'world cinema':

For what makes it 'world music' . . . is precisely its latent capacity to contribute to the dismantling of the cultural logic of Western popular music, a cultural logic resting squarely upon the political economy of empire. To listen to world music dialogically . . . seems to me a distinctively subversive practice: for it is to allow oneself to take seriously the suggestion of a world free of imperial domination. Free of imperial domination, note – not 'on the other side of the imperial divide'; the implicit proposal is not that we (in the West) listen to World Music for what it can tell us about life 'over there', but that we listen to it for what it can suggest to us about radically different ways of living 'over here', ways of living that are unimaginable under prevailing social conditions. (1999: 225)

Yeelen may have been made primarily for a Malian (and wider African) audience but in its travels around the world it also inevitably speaks to non-African audiences. If spectators in the West engage with such films 'dialogically', they can, as Lazarus suggests, shift perceptions not only of life 'over there' but also of how life 'over here', and our relationship to other places, might be imagined differently. There is undoubtedly a strong idealistic impulse in Lazarus's concept of 'dialogical' reading but, even if the reality falls short of this ideal, it none the less provides us with a different (and invaluable) model for reading African culture to the exoticism of capitalist commodification. *Yeelen* may be an example of the 'postcolonial exotic' but it also contributes to the oppositional discourse of postcolonialism.

Notes

1 Ukadike rightly comments on the 'exquisite attention to detail' in *Baara*'s examination of life in Bamako, but his assertion that '*Baara* would impress [factory workers] as a film that could also pass for an industrial training program' is rather misleading (1994: 188). There are several instances within the film in which good relations between workers and employers are depicted in a partisan and quite idealistic fashion, but to define *Baara* in terms of the approach in such sequences is to overlook the very different stylistic registers adopted elsewhere in the film.
2 Ukadike (1994: 254–62) sees *Yeelen* as an attempt to develop a specifically African aesthetic, while Boughedir (2000: 119) views it as a retreat from the 'committed' social realist cinema of the 1960s and 1970s.
3 See Ukadike (2002: 26–7) for Cissé's account of the financial difficulties that he faced in making the film.
4 Cissé's brief imprisonment and the withholding from release of *Den Muso* appear to have been the result of a contractual dispute rather than an act of government censorship.
5 Thackway provides an insightful reading of the film as political allegory (2003: 70–1).
6 Dudley Andrew links Cissé's style in *Yeelen* with that of French new wave filmmakers, claiming that both are explicitly reacting against the artistic limits of an earlier *cinéma de papa* (1995: 122–3).

7 See Diawara (1992: 160) for an interesting, if problematic, discussion of the genre of 'return to the source' films. Chapter 6 on Flora Gomes will examine the question of a 'return to the source' from a somewhat different perspective.

8 See Murphy (2000b) for similar ideas.

9 For example, Ukadike includes *Yeelen* in a list of African films (alongside *Yaaba*, *Tilaï, Zan Boko* and *Finzan*) which are deemed to 'offer meticulous anthropological renditions of African cultures. The films are true to life and do not attempt to re-arrange natural settings or modernize them to look foreign' (Ukadike 1994: 252).

Filmography

L'Homme et les idoles (Man and Idols) (1965)
Sources d'inspiration (Sources of Inspiration) (1968)
L'Aspirant (The Candidate) (1968)
Degal à Dialloubé (Degal in Dialloubé) (1970)
Fête du Sanké (The Festival of Sanké) (1971)
Cinq jours d'une vie (Five Days in a Life) (1972)
Dixième anniversaire de l'OUA (Tenth Anniversary of the OAU) (1973)
Den Muso (The Young Girl) (1975)
Baara (Work) (1978)
Chanteurs traditionnels des îles Seychelles (Traditional Singers of the Seychelles) (1978)
Finyé (The Wind) (1982)
Yeelen (The Light) (1987)
Waati (Time) (1995)

Films about Cissé

Etienne Carton de Grammont), *A be munumunu* (1987)
Rithy Panh, *Souleymane Cissé* (1991)

Chapter 6

Flora Gomes

Introduction

Over the last 15 years, black cultural critics – in particular, black British cultural critics such as Paul Gilroy and Kobena Mercer – have analysed the problem of 'the burden of representation' constituted by the piecemeal emergence of cultural producers from the black communities and the consequent potential obligation to represent the entirety of those communities (Gilroy 1989; Mercer 1994). While these arguments are formulated above all in relation to postcolonial populations in the metropolis, they carry an obvious relevance for African filmmakers – although, by and large, it is a debate still waiting to happen in the field of African cinema.

Whether or not he feels especially burdened by the fact, Florentino 'Flora' Gomes certainly occupies a lonely position as the only internationally recognised filmmaker from his country of Guinea-Bissau. Born in 1949, in Cadique, in the south of the country, he was – inevitably, in view of the socio-cultural and political circumstances of life in a Portuguese colony, which are discussed in greater detail in the following section – obliged to go abroad in order to study cinema. In fact, on his own account, it was when he was finishing high school in Cuba that the decision of a friend of his to study filmmaking convinced him to do the same. Although Gomes does not mention the name of his friend in the interview, it may well have been his contemporary Sana na N'hada, director of almost the only other feature film to date from Guinea-Bissau, *Xime* (1995), with whom Gomes worked on two of his own early short films, *Regresso de Cabral* (1976) and *Anos os oca luta* (1978), and who, like Gomes, studied at the prestigious ICAIC (Instituto Cubano de Arte e Industria Cinematograficos) in Havana.

After his studies in Cuba, Gomes spent two years in Dakar with the pioneering Senegalese filmmaker Paulin Soumanou Vieyra. At this time, along with a number of African directors like Sembene and Hondo, and established figures from Latin America, such as Fernando Birri from Argentina and Santiago Alvarez from Cuba, Gomes was one of the participants in the enormously important 1973 meeting of Third World filmmakers in Algiers – even before he himself had become a filmmaker – and was a member of the Committee on People's Cinema examining 'the role of cinema and filmmakers in the Third World against imperialism and neo-colonialism'. The Resolutions

of the meeting contained both a radical and, particularly for the time, a sophisticated analysis of the relationship of imperialism and filmmaking, and have
become a key document in the history of the emergence of postcolonial
cinema.

Gomes returned to Guinea-Bissau in 1974 in order to take part in the celebration of independence, in particular, as he has said, to film the proceedings.
In the previous twelve months, his country had experienced both the delight
of the successful conclusion of its long and bitter fight for liberation from the
Portuguese, and sorrow at the assassination, by Portuguese agents, of the man
who had led them to independence, Amilcar Cabral. Whether in fact Gomes
managed to document his country's independence celebrations is not clear,
since nothing from that precise period features in his filmography (his first
film, a short piece from 1976 entitled *Regresso de Cabral – The Return of
Cabral* – may be what resulted). Nevertheless, Gomes's relationship of fidelity
to his country and its aspirations for political and cultural liberation, as well
as to the man who incarnated their desire to be free, has remained fundamentally unchanged in the intervening years – in spite of everything. When
the civil war broke out in Guinea-Bissau in 1998, rampaging soldiers looted
the Cinema Institute – established by the government in the aftermath of independence, but never appropriately funded and therefore virtually inopera-
tive – and in so doing destroyed Flora Gomes's personal archive, the only
prints of his films and all the painstakingly assembled footage (72 cassettes,
eight videos) which was to have formed the basis of his life-long project: to
make a full-length film specifically about Cabral. Despite these in many ways
irreparable losses, Gomes still harbours hopes of one day realising his aim. At
the end of an interview with Olivier Barlet in which he talked, among other
things, of these losses, Gomes was asked 'One last word?' and replied, 'You
have to keep on hoping' (Gomes 2004). This typifies both his personal credo
and, as we shall see, one of the structuring themes of his cinematic output.

Historical and cultural contexts

As Frank Ukadike comments in the introduction to his interview with Flora
Gomes, 'Few people in the United States are familiar with the work of Flora
Gomes, the most prominent figure in Guinea-Bissau's film industry, because
none of his feature films or documentaries has been distributed in this
country. Indeed, little is known in the West about either the cinema in
Guinea-Bissau or the country itself' (Ukadike 2002: 101). The invisible or
forgotten nature of Guinea-Bissau is a perfect expression of the legacy of five
hundred years of Portuguese colonialism. Although, as Basil Davidson
points out, 'the Portuguese have long been notable historians of themselves',
that emphatically did not apply to their colonised subjects:

the Africans have evidently remained for them a faceless mass of 'natives', a cultural zero, a historical nothing; indeed the present Prime Minister of Portugal,

when a professor at Coimbra, emphatically declared in terms that matched his master's voice that the Africans 'have invented nothing useful, discovered no profitable technology, conducted no conquest of value to the evolution of mankind'. (Davidson 1994: 186)

This historiographical and discursive obliteration of Africans by the Portuguese reached its high point under the fascist dictator Salazar, who, as Cabral recalls, 'would repeat over and over to anyone willing to listen that "Africa does not exist" (an assertion which clearly reflected an insane racism but which also perfectly summed up the principles and practices which have always characterised Portuguese colonial policy)' (Cabral 1976: 26).

The practical counterpart of this deliberate forgetting was the systematic impoverishment and underdevelopment of Portugal's colonies; indeed, André Gunder Frank's famous phrase 'the development of underdevelopment' might have been formulated specifically in relation to the Portuguese Empire. In addition to the absence of anything resembling a functioning economy or a social infrastructure, five centuries of Portuguese rule in Guinea-Bissau had resulted in the production of a population where, at the time of the liberation struggles, precisely 0.3 per cent were '*assimilados*' – assimilated, educated, fit almost to stand alongside indigenous Portuguese – while the remaining 99.7 per cent were illiterate, and quite literally 'savages' in the eyes of their white rulers. Cabral was one of only three Africans from Guinea-Bissau to have gone to university; as an agronomist, he was literally one of a kind. This was the situation in which Flora Gomes grew up.

Although it might be imagined that Portugal would be all too ready to divest itself of colonies on which it evidently expended so little time and effort, nothing could be further from the truth, and, with the possible exception of Algeria, it was the liberation struggles in the Portuguese territories which were the most protracted and bitter, and their legacies, therefore, frequently the most painful. While the contradictory refusal to let go of unregarded lands full of savages might look like simple bloodymindedness on the part of the Portuguese, it had much to do with the fact that, as Cabral pointed out, Portugal was 'the most under-developed country in Europe'. Its own under-development meant that Portugal was economically incapable of emulating the other imperial powers and moving from the phase of colonialism to that of neocolonialism.

This was not the only contradiction of Portuguese colonialism. Alongside Portuguese assertions of African inability to produce anything, it is worth noting, for example, the Portuguese inability to build aircraft ('not even toy ones!' as Cabral gleefully commented); and the fact that they did possess an air force with which to attack their colonised subjects was due to the complicity of fellow NATO members such as Germany who supplied them with fighters and helicopters. Similarly, while Portuguese generals and politicians claimed 'we are the only civilising influence', their 'civilising' consisted, in classic colonial style, of the use of napalm against Africans, the herding of

Africans into concentration-camp-like 'peace villages' and the use of assassination, most notably that of Cabral in January 1973.

Meanwhile, faced with the Portuguese who had five hundred years in which to do something in Africa and did almost nothing at all, the Africans who supposedly 'conducted no conquest of value to the evolution of mankind' in fact carried out remarkable feats in terms of the liberation and emancipation of their fellows. In the case of Guinea-Bissau, this began, according to Basil Davidson, with ten men and three rifles, and ended in the defeat – in guerrilla terms, rather than in pitched battle – of the Portuguese army. At the same time, the mass movement launched by the armed struggle transformed the country at the level of social justice, education and participatory democracy. While this was – in large measure thanks to both the vision and the organisational ability of Cabral – arguably more principled, and more thoroughgoing, than in any other comparable liberation struggle, sadly many of its better qualities did not long survive Cabral's assassination. The difficult, painful combination of, on the one hand, the almost unrivalled potential for social progress in Guinea-Bissau created by the processes set in motion by the fight for freedom and, on the other, the harsh realities of the postcolonial or neocolonial world which resulted in the potential remaining largely unrealised, form the principal context for Flora Gomes's filmmaking.

Although the PAIGC (Partido Africano da Independencia da Guiné e Cabo Verde), founded and led by Cabral, was in power from independence in 1974 to the end of the civil war in 1999, President Vieira's 20-year rule was one in which the fledgling egalitarian structures and democratic policies instituted by Cabral were comprehensively ignored and undermined. Although it hardly ranks as the worst mistake of the Vieira government, it is none the less indicative in terms of possibilities which were stillborn that the Film Institute which was set up in Guinea-Bissau after independence never subsequently received the level of funding which would have allowed it to actually make films.

The films

Although Flora Gomes does not deliberately assume the role of (solitary) representative of his country and culture, his films nevertheless offer an almost paradigmatic example of the historical, cultural and ethnic representation of one country in the postcolonial context via a range of cinematic genres and stylistic modes. Gomes's four feature films – *Mortu nega* (*Those whom Death Refused*) (1988); *Udju azul di Yonta* (*The Blue Eyes of Yonta*) (1992); *Po di sangui* (*Tree of Blood*) (1996); and *Nha fala* (*My Voice*) (2002) – trace, in chronological sequence, different aspects of the last 30 years of Guinea-Bissau's history, from the height of the anticolonial struggle to the present day. As such, they constitute the visual equivalent of the work of postcolonial writers such as the Kenyan Ngugi wa Thiong'o in delineating the difficult rise and partial fall of the independent African nation state.

As with Ngugi's novels, Gomes's films move gradually from a realistic mode of representation and linear narrative structure to more mixed, or less conventional, approaches. Thus, *Mortu nega* is straightforwardly realist, even socialist realist, filmed using a muted tonal palette to match the characters' lives of struggle. *The Blue Eyes of Yonta* is a broadly realist narrative framed by moments which are both symbolic and, particularly in the case of the closing scene, quite surrealist. Its brighter colours and use of both pattern and fabric reflect its interest in both youth culture and African culture more broadly. *Po di sangui* then partially abandons quotidian realism as it operates in a mode where the supernatural constitutes an ordinary part of daily life. Its frequently bleached colours are appropriate in a land where the power of the sun appears to be slowly destroying all forms of life. However, whereas a film like Souleymane Cissé's *Yeelen* exists more or less entirely in the world of the spiritual and the supernatural, *Po di sangui* is, at least in part, firmly rooted in the unpleasant realities of the late twentieth century. Finally, *Nha fala*, as a musical, eschews realism in a different way, while its upbeat tone is visually matched in the vibrancy of colour and cloth.

Gomes's analysis of postcolonial Guinea-Bissau is organised around a number of themes which weave their way through his films. These include: Cabral and his legacy; modernity and tradition (both of which are discussed at length in the main section of this chapter); the problems faced by the nuclear couple; the journey or quest; the ideas or ideals we are to organise our lives and our society by, and how realistic or otherwise they are; children; and the question of human dignity. Almost all of these intersect with the others in various ways, but it is worth separating out and examining one or two in a little detail, focusing particularly on Gomes's second film, *The Blue Eyes of Yonta*.

As Fredric Jameson famously argued, 'Third world texts – even those which are seemingly private and invested with a properly libidinal dynamic – necessarily project a political dimension in the form of national allegory: *the story of the private individual destiny is always an allegory of the embattled situation of the public third world culture and society*' (Jameson 1986: 69). Whether or not Gomes's couples constitute national allegories, (and 'not' is probably the answer), there is certainly a significant relation between the central couples and characters in his films and the wider fate of the postcolonial society. This is perhaps clearest in *Mortu nega*, the story of Guinea-Bissau's fight for freedom from the Portuguese, and of its struggles in the postcolonial period. In the context of the cultural and ideological imperatives of the fight to liberate and build the nation, it is more to be expected that the narrative function of the central couple should be closer to Jameson's model. Even then, however, Diminga and her husband Sako, one of Cabral's army of liberation, are not reducible to figures of national allegory.

In Gomes's next film, *The Blue Eyes of Yonta*, Yonta herself is at the centre of two potential couples, neither of which in the end is able to resolve itself into a stable pairing. The young student Zé is attracted to Yonta, but she is unaware of the fact. She in turn is attracted to the older Vicente, friend and former comrade in arms of her father in the independence struggle, but his interest in her seems friendly and avuncular, rather than romantic. While Zé and Yonta are the obvious couple – the same age, similar interest in music and dancing, etc. – it is the possibility of a relationship between Yonta and Vicente with which the film tantalises the viewer. These non-couples are also contrasted with Yonta's friend Mana and her fiancé, whose lavish wedding party ends the film on a note of fairytale romance.

The central dysfunctional triad symbolises tendencies, and tensions, within contemporary urban society in Guinea-Bissau, as well as possible sets of values to live by: Zé can be seen as embodying a substantial degree of assimilation, as he copies out European love poems in praise of the blue eyes Yonta clearly does not have; Yonta is part of the younger generation of Africans who, while attracted to aspects of Western culture, have not neces-sarily thereby completely abandoned their own; Vicente is an example of the sincere, committed, socially responsible individuals who fought for freedom, but have been able neither properly to construct the society in whose name they struggled nor properly to adapt to the one which has emerged in its stead. As Yonta's mother comments, 'Vicente is a dreamer, he can't accept that things change.' The profound contradiction he represents is indicated by the fact that in the wholesale fish business he runs he is referred to as 'comrade boss'.

Vicente also embodies contradiction in his relation to African culture and the values it embodies – another variation on the issue of tradition and modernity. On the one hand, Vicente is the character most clearly concerned with traditional aspects of African culture: on his return from his business trip to Europe, for example, he talks to the carved figures of ancestors in his apartment: 'I felt strong and protected in my travels, but I wanted to return to listen to your silence again.' Despite this, in the eyes of Nando, his long-lost comrade from the liberation struggle, Vicente is clearly over-identified with Western conceptions of modernisation and progress. When Vicente says, 'What we fought for isn't in your village – good roads, electricity, proper houses . . .', Nando responds, 'Our land, our ideals, the progress we dreamed of . . .', but for Vicente it is a question of 'No more dreams. This is reality. Not for everyone, but it *is* progress.'

Although Yonta's desire to choose for herself, particularly in terms of a possible husband, is a mark of how modern she is, that same desire exists in the altogether more traditional and rural setting of Gomes's next film, *Po di sangui*. Here, social norms pressure the recently returned Dou to take the practical, and traditional, step and marry his brother's widow, and take care of her and her child; he, however, very much wants to make the more 'modern', and romantic, choice and marry his sweetheart Saly. This question of how to constitute the central couple in part instantiates the constantly recurring problem of modernity and tradition to which we will return later in the chapter, and it is significant that Dou, in the context of a general reaffirmation of the importance of the traditional in the film, makes the 'modern' choice.

'No more dreams. This is reality', says Vicente, but in the wake of Nando's rejection he is left confused as to the nature and content of each. As he says to the ancestor figurine: 'Look at the vultures . . . It will always be like this . . . Nha Pradidor, help me – deliver me from the weight of my past. And tell me whether the future I dream of is still possible.' Now, it seems, divisive capitalist values are the reality, while the communal, progressive ones are relegated to possibly unrealisable insubstantiality. In a similar inversion, the past, previously a source of strength, comfort and inspiration, has become something to be repudiated and escaped from, in a way even more negative than Yonta's 'We respect the past, but we can't live in it'. That such thoughts are articulated by the character who most embodies Cabral-type socialist ideals is a mark of the changes for the worse in postcolonial Guinea-Bissau. They are also an indication of the need for what Cabral called the 'return to the source', which is the focus of the final section of the chapter.

The closing, somewhat surreal, scene of the film offers its final take on dream and reality. On the morning after the wedding, guests sprawl on chairs around the swimming pool, fast asleep, while the happy couple, in the absence of musicians or companions, dance on alone, wrapped in their dream of marital bliss; Amilcar's huge inflated inner tube from the film's opening scene, with two sleeping children on it, floats in the swimming pool, where a fisherman aimlessly casts his net. Meanwhile, Yonta and the children dance in line, out of this world of dream-induced stasis, and eventually out of shot, into a future which may not be the one Vicente and his comrades dreamed and fought for, but will still be a reality more humane than that of the gathering vultures.

Return to the Source: Cabral and Flora Gomes

'Traditions inspire us, but we must not let ourselves be imprisoned by them' (Flora Gomes). 'One must have tradition in oneself, to hate it properly' (Adorno, *Minima Moralia*). The remainder of this chapter will focus on the relationship between the ideas and texts of Cabral and Flora Gomes. As such, the aim is simple, but one of the lessons of Cabral is that things are not always as simple as they seem. This section also offers yet another revisiting of the overworked – and in certain respects unworkable – pairing of tradition and modernity, but another of the lessons of Cabral as we shall see, particularly at the end, is that certain repetitions are essential, indeed, inescapable.

It is, of course, important to emphasise yet again that the idea that 'modernity = Western = dynamic and progressive', while 'tradition = non-Western = static and conservative', is a colonialist ideological construct. Such a construct ignores the existence of both modernity and tradition in both the West and non-West (though not in the same way, or to the same extent). It also ignores the (potentially) radical or progressive nature of tradition – something that has always been clear to Marxists, even if the quotation above from Adorno appears to construe tradition as simply something to be rejected. For Walter Benjamin, for example, tradition was to be understood in opposition to history: the latter first and foremost the preserve of official or dominant knowledge; the former above all the repository of the experiences of the oppressed in society, and as such the basis for their oppositional, or ultimately revolutionary, activity. Nevertheless, tradition is neither an unproblematic given, nor simply and straightforwardly radical: for Benjamin, again, 'The danger affects both the content of the tradition and its receivers. The same threat hangs over both: that of becoming a tool of the ruling classes. In every era the effort must be made anew to wrest tradition away from a conformism that is about to overpower it' (Benjamin 1982: 257).

The relationship between tradition and modernity, and the awareness that the former is constantly menaced by the powers of conformism, continues to be useful for Flora Gomes, an integral aspect of the structuring of his films and as necessary to his view of the world as the similarly 'old-fashioned' theories of his fellow-countryman Cabral, and to that extent its use requires close critical examination. Although for some people returning to these apparently passé topics can only be done apologetically or dismissively, there is an important sense in which the opposite is, or should be, the case, given that 'Those who cannot defend old positions will never conquer new ones' (Trotsky 1966: 222) and it is this movement to defend the 'old' positions which the films of Flora Gomes instantiate.

In certain contexts, of course, the 'old-fashioned' carries very different implications, and for a great many postcolonial writers and theorists, the moment of historical reclamation represents something like, to borrow Fredric Jameson's formulation, a 'transhistorical imperative': Achebe's stated determination to use his novels to counter the prevailing racist image of his people and their past offered by Western texts is just one of many famous examples of anticolonial resistance at the level of history. For Cabral, too, 'The foundation for national liberation rests in the inalienable right of peoples to have their own history' (Cabral 1976: 43). The search for an acceptable national past is often intimately linked to the search for cultural authenticity, particularly via the ('old-fashioned') category of tradition. Here again, the understandings, effects and political valencies of the traditional and the authentic vary enormously: cultural nationalists – Chinweizu and his co-authors in *Toward the Decolonisation of African Literature* might serve as representative examples – are typically criticized for essentialising and dehistoricizing the authentic and the traditional; a progressive like Cabral, on the other hand, can fully understand the impetus behind a cultural nationalist movement aiming at an ahistorical version of tradition and authenticity such as Negritude, but simultaneously consider it to be theoretically deeply flawed. For him, culture can properly be understood only historically, which also means politically and economically:

> Whatever may be the ideological or idealistic characteristics of cultural expression, culture is an essential element of the history of a people . . . Like history, or because it is history, culture has as its material base the level of the productive forces and the mode of production. (Cabral 1976: 42)

For some, cultural nationalism or nativism remains profoundly problematic, however hard one tries to understand or explain it:

> To say, as Deane does, that [the nativist enterprise] is incoherent and yet, by its negation of politics and history, also heroically revolutionary seems to me is to fall into the nativist position as if it were the only choice for a resisting, decolonising nationalism. But we have evidence of its ravages: to accept nativism is to accept the consequences of imperialism, the racial, religious, and political divisions imposed by imperialism itself. To leave the historical world for the metaphysics of essences like *négritude*, Irishness, Islam, or Catholicism is to abandon history for essentialisations that have the power to turn human beings against each other. (Said 1993: 276)

In this view, nativism, far from representing a return to indigenous authenticity, actually involves the acceptance of the thoroughgoingly inauthentic – and alien – ideas, images and identities put forward by imperialism in the pursuit of its own ends. There is the profound (historical) irony that the movement which aims to leap out of the clutches of imperialism unwittingly reproduces a range of profoundly imperialist categories. (This, it should be noted, is not the same as the pointlessly self-defeating argument which says that if anticolonial movements use, for example, Marxist arguments to attack colonialism they remain trapped within Eurocentric categories.)

In the search for authenticity, the image of the 'return to the source' is fundamental, and it is this image which this section will examine: in relation to film studies, via the work of Manthia Diawara; in relation to political struggle, via Cabral; and in relation to both, via the films of Flora Gomes. In Diawara's book *African Cinema: Politics and Culture*, the Return to the Source is one of the three (variously problematic) categories taken to constitute contemporary African filmmaking, the others being Social Realism and Colonial Confrontation. Films in this category are concerned above all with articulating African identity, and doing so in a manner which prioritises filmic style and form over politics and content. For Diawara, the Return to the Source is an altogether positive movement:

> Unlike the films about historical confrontation that are conventional on the level of form, these films are characterised by the way the director looks at tradition. It is a look that is intent on positing religion where anthropologists only see idolatry, history where they see primitivism, and humanism where they see savage acts . . . Pointing to their aesthetic appeal, some filmmakers and critics have acclaimed the return to the source movement as the end of 'miserablism'

in African cinema and the beginning of a cinema with perfect images, perfect
sound and perfect editing. (Diawara 1992: 160)

Although there are a number of problems with this, not least the claims for
perfection and the assertion that 'historical confrontation' films are formally
conventional whereas 'return to the source' ones are not, the emphasis on a
different directorial 'look' at the question of tradition is important. Not
everyone is as enthusiastic, however: other critics, such as Clyde Taylor,
have, while acknowledging the improved production values of these more
recent works, expressed anxiety over the ways in which, in an apparent bid
for international acceptance, they effect 'an abandonment of the original
mission of presenting reflective and self-empowering narrative to African
audiences – the only mission that justifies treating African cinema as a movement' (Taylor 2000: 139). More importantly, filmmakers including Med
Hondo, Haile Gerima and Ferid Boughedir have strongly criticised Return
to the Source films for peddling precisely the kind of timeless, exoticised,
'authentic' Africa that appeals to Western audiences and avoids the contemporary realities of the continent, though Boughedir does at least acknowledge that the pressure exerted by the Western audience and its tastes can
distort the aims or effects of African films (Boughedir 2000).

In the face of these somewhat polarised positions, it is important to appreciate Cabral's understanding of the concept, which is simultaneously more
nuanced, wider-ranging and more political. The first thing to emphasise is
that, for Cabral, culture is anything but simple, static, 'authentic' or racial:

> From this we see that all culture is composed of essential and secondary ele-
> ments, of strengths and weaknesses, of virtues and failings, of positive and neg-
> ative aspects, of factors of progress and factors of stagnation or regression. From
> this also we can see that culture . . . is a social reality, independent of the will of
> men, the colour of their skins or the shape of their eyes. (Cabral 1976: 50–1)

The complex nature of culture requires a correspondingly complex
approach, both to understand it and to interact with it. (The absence of this
is one reason why colonialists have, in Cabral's eyes, been unable either to
control or to eradicate African culture as completely as they would have
wished.) Unlike cultural nationalist commentators, for whom the return to
the source is something incumbent on all formerly colonised individuals,
communities and cultures, Cabral is acutely aware of the profound difference that location – both in class terms and in spatial ones – makes:

> Repressed, persecuted, humiliated, betrayed by certain social groups who have
> compromised with the foreign power, culture took refuge in the villages, in the
> forests and in the spirit of the victims of domination. Culture survives all these
> challenges and through the struggle for liberation blossoms forth again. Thus
> the question of a 'return to the source' or of a 'cultural renaissance' does not
> arise and could not arise for the masses of these people, for it is they who are
> the repository of the culture and at the same time the only social sector who can
> preserve and build it up and *make history*. (Cabral 1976: 61)

Among the important aspects to highlight here is the fact that the oppressed colonised culture may be forced to retreat or hide, but it is never destroyed. As a result of this, significant sections of the population – above all, the rural masses – never lose their culture, and therefore have no need to rediscover it in the movement of the return to the source. The corollary of this is, however, that other sections of the population – in particular the petty bourgeoisie – do indeed need to make the movement of return.

One of the problems that Cabral, like Fanon, wrestled with was the question of who would govern the liberated postcolonial nation. The situation in Guinea-Bissau was even worse than that in Algeria in terms of the absence of a broad educated class capable of occupying positions of power in the new government, and, above all, there was nothing like an oppositional intelligentsia. Instead there was a petty bourgeoisie, assimilated as far as the Portuguese colonialists had managed (which was not very far at all), and whose involvement was essential for the future of the country. In Cabral's terms, they needed to commit 'class suicide' – in other words, to renounce the status, privilege, ideologies and assumptions acquired from their position in the colonised state, and to join with the mass of their fellow citizens in creating the new, liberated society. This, then, is the full meaning for Cabral of the return to the source: it is the return of the alienated and the inappropriately westernised to the place where they belong – side by side with their fellow countrymen and women, not distanced from them and harbouring false ideas of superiority towards them. In addition, the importance of the historical situation, of the need of the new nation, is such that the return almost ceases to be a question of choice, and becomes rather something required as a matter of historical necessity. As such, the culturally and politically progressive nature of the return places it in stark contrast to that other form of 'back to the roots' which is motivated by the West's desire for an appropriately 'authentic', consumable, non-threatening indigeneity.

Flora Gomes is – inescapably – one of Cabral's indigenous, variously alienated, petty bourgeoisie, and as such required to make his own return to the source. The ways in which he does this in his films are both varied and fascinating, comprising what one might call 'doing tradition differently', or even perhaps, in an echo of the quotation from Adorno above, 'doing tradition properly', since there is an important sense in which you need to have tradition within yourself to do it properly, as well as to hate it properly. Here again, the lessons from Cabral are both simple and far-reaching. Firstly, tradition *looks* fixed and immutable (that is why it *is* tradition); the lesson of Cabral is that it is not either of these things. Secondly, tradition *looks* like the essence of authenticity (what could be more authentic?); the lesson of Cabral is that the more it tries to be immovably, essentially traditional, the less actually authentic it is. 'Doing tradition differently' is an important trope in Flora Gomes's films, even those which, on the face of things, seem to be little concerned with the traditional. Gomes's first feature film, *Mortu nega*, is, as mentioned, the story of Guinea-Bissau's fight for independence from the Portuguese and for survival after independence, struggles personified in the central character Diminga and her husband Sako, the wounded guerrilla fighter. Diawara classes *Mortu nega* as a film of Colonial Confrontation, and that is certainly true of the first part, which concentrates on the fight for national liberation led by Cabral, but its final minutes contain a powerful example of the complexity of a return to the source.

Among the variety of problems facing the newly independent nation is that of drought (both real and symbolic), and Diminga has a disturbing dream which is interpreted as requiring that the ancestors be consulted. Accordingly, the ceremony is held and the ancestors and the deity Djon Cago (more usually known as Diancongo) are invoked, their instruction and guidance asked for. On the face of it, this looks like a society which has so painfully fought for its place in the modernity of independent nation states, and buttressed that independence through progressive social policies – such as the radical democratic education we see being enacted in the post-independence section of the film – doing what, after all, the West expects of Africa, and rapidly slipping back into 'primitivism'. In fact, something very different is happening here: although the structure of the ceremony is traditional, the discourses and procedures employed are modern. For instance, there is a fundamental shift in gender roles, and a ceremony at which men usually preside is organised and conducted entirely by women. Also, the purpose of the gathering is political, not mystical or spiritual as one might expect from a conversation with the ancestors; the help of the latter is sought for in order to unmask the enemies within, those who 'desire the death of the baobab'. Once again, as with the drought, the simple, natural, 'traditional' image serves a modern political purpose, as the baobab, the tree of life, represents the young growing nation and its revolutionary struggle, which, as the film's audience is by now well aware, is under threat from a range of enemies. To counter that, the inclusive, multi-ethnic image of the nation – which was, above all, the one for which Cabral fought, and which is fundamentally opposed to the divisiveness of ethnicity as 'traditionally' understood – is reaffirmed.

The relationship here is, significantly, tradition *and* – or, even more so, *as* – modernity, and categorically not, as it is usually represented, tradition *versus* modernity. In this respect, Flora Gomes's work figures as an example of the way in which, as Paul Gilroy argued in *The Black Atlantic*, the histories of black people and their modes of cultural production require at the very least a re-evaluation, if not a fundamental restructuring, of typical conceptions of modernity. For Gomes, modernity and tradition are inseparable: significantly, fifteen years after making *Mortu nega*, he continues to stress the importance and, indeed, the living presence of the traditional and the spiritual at the heart of the modern. As he goes on to say, however:

This must not prevent us from developing and mastering science and technology. We are part of the modern world, and must make use of its progress, but

the fact of using a camera, a zoom or a cutting table in no way stops me asking
questions about my origins. Our inspiration should come from the positive
aspects of our society, as Cabral said. (Gomes 2002a)

In this case, the return to the source, the positive aspects of traditional practices applied in pursuit of progressive political aims, yields positive results:
Diminga and Sako awaken to the sound of rain, marking the end of the
(multi-level) drought. Doing tradition differently works.

Three points remain to be made briefly. Firstly, it is worth noting that,
despite Manthia Diawara's claim in *African Cinema* that, during the invocation of Djon Cago, Diminga prays for rain, she does not: the purpose of
the ceremony is, as already indicated, something other than this altogether
traditional one. Secondly, while the film does not portray onscreen a return
to the source in the sense in which Cabral articulates this, given that the
characters belong to the rural masses rather the assimilated or alienated
petty bourgeoisie, it clearly nevertheless represents such a movement on
the part of the (notionally assimilated or alienated) filmmaker. Finally,
although the film ends on an optimistic note, the fact that those alienated
individuals who are in positions of authority in the postcolonial state show
no signs of making the necessary return to the source points towards future
problems for Guinea-Bissau, problems which Gomes's subsequent films
address.

Gomes's later film, *Po di sangui*, released in 1996, presents an entirely different cinematic approach to traditional Africa and its cultural heritage,
although many of the basic issues remain the same as in earlier films:

In [*Po di sangui*] I wanted to ask questions: do we want to keep *all* our traditions?
Do we want to sacrifice part of ourselves, part of our tradition, and link up with
Western thought, from the so-called developed countries? (Gomes 2002b)

Po di sangui is simultaneously more modern (in terms, particularly, of higher
cinematic production values) and more traditional (the film is set in a deliberately allegorically stylised African village, whose name means 'tomorrow
is far away'). More important, however, is the weight given to traditional
culture: if *Mortu nega* offered something in the way of balance or equiva-
lence between tradition and modernity in its final scene, *Po di sangui* is tilted
very strongly in the direction of the traditional. At that level, the film could
hardly be more of a return to the source.

As we have already seen, however, it is not the simple fact of representing
traditional Africa in a return to the source which is crucial but the nature
(political or ideological) of the representation. On one level, the village in *Po
di sangui*, in its (apparently) timeless simplicity, is strikingly reminiscent of
that in Idrissa Ouédraogo's *Yaaba*, one of the paradigmatic Return to the
Source texts. However, whereas the latter film has been criticised for presenting a romanticised idyll of rural African life, that is something of which
Po di sangui is clearly not guilty, based as it is on a narrative of exile and
catastrophe. In addition, if the idyll represents something like a flight from

the real, then *Po di sangui* might be seen as simultaneously more and less culpable. On the one hand, its (deeply traditional) mythic dimension – anthropomorphised narratives of the Sun falling in love with a beautiful young woman, for example – is both more powerful and more persistent than anything in *Yaaba*; on the other, Ouédraogo's film has nothing to compare with *Po di sangui*'s critique of rapacious capitalism masquerading as benevolent development, making the latter film arguably more real, more political and more modern.

The impact of capitalism means that, rather than working or negotiating with modernity, in *Po di sangui* tradition finds itself reluctantly in the position of having to fight modernity – at least in so far as capitalism and modernity are synonymous. The 'modern' attempt to work with the modern world – cutting down the all-important trees in order to sell them off as charcoal – fails, and tradition remains as the only available site and means of resistance to the forces which then threaten the village of Amanha Lundgu. Although this might look regressive – a retreating into the archaic rather than an embracing of the modern – it is probably better understood as another example of the kind of necessary cultural resistance to imperialism theorised by Cabral. Indeed, it is interesting to note how 'development' in the film follows an archetypal colonialist or imperialist pattern: beginning with 'progressive' information gathering – the cataloguing of the natural world presented as non-threatening or even straightforwardly beneficial – the process of knowledge formation rapidly shifts to enable invasion of the people's territory, undesired commercial exploitation and ultimately destruction of the environment.

If, as suggested by the quotation from Flora Gomes above, signing up to modernity comes at a price – giving up a part of ourselves, in the shape of traditional culture and beliefs – then resisting it may come at an even higher price. In *Po di sangui*, as the unseen, but all-too-audible and seemingly apocalyptic threat draws near (the screeching chainsaws of the logging company, felling the village's sacred trees – simultaneously very real and presented as almost supernatural), the people of Amanha Lundgu are instructed by their wise man Calacalado to leave, while he will stay to defend the village on their behalf against the encroaching menace. The inhabitants then set off on a journey of exile and wandering, from which they eventually return (to their source, as it were) to discover the village reasonably intact – though looking somewhat like a battle-zone – and Calacalado dead.

There are a number of possible ways of interpreting the villagers' journey. One, perhaps not the most fully convincing, would be to see it as a form of collective alienation from which they must collectively return. Another would be to regard it as a sort of pedagogical space, a series of lessons from Calacalado. Among these would be a 'back to the future' combination of regression as intimation of things to come: here, the return to a kind of absolute source – absolutely denuded nature, harsh, threatening and unsupportive, a nature without human beings – which represents one possible future if things continue as they are at present. Alongside this is a lesson about the importance of human solidarity. Calacalado sends the villagers away as a united group: 'All one. No one apart' – something which is severely tested by the rigours of their travels; then, when their journey is at its harshest, they meet another wandering, searching group, whose members, despite being strangers, treat them kindly; perhaps the highest form of solidarity, however, is the one exhibited by Calacalado: to give your life for others, though a final lesson contained in his actions is that his death is necessary only because the rest of the community have forgotten how to behave appropriately towards one another and towards the natural world.

Calacalado's heroic and self-sacrificial fight is at one and the same time the defence of traditional culture, the traditional way of life, and the natural environment, since in the perspective embodied here all of these are indistinguishable or inseparable. Flora Gomes here suggests an ecology of liberation, or, indeed, ecology *as* liberation (liberation ecology, as opposed to liberation theology, perhaps), but the symbolic, and real, importance of the natural world has been present in all his films, as witnessed, for instance, in the significance of the drought in *Mortu nega* mentioned earlier. In *The Blue Eyes of Yonta*, a similar parallel between problems in the natural world and those in human society is expressed by the central character Vicente as he is forced to realise that even his partially positive assessment of the state of postcolonial Guinea-Bissau is over-optimistic: 'See the town? How it is dying? It weeps over its divorce from the River Geba. Now, it is married to the container ships. And the huge mango trees along the streets are gone; they reminded us of the jungle . . .' Cabral, too, as his country's first agronomist, had a very clear understanding of the importance of the natural world, again ranging from the symbolic or metaphorical – for example, his use of the (non-existent) mountains of Guinea-Bissau in a series of political images – to the fundamentally real – as in the countryside's potential as the source of food for his people, or camouflage for his fighters.

In *Culture and Imperialism*, Said talks about the idea of 'third nature', where an approach to the natural world which is non-essentialising, historically informed and progressive is articulated:

> Following Hegel, Marx, and Lukacs, Smith calls the production of this scientifically 'natural' world [of imperialism and expansionist capitalism] a *second* nature. To the anti-imperialist imagination, our space at home in the peripheries has been usurped and put to use by outsiders for their purpose. It is therefore necessary to seek out, to map, to invent, or to discover a *third* nature, not pristine and pre-historical . . . but deriving from the deprivations of the present. (Said 1993: 272)

Importantly, Said recognises the extent to which the reclamation of the natural world still involves the question of authenticity:

> One of the first tasks of the culture of resistance was to reclaim, rename, and reinhabit the land. And with that came a whole set of further assertions, recoveries,

and identifications, all of them quite literally grounded on this poetically pro-
jected base. The search for authenticity, for a more congenial national origin than
that provided by colonial history, for a new pantheon of heroes and (occasionally) heroines, myths, and religions – these too are made possible by a sense of
the land reappropriated by its people. (Said 1993: 273)

A range of complex and potentially contradictory or conflictual articulations
of relationships to the land or nature within notionally postcolonial space
are involved here. The second quotation outlines a classic anti-/postcolonial
stance, whose potential weakness lies in an oversimplified appropriativeness:
as far as this approach is concerned, reconquest is all. That oversimplification may be compounded by a similar lack of self-reflection in relation to the
notion of the authenticity being claimed. In contrast to that, the elaboration
of a concept of 'third nature', while also postcolonial, presents fewer problems in terms of foundationalist or originary claims, and operates within the
space of a Cabralian emphasis on the real, constituted, in Said's words, by
'the deprivations of the present'. The sobering facts of deprivation make any
slippage into romanticised notions of natural plenitude all the more unlikely,
while a concentration on the present avoids problematic returns to the time-
lessness of the 'pre-historical'.

The self-reflexiveness involved in the articulation of a concept of third
nature aligns it with the potentially more oppositional form of liberation
ecology. Although a concern with ecology may look to some like modernity
gone soft – in particular, the middle classes of the over-developed world
getting over-sensitive or sentimental about nature – it in fact involves a significant 'return to the source'. Whereas modernity is characterised by an
increasingly intensive, capitalist-driven and exploitative stance towards the
natural world, one which grows ever more rapacious and destructive – and
is therefore the complete antithesis of the ecological – traditional societies
have, of necessity, lived in a relationship with nature which is more sparing,
respectful or harmonious; in other words, ecological. In that respect, a
postcolonial politics of a 'third nature' will involve a conscious return to
tradition-as-ecology as part of the formulation of a more liberated, and liberating, relationship with the natural world. Among the best-known examples of recent ecological interventions characterised by an oppositional
political stance are the Chipko movement in India, famous for its protective
encircling of trees by women, and the Narmada Dam movement, also in
India. In turn, Chipko has inspired, and is echoed by, the Green Belt movement of recent Nobel Peace Prize winner Wangari Maathai, involving
Kenyan women fighting in similar ways to protect trees in Africa.

If *Mortu nega* represents a classic example of the people, in the shape of
the armed liberation struggle, fighting, as Said expressed it, 'to reclaim,
rename, and reinhabit the land', then *Po di sangui* offers a different perspective on the relationship between humanity and nature, one which is
more intimate and more mythic (but not, therefore, necessarily de-realised).
At the heart of this is the symbiotic connection between people and trees,

indicated in the film's title, variously translated as *Tree of Blood*, or, in the French version, *Tree of Souls*. In the culture of Amanha Lundgu, at the birth of a member of the community a tree is planted which is then seen as intimately connected to, in some ways mirroring, the life of the human being. (It is a mark of the fact that the world of the village is moving dangerously out of kilter that when, at the opening of the film, the wanderer Dou returns to the village, he finds that his twin brother Hami is dead, but also that his own tree, not his brother's, has died.) As Calacalado later explains, the reason why the charcoal-making venture fails is because the men who have embarked upon it have perpetrated a kind of murder – turning living trees into dead wood – and have done so for money. One of these men was Dou's twin Hami, and his death is a consequence of the 'deaths' he has caused. In that context, Calacalado's fight is more than just to protect trees from the logging company: it represents quite literally a battle for the soul(s) of his people and their culture. It is also a battle whose lines extend far beyond the lands around Amanha Lundgu; writing about the stories of Mahasweta Devi from Bengal, Gayatri Spivak comments:

> In this context, it is important to notice that the stories in this volume are not only linked by the common thread of profound ecological loss, the loss of the forest as foundation of life, but also of the complicity, however apparently remote, of the power lines of local developers with the forces of global capital. This is no secret to the initiative for a global movement for non-Eurocentric ecological justice. But it is certainly a secret to the benevolent study of other cultures in the North. (Spivak 1995: 198)

Notwithstanding the ramifications of this global battle, the implication, in Flora Gomes's typically quietly optimistic ending, is that Calacalado's fight has been successful. The villagers have returned to their place of origin. A new baby is born, and a new tree will be planted for it. The story, like a good traditional/mythic tale, has returned to its starting point. Neither the people nor the narrative are quite the same, however, and it is this difference which is significant. The film begins with the 'once upon a time' real-but-mythic tale of Hami and Dou told to the children; it ends with the villagers (visually) representing their experiences, and this – real history, rather than myth – is narrated and explained *by* a child. The capacity for making small but crucial shifts in attitude or social practice, for 'doing things differently' – including tradition – is the source to which Flora Gomes returns time and again in his films. It is a source of hope, embodied above all in children, but also in a faith in people, in his own people – as Cabral taught.

Nha fala (*My Voice*), Gomes's latest film (2002), is in many ways the opposite of *Po di Sangui* (though in one respect at least, it is a direct outgrowth of it). For instance, while the latter is a serious examination, in the shape of an allegorical quest, of a traditional society grappling with modernity, the former is a light-hearted treatment, in the shape of a musical, of contemporary society grappling with tradition. As the most recent of his films,

Nha fala marks the latest stage in Gomes's chronicling of the postcolonial history of his country, and in this respect, if in no other, is the most modern. The other face of this modernity is, however, that *Nha fala* looks rather like that most traditional of narrative modes, a fairy story – though a fairy story for twenty-first-century Africa. The events of the film are also simultaneously grounded in the traditional and the modern: the context is the problematic state of contemporary post-independence society in Guinea-Bissau – the corruption, the profiteering, the consumerism; the motor of the plot is, however, traditional, in the shape of a potentially fatal curse affecting the central character Vita and her family, and everything hinges on how this traditional belief is interpreted and dealt with, by her and others.

The question of return (to the source, or perhaps not) resonates through the film in various ways. For Vita, the story is one of departure and return (to Paris and back), though her return to Africa also signals a different kind of departure, in this case, freeing herself from the constraints of tradition, as she prepares to face up to the consequences of her rejection or defiance of the curse. The importance of a careful assessment of the value of traditional culture is something stressed by Cabral, as noted earlier, since:

> all culture is composed of essential and secondary elements, of strengths and weaknesses, of virtues and failings, of positive and negative aspects, of factors of progress and factors of stagnation or regression. (Cabral 1976: 50–1)

Vita is brought to see how the curse is part of the 'factors of stagnation or regression' in her culture, and how she, in the words of the final song of the film, has to learn to 'dare', in order to overcome its effects. The daring, in Vita's case, consists of, once again, doing tradition differently, as she – flagrantly, transparently artificially – stages her own traditional wake and funeral; and her 'death' and rebirth, her return to and from the source, liberates more than just her. The obvious counterpart to this is doing modernity (especially its capitalist variant) differently, and, by the time Vita returns home to Africa, her sharp-suited, mobile-phone-wielding, would-be boyfriend has abandoned his shady profiteering deals and, in a way reminiscent of Vicente, is involved in business with a social conscience. If, for Flora Gomes, the answer to the opposition (apparent or actual) between modernity and tradition is neither one nor the other but both, then that syncretic resolution is for him only the sign of a larger reality: 'The future of this planet is hybridity. No one can prevent it' (Gomes in Benabdessadok 2003). Perhaps no one can, though achieving that all-important mixture may still require courage: in the words of the song from *Nha fala*, 'What do we have to do to be together and different? We have to dare!'

The other significant return in the film – ironic, in many ways, given his position as theorist of the return to the source, but also entirely appropriate – is that of Cabral himself. As the film opens, a lorry brings what turns out to be the first statue of Cabral to be erected in the town. This is an additional irony – or condemnation – namely that, a quarter of a century after independence, there is still no monument to the father of that independence. The irony or condemnation is further compounded by the fact that a number of people are unable to recognise the statue, and yet further by their inability to decide where to put it. The problem of 'Where do we put Cabral?' is clearly one with more than local or merely rhetorical signifi-cance, but, in the absence of any initial decision on that in the film, the statue is wheeled around town in a baby's pram. Although in one sense this reduces Cabral to an almost ridiculous level, as the film progresses so the pram's fol-lowing grows, becoming part religious procession, part political march, and part carnival – a mass or popular event, bringing all types of people together in a manner of which Cabral would have heartily approved. In the final section of the film, problems – the curse included – are overcome, wounds are healed, the alienated petty bourgeoisie – capitalist profiteers – see the light, and a place is found for Cabral's statue. Or rather, Cabral's statue finds its own place, as in the last scene it somehow ascends to a position of rightful prominence on an empty plinth. Not terribly realistic, but then that is not something this film worries about very much.

As was mentioned above, the title of Flora Gomes's first short film, made in 1976, was, significantly, *The Return of Cabral*. One of the implications of his latest film is that the return is not a once-and-for-all event, that it needs to be repeated in order to achieve its full meaning – the return not so much *to* the source, as *of* the source, perhaps. It is also an important reminder that, just as in the Benjamin quotation where tradition must be repeatedly defended against the powers of conformism, so here the lessons and the legacy of Cabral must be repeatedly defended against the threat of oblivion, and restored to the present where they offer the possibility of doing things very differently – the necessary condition for a better, 'modern' future:

> The cultures that defenders of tradition look back to with such nostalgia are the dream-form of the societies that gave them birth. Precisely for that reason, in their time they functioned ideologically . . . If the Left returns to the past, it is not to redeem some sort of original ideal world from which we have been ban-ished . . . so the nostalgia is really for *the possibility of something else today.* (Buck-Morss 2003: 104, 125)

Filmography

Regresso de Cabral (The Return of Cabral) (1976)
La Reconstruction (Reconstruction) (1977)
Anos os oca luta (The Years of Struggle) (1978)
Mortu nega (Those whom Death Refused) (1988)
Udju azul di Yonta (The Blue Eyes of Yonta) (1992)
A mascara (The Mask) (1993)
Po di sangui (Tree of Blood) (1996)
Nha fala (My Voice) (2002)

Chapter 7

Idrissa Ouédraogo

Introduction

Idrissa Ouédraogo is a key figure in the 'second wave' of African filmmakers who came to the fore in the 1980s, and he is often argued to have forged a new cinematic style in which political issues have given way to smaller, 'human' stories. Frank Ukadike describes Ouédraogo as 'dean of the "new wave" in African film', arguing that the director 'deliberately eschew[s] the *traditional films of protest* initiated by the pioneers and opts[s] instead for narrative forms in which the humanistic and the universal coalesce into a pleasing aesthetic formula that in turn translates into acceptability and commercial viability' (2002: 151–2; our emphasis). Within this assessment, one finds a curious mixture of praise for Ouédraogo's innovativeness in creating a new type of filmmaking and a rather 'watery' appraisal of this style as 'pleasing', 'commercial' fare. This assessment is primarily based on the rather contentious claim that prior to Ouédraogo – and Gaston Kaboré, his compatriot, with whose work Ouédraogo's is often compared – most (sub-Saharan) African films were 'traditional films of protest', which, as has been argued throughout this volume, provides a rather misleading vision of African cinema history. Although Ukadike's critical appraisal of Ouédraogo's work is less than fulsome, he acknowledges that: 'From the mid-1980s to the early 1990s, the films of Idrissa Ouédraogo, more than those of any other African filmmaker, made an enormous impact internationally, in terms of both universal acceptability and commercial viability' (2002: 151). Considering how dramatically Ouédraogo's critical and popular reputation has waned over the past decade, Ukadike's comment acts as a timely reminder of the pivotal role played by the director in charting new territories for African filmmakers and finding new audiences for African films. His third feature film, *Tilaï*, won the special jury prize at Cannes in 1990 (his previous film *Yaaba* had won the Critics' Prize at Cannes the previous year), and its success, coming just three years after that of Souleymane Cissé's *Yeelen*, seemed to herald a new era for African cinema on the international stage. Moreover, *Tilaï*'s depiction of an isolated rural community and its focus on generational conflict reinforced the connections between the two directors, who soon saw themselves cast by critics as the main exponents of the 'return to the source' genre of filmmaking with its emphasis on the values and knowledge

associated with rural communities (for further discussion of the concept
of a 'return to the source', see Chapters 5 and 6 on Cissé and Gomes
respectively).

Born in Banfora in Burkina Faso in 1954, Ouédraogo is part of the second
generation of African filmmakers, those who explicitly set out to become
directors and who received an 'official' film education – unlike Sembene,
Mambety, Cissé and the other 'first generation' filmmakers who either developed their skills on the ground or picked up training later in life. Ouédraogo
studied cinema at the Institut Africain des Etudes de Cinématographie in
Ouagadougou (the capital of Burkina Faso), during which time he made the
short film, *Poko*, which won the prize for best short film at FESPACO in
1981. After a brief spell working for the state film production office, he
studied cinema briefly in Kiev (in the former Soviet Union), before obtaining
a place at the prestigious Institut des Hautes Etudes de Cinéma (IDHEC) in
Paris, from which he graduated in 1985.

Ouédraogo is a very prolific director who has made eleven feature films and
a similar number of short films and documentaries in just over two and a half
decades.[1] This output seems all the more remarkable given the difficulties
faced by African filmmakers in financing their films: in comparison, the
'father' of sub-Saharan filmmaking, Ousmane Sembene, has made only nine
feature films in almost five decades; while Souleymane Cissé has made only
five feature films in over thirty years. As is clear from interviews that he has
given over the years, Ouédraogo very much identifies himself as a 'working
director' who is willing to explore a range of styles, genres and media in order
to continue producing work and reach new audiences. For example, in the
late 1990s, he turned his hand to television, making the *Kadi Jolie* series,
which was screened across Francophone West Africa. The series focuses on
the 'adventures' of its eponymous heroine, and its broad mix of comedy and
drama has proven very popular with television audiences. Also, he has
recently announced that his future film projects will be shot using digital
cameras, the reduced technological cost of which he believes will allow
Burkinabe filmmakers to target their relatively limited national audience (De
Rochebrune 2005: 58–9). As will be argued in greater detail below, this willingness to explore a range of forms that might allow him to reach new audiences has been looked on with suspicion by many critics who see in his work
a 'betrayal' of the radical nature of postcolonial African filmmaking.

During his film training, Ouédraogo made seven short films, which are shot
in a wide range of styles and genres, indicating a willingness to experiment in
search of a cinematic 'voice', a process that has also marked his later career.
His first (very) short film (four minutes), *Pourquoi* (1981), might be seen as a
student engaging in an *exercice de style*, and attempting to render (not very
convincingly) a man's nightmare of frustration and anger, during which he
murders his wife, only to wake up at the end of the film to discover her playing
with their baby daughter. In *The Bowls* (1983) and *Ouagadougou, Ouaga
deux roues* (1984), he tries his hand at naturalistic documentary to great

effect. The former film is set in an isolated Mossi village (in the north of Burkina Faso) and it traces the making of the eponymous bowls from cutting down a tree for wood, through the painstaking work of shaping them, until finally they are put to use by the village women or sent for sale to the local market. Even in such a short work, Ouédraogo displays his capacity for uncovering powerful 'human stories': the young people are deserting the village for the towns, leaving it to the old people to keep alive artisanal trad-itions such as those we see in the film. Although classified as a documentary, it might better be described as 'docu-fiction', as indeed might all of Ouédraogo's 'documentaries'. This is underlined by the presence within the film of his 'fetish' actor Rasmane Ouédraogo, who plays the trader, who takes the bowls to the market. (Ouédraogo is an excellent Burkinabe actor, capable both of giving highly nuanced performances and of playing exaggerated types.) Indeed, the blurring of the boundaries between fiction and documen-tary has been a common feature of African cinema, as for example in the work of Safi Faye and Jean-Marie Téno, and it seems indicative of a desire on the part of certain directors to embed their narratives within specific socio-cultural realities, while also keeping open the narrative possibilities of the fiction film.

At its name suggests, *Ouagadougou, Ouaga deux roues* is set in the capital city and traces the national obsession with bicycles and scooters, a subject to which Ouédraogo would return in his later documentary, *Le Marché des deux roues à Ouagadougou* (2001). Unusually for Ouédraogo, the film does not really attempt to construct a narrative: it is simply a series of fragmented episodes in the streets of the city, some of which provide more 'narrative' interest than others: the aftermath of a collision between two bicycles; a man with a pile of live goats in a basket on the back of his moped. However, the film does underline an important but neglected aspect of Ouédraogo's work, namely his ability to evoke a sense of place. His 'human stories' generally take place within a carefully defined environment: the barren savannah and enclosed space of the village in *Tilaï*, or the lush, open spaces of the Zimbabwean countryside in *Kini and Adams*.

Alongside these 'documentaries', Ouédraogo had also turned his hand to several short fiction films. *Poko* (1981) falls very much within the social realist category, tracing the hazardous journey of a young couple expecting their first child from their village to the hospital in town. As with many other films of that era, it is a film with a 'message' about the hardships of rural life and the failings of post-independence societies. However, in later short films, such as *Issa the Weaver* (1984) and *Tenga* (1986), Ouédraogo mixes a natur-alistic style, which documents the lives of his main characters in meticulous detail, with a concern for the inner life and dreams of his characters. Indeed, it is curious to think that *Issa, the Weaver* won the 'Cauri' for best docu-mentary at FESPACO in 1985, for it deliberately blurs the boundaries of documentary by including explicitly fictional elements: as his wife passes him a drink, Issa drifts off into a daydream of a better life in which his financial

woes have been placed behind him. In *Tenga*, the daydream is of a return to
a simpler life in the country: the eponymous Tenga is sitting in a canteen in
the city when he hears a traditional air and is transported (in a flashback) to
the rural life that he has left behind. Both Issa and Tenga are struggling to
come to terms with the modern, urban capitalist world: Issa's 'traditional'
weaving skills are increasingly useless in face of the onslaught of cheap, mass-
produced goods, while Tenga's rural knowledge is worthless to him in the big
city. In both cases, Ouédraogo chooses to explore the hopes, dreams and feelings of his characters rather than focusing solely on their material concerns.

This approach has marked Ouédraogo's subsequent career and it clearly
feeds into his first feature film, *Yam Daabo* (1986), which, although it is concerned with wider social issues (drought, migration from the land), places
the exploration of family relationships at the heart of its story. Ostensibly a
story about famine and international aid, the film presents a complex portrait of a family torn apart by tragic circumstances and generational conflict.
As in *Issa the Weaver* and *Tenga*, it is the movement from village to town
that sparks the drama of the narrative, but Ouédraogo seems more interested
in the human relationships and the dynamics of family bonds than in the
wider social issues of poverty and aid. As with many other African films, the
exploration of character continually veers between naturalistic and 'stock'
elements: in particular, Ouédraogo often gives his characters defining 'tics'
that are designed to provoke laughter or anger in his audience: for example,
in *Yam Daabo*, Rasmane Ouédraogo plays Tiga with great comic brio as a
spiteful but ineffectual buffoon.

Ouédraogo's major artistic and commercial breakthrough came with
Yaaba (1989), which relates the story of Sana, an elderly woman who is
accused of being a witch: she is cast out by the villagers, and her only friends
are two young children, Bila and Nopoko. The film uses these characters as
a way of exploring the 'margins' of this society: the oldest and the youngest
are able to forge a space in which certain norms can be challenged. As in *Yam
Daabo*, Ouédraogo is not so much interested in developing a 'believable'
character study: rather, he presents the grandmother and the children as
character 'types': the 'wise' grandmother and the 'roguish' but 'lovable' children. (Mambety's documentary on the making of the film, *Let's Speak,
Grandmother*, beautifully captures the essence of Ouédraogo's portrait of
childhood friendship and the dignity and wisdom of the old woman: see
Chapter 4.) At times, this leads to a quite sentimental approach to his subject
matter but, as will be argued below, Ouédraogo's primary concern has
always been to make popular rather than art house movies. Such was the
popularity of *Yaaba* that Ouédraogo quickly made *A Karim na Sala* (1990),
which reunites the child leads who had so entranced audiences both in Africa
and in the West.

Even greater critical and commercial success was to come the director's
way with *Tilaï* (1990). Although often categorised as a 'simple', 'village' film,
Tilaï is, in fact, an extremely complex tragedy, which explores the conflicting

forces of family, social convention and love. Saga returns to his home village after two years away to discover that Nogma, the girl who had been promised to him, has in fact been married to his father. When Saga and Nogma are discovered to have disobeyed the rules of society and of the family by committing adultery or incest, this sparks a chain reaction of events that eventually lead to death and the destruction of social and family ties. As in *Yaaba*, Ouédraogo focuses on the story of those seen to transgress society's rules. However, unlike many of his predecessors, Ouédraogo adopts no specific position in relation to his story. Even though the spectator is visually and emotionally aligned with Saga and Nogma, Ouédraogo acts neither as the voice of modernity in calling for change nor as the voice of tradition in calling for the rules to be upheld. Rather, his film contents itself with revealing the forces unleashed when the rules are broken as well as their effect on individuals.

The theme of transgression remains to the fore in the last of Ouédraogo's critical successes, *Samba Traoré* (1992), which won the Golden Lion at the Venice Film Festival. The film focuses on the torment of the eponymous hero who has been involved in a hold-up at a garage, and who attempts to rebuild his life in his home village. It is in many ways a morality tale, which traces the tragic consequences of one man's past actions. Once again contrasting rural and urban life, Ouédraogo presents the city as a site of menace and temptation for those in the country.

The films *Obi* (1991) and *Afrique, mon Afrique* (1994) represent another aspect of Ouédraogo's career: they are both specially commissioned films, dealing with 'topical', 'social' issues but in radically different ways. *Obi*, which was made for a series called 'Families' on Channel 4 (UK), saw Ouédraogo return to docu-fiction, and he plays with the boundaries of genre to great effect. An extremely impressive but overlooked work in Ouédraogo's canon, the film is a very intelligently constructed portrait of Obi, a woman who forges a life for herself and her four children after she has been abandoned by her husband. Much of the film is shot without dialogue, as we follow Obi through a range of jobs – waitress, miner, market trader – and see her caring for her children. Then, in a series of 'interviews' with an off-camera figure, she tells the story of her life in highly unsentimental terms. Mixing realism and optimism, the films ends with Obi finding wealth and prosperity – she discovers (her crock of?) gold at the mine – and she chases the camera away, telling the crew that their presence will not earn her a living. Ouédraogo adopts a very different approach in the AIDS-awareness film (made for the NGO, Plan International), *Afrique, mon Afrique*. Starring the well-known Senegalese singer Ismael Lô (an enthusiastic if rather wooden actor), the film is a didactic, educational work that uses broad comedy, song and often quite mawkish sentimentality to make its point. The film illustrates Ouédraogo's keen awareness of the audience(s) that he is trying to address in his films: *Afrique, mon Afrique* is an attempt to reach as wide a public as possible in Francophone West Africa, and it uses every populist trick in the book to appeal to this intended audience. A similar approach is adopted in the three short films on AIDS, which he made for the British NGO, Global Dialogue Trust in 1997.

Ouédraogo's next feature-length film, *Le Cri du coeur* (1995), was a commercial and critical failure, which marked the beginning of a decline in his reputation from which he has not yet recovered. Although it features many of the elements that had made Ouédraogo's earlier films critically and commercially popular – the 'cute' child, uncomprehending parents, the trauma of moving from village to town – the film is strangely disjointed and full of loose ends and non-sequiturs. However, it is curious that many critics of the film have focused not on its shortcoming as a piece of cinema but rather on Ouédraogo's decision to move away from his West African homeland to make a film about an African family in France (Lyons). Once again, culturalist arguments are given precedence over cinematic arguments, a process that was examined at length in the introduction to this volume, and will be addressed once again in the final section of this chapter.

With *Kini and Adams* (1997), set in rural Zimbabwe and shot in English using a mainly South African cast, Ouédraogo continued to roam far beyond West Africa. Although the film met with a similar critical and commercial response to *Le Cri du coeur*, it is an altogether more accomplished work, which deserves to be considered alongside *Tilaï* as one of his finest achievements. A film about the joyful but ultimately destructive nature of the friendship between the two eponymous male leads, it is, by turns, both thoughtful and exuberant, in a film that seeks both to be 'popular' and 'complex'.

Ouédraogo's two most recent feature films have seen the director return to his homeland to develop narratives that are firmly embedded within the rural culture of Burkina Faso: *Le Monde à l'endroit* (2000) is the gently comic story of gender relations within a small, rural community, which contains echoes of Malian director Adama Drabo's hilarious topsy-turvy tale of male–female role reversal, *Taafe Fanga* (1997); while *La Colère des dieux* (*The Wrath of the Gods*, 2003) is the compelling tale of a nineteenth-century African monarch who steals the throne from the rightful heir (his uncle), an act that leads to a cycle of revenge. (In 2002, he made a short a comic fable, set in Ouagadougou, as part of the portmanteau film *11/09/01 – September 11.*) Simple (but not simplistic) moral tales about power and authority, these films are clearly on a par with *Yaaba* and *Tilaï* but they have not received much attention from critics and have not been screened widely. Although these works have failed to revive Ouédraogo's critical and commercial fortunes, they are clear evidence of his boundless capacity for reinvention as a director. As was mentioned above, he has now turned his attention towards developing a cheap, but high-quality, digital cinema for the national market in Burkina Faso, investing heavily in digital cameras for filming, and projectors for screening in a number of cinemas across the country (De Rochebrune 2005: 58–9): clearly, another chapter in Ouédraogo's process of reinvention is about to be opened.

Social, cultural and political contexts

The territory now known as Burkina Faso was originally founded as a colony by the French in the early twentieth century, under the name of Upper Volta. A vast, landlocked territory of no real commercial importance to France, it had little in the way of infrastructure by the time it gained its independence in 1960. The first president, Maurice Yaméogo, oversaw a downturn in the country's already dire economic situation and grew increasingly authoritarian in a bid to retain power. He was finally overthrown by a *coup d'état* in January 1966, led by the army chief of staff Sangoulé Lamizana. Although the military claimed that their intervention was designed to pave the way for a quick return to civilian rule, the country was to be governed by various forms of military authority for the next twenty years.

The most charismatic of this succession of military rulers, and the one who was to have the most significant impact on the country, was Thomas Sankara, who seized power in August 1983, at the age of only thirty-four. Promising to put an end to the corruption that had marked previous regimes, Sankara was a radical and an idealist who inspired many of his compatriots with an anti-imperialist rhetoric and a firmly held belief in equality: his most symbolic gesture was to rechristen the country 'Burkina Faso' (in a hybrid of the More and Dioula languages), meaning 'the land of men of integrity'. Although Sankara's actions and rhetoric placed strain on the relationship between the country and its former colonial ruler, within Africa he was seen as an inspirational figure (despite disquiet at some of his methods). However, within Burkina Faso, he had created many enemies and his short reign came to an end in October 1987 when he was killed in a messy and bloody coup that saw his fellow officer and partner in government, Blaise Compaoré, take power. A distinctly uncharismatic leader, very much in the 'strong man' mould of African politics, Compaoré is often perceived as a Machiavellian figure, suspected of involvement in the death of Sankara, and of aiding opposition rebels in neighbouring countries, such as Liberia and more recently the Ivory Coast. However, Compaoré at least had the organisational and political skills lacking in his former friend: he managed the (uneasy) transformation to multi-party democracy in the early 1990s, stabilised the country's dire economic performance, and remains in power to this day.

Given this extremely troubled recent history, it seems remarkable that such a poverty-stricken and unstable country should have managed to create an embryonic national film 'industry': its film production may lag well behind those of countries with a genuine film industry but, for a country of its size and wealth, the ability to produce a small number of films annually is, in the African context, quite remarkable. This situation can be traced back to 1970 when the country's film theatres were nationalised. Borrowing from French policies for the development of its cinema, the Burkinabe government placed a tax upon all film tickets with the revenues being ploughed back into filmmaking by indigenous directors. This did not change the country's cinematic culture overnight but it did encourage the development of filmmaking, a process reinforced by the decision to create a national film school in Ouagadougou. As well as fostering film production, the country also sought to develop an audience for African films within the country, releasing locally produced films in its nationally owned theatres. Furthermore, the establishment of the biennial film festival FESPACO as the prime event on the African film calendar meant that this isolated and sparsely populated country had by the end of the 1970s become a major force in African cinema.[2]

However, it had not as yet produced any directors of continental renown. This all changed with the international success of Gaston Kaboré's *Wend Kuuni* (1982), which in many ways launched what became known as the 'Return to the Source' genre. Set in the precolonial Mossi Empire, the film focuses on the mysterious story of a young boy who is found unconscious on the roadside by a passing trader. The man takes him to the nearest village, where he is immediately adopted by a new family who refer to him as a 'gift from god' (or 'wend kuuni'). Beautifully filmed and intelligently acted, the film gradually reveals the circumstances of the mysterious child's hidden origins: he is an orphan whose parents have both been killed. The film deals with loss and pain but in a way that emphasises the security and love offered by the family unit: Wend Kuuni may have lost a family but the film focuses primarily on the way in which he gains a new one.

This story of family life was heralded by most critics as an innovative and largely successful attempt to forge a cinematic aesthetic based on the structure of oral narratives. However, its focus on the 'human' story of one small boy seemed to many of these same critics to be an abandonment of the fundamentally political dimension of African filmmaking. This criticism of the so-called 'Return to the Source' films is interrogated and criticised at length at various points in this volume, not only for the reductive genealogy of African cinema that it posits (i.e., suggesting that all African films before *Wend Kuuni* were explicitly political films) but also because of the insinuation that such films are less 'African' than more political works, and are somehow pandering to Western tastes. Such an approach ignores the fact that, although *Wend Kuuni* enjoyed a certain art house success in Europe, it was also phenomenally popular in Burkina Faso (and further afield in West Africa), which indicates that its narrative style and its subject matter were clearly attractive, on some level, to a substantial local audience.

For Ukadike, Kaboré's movie marks the 'revival of the family-oriented film fashioned after the African oral tale tradition' (1994: 207), an assessment that seems a very useful way of understanding the development of Burkinabe filmmaking as a whole. Thanks to the nationalisation of the film theatres, filmmakers from Burkina Faso know that their films will usually get a chance to play to a local audience, even if this local audience is very small by Western standards. This means that Burkinabe directors have, over the past few decades, been involved in the type of dialogical relationship with their local audience that has been denied to directors in other

African contexts. There has also developed an informal troupe of actors with whom directors such as Ouédraogo, Kaboré and Fanta Régina Nacro work regularly: the likes of Rasmane Ouédraogo and Roukiétou Barry have become familiar faces to Burkinabe audiences who have, in turn, established a 'relationship' with these actors (which constitutes something of a break with the demand for non-professional actors in the first decades of African cinema). This is in no way to claim that all films from Burkina Faso are shaped solely by the expectations and demands of the audience but it does seem highly significant that Burkinabe films have consistently adopted certain narrative devices and styles that have played well with local audiences – for example, *Yaaba*, Ouédraogo's tale of lovable children and an ostracised woman, can be situated within the same (slightly sentimental) tradition as *Wend Kuuni* – and it now seems possible to speak of a certain type of Burkinabe film aesthetic – human stories, lack of explicit political engagement, influence of oral tradition – in which Ouédraogo's work has played a central role.[3]

The final section of this chapter will consider at greater length the popularity of Burkinabe 'national' cinema. However, one cannot look solely to audience expectations when seeking to explain the relative absence of direct political engagement in Ouédraogo's films (and in Burkinabe filmmaking more generally). For a start, the status of a *national* film industry places the director in a difficult position when it comes to making direct comments about the regime in his or her work. Alongside the fear of direct censorship, there is the danger of self-censorship: should the director risk offending the government if future funding will depend upon its goodwill?[4] Equally, one can argue that Burkinabe filmmaking came to the fore in a period (the early 1980s) when politically radical filmmaking was on the wane. However, this is not to suggest that Ouédraogo's films are completely unconcerned with social or political issues. It is simply that such issues are subsumed within the human stories of the narrative: for example, *Tilaï*, *Le Monde à l'endroit* and *The Wrath of the Gods* all explore the abuse of male authority; *Afrique, mon Afrique* is an AIDS-awareness film; *Yaaba*, *Obi* and *Kini and Adams* focus on characters who are marginalised by their societies; *Yam Daabo* and *Samba Traoré* are concerned with the rural exodus towards the cities and the moral and personal difficulties that this can bring about. This latter point is a crucial one to bear in mind when considering the choice of style and subject matter in Ouédraogo's films. For Burkina Faso remains a very rural country and much of his local audience in the towns and cities is constituted of people who have either just come from the country or who still have a close attachment to the land. Consequently, the oral tradition, as well as rural values and customs, remain extremely influential forces, and Ouédraogo's work consistently engages with them in ways that can be both sentimental and extremely challenging. The remaining sections of this chapter will examine the nature of this engagement in much greater detail.

The films

Ouédraogo's critical and commercial reputation was forged primarily by the hugely successful films, *Yaaba* and *Tilaï,* which have come to be seen as emblematic of his work as a whole: essentially, this has meant that Ouédraogo is generally seen as the purveyor of simple or simplistic – depending on the critic's point of view – 'village films', which eschew the overt political radicalism of Sembene, Hondo and – in his early work – Cissé. As was indicated in the opening section of this chapter, these appraisals fail to do justice to the sheer diversity of Ouédraogo's career as a filmmaker. However, as is often the case with such generalisations, there is more than a grain of truth in their depiction of his cinematic output, for much of Ouédraogo's work has focused on individual moral dilemmas and interpersonal conflict, which he often treats in sentimental or gently comic fashion.[5] The aim of this section is thus to trace the elements of this aesthetic that have most often been commented upon by critics. It will then consider the ways in which elements of Ouédraogo's films might be seen, in fact, to challenge, interrogate and ultimately confound certain aspects of these critical appraisals. The final section of this chapter will move on to examine the 'popularity' of Ouédraogo's breakthrough film, *Yaaba,* in an attempt to uncover the nature of critical attitudes towards the very notion of a popular African cinematic aesthetics.

As was mentioned above, Ukadike's notion of a specifically African style of 'family-oriented film' seems like a very useful way to engage with key aspects of Ouédraogo's major works. Firstly, it is remarkable just how many of his films are seen primarily through the eyes of children. In *Yaaba,* Ouédraogo focused on the adventures of a young boy called Bila and his female cousin Nopoko in a film that proved hugely popular with both West African and Western audiences. Indeed, such was the popularity of the two child leads that he brought them back for a follow-up film, *A Karim na Sala,* a rather contrived but entertaining 'vehicle', which cast the pair as rich girl from the city and poor country boy who runs away from his 'evil' stepfather. Perhaps Ouédraogo's clearest attempt at creating a 'popular' family comedy, *A Karim na Sala* is full of childish pranks and cartwheels, and stock characters with easily identifiable tics. Even Ouédraogo's contribution to the portmanteau film *11/09/01 – September 11,* featuring the perspectives of eleven directors from around the globe on the attack on the World Trade Center on 11 September 2001, is played out as a childlike fable. A (cute) young boy is forced to abandon his schooling in order to earn money to support his gravely ill mother. Shortly after 11 September, he convinces himself that he has seen Osama bin Laden in downtown Ouagadougou and, together with a group of his former school friends, they attempt to capture him so that they can claim the $25 million reward: what follows is a series of boyish pranks that concludes with a freeze frame of the boys jumping in the air as they find another solution to their friend's money worries (the plan to capture 'Bin Laden' having ended in failure).

A slightly darker portrait of childhood is to be found in *Le Cri du coeur*: in the early stages of the film, we are shown idyllic scenes of Mokhtar's childhood in Burkina Faso (stunning landscapes, playing with friends, talking to his beloved grandfather). However, after he moves to France, Mokhtar becomes an anxious and lonely child, haunted by nightmares in which he is stalked by a hyena with deadly, glowing eyes. In *The Wrath of the Gods*, we see what is perhaps Ouédraogo's most complex portrait of childhood. Salam is heir to the throne and often behaves like a spoilt young brat, but he is also the object of the other children's derision, as he has an enormous 'buck' tooth, and, more generally, he is feared as an omen of bad luck by the people of the kingdom. In the end, it is his stubborn, headstrong defiance that allows him to survive and eventually to become king but his wilful actions will ultimately bring about his downfall.

In many ways, the portrait of the boisterous, but essentially innocent, children in *Yaaba* set the pattern for the rest of Ouédraogo's career. From the opening sequence, the camera focuses on Bila and Nopoko running across the wide-open space of the savannah. They are depicted as lovable rogues, who echo the mischievous but precocious children of the oral tradition: they are fundamentally well-meaning 'tricksters' who challenge the wisdom and authority of their elders (yet another example of the space for debate provided by the oral tradition). Bila is the archetypally unruly boy who plays tricks and seeks to impress his companions, especially Nopoko. The first encounter with Sana, the old lady (or 'yaaba' of the title), comes when Bila plays hide-and-seek with Nopoko: Sana helps Nopoko to find Bila, much to his chagrin, as he now has to pay his cousin a 'reward'. The gentle comedy of the moment is reinforced by a standard Ouédraogo trope: a close-up of Sana laughing at this scene. (The significance of these close-ups of people laughing will be considered in greater detail below.) Later in the film, Bila and Nopoko bathe at the river, and he holds his breath under the water in order to make his cousin believe that he has drowned. Nopoko gets her revenge by pretending to be asleep when Bila approaches.

Essentially, these actions are portrayed as those of lively children fooling around in a harmless fashion. This notion is reinforced by the opposition between Bila, Nopoko and the three boys who throw stones at Yaaba: Bila and Nopoko have direct personal experience of Yaaba and know her to be a kindly woman, whereas the other boys simply believe the rumours that have spread amongst their elders. Consequently, it is through Bila's (and to a lesser extent Nopoko's) friendship with Yaaba that the film gives a gently subversive role to children who are able to confront the received ideas of their elders when these contradict their own lived experience. The moral lesson learned by Bila and Nopoko stems from Yaaba's injunction not to judge others, for everyone has his or her reasons for acting as they do: we learn that Koudi commits adultery because she is unhappy with her marriage to the drunken Noaga (played with customary brio by Rasmane Ouédraogo); while Noaga's problem with alcohol is balanced by his willingness to

challenge the superstitious beliefs of his fellow villagers. It is highly significant that it is Noaga who helps the children to bury Yaaba after her death,
and it is he who reveals the secret of the old lady's banishment from the
village: her mother had died in childbirth and her father had immediately
died of grief, leading the villagers to see the child as a witch.

Such friendships between children and an older, often marginalised, character are central to several of Ouédraogo's other films. In *Le Cri du coeur*,
Mokhtar is very close to his grandfather, and, when he moves to Lyons, he
is befriended by the failed magician (played by well-known French actor
Richard Bohringer). Equally, in *The Wrath of the Gods*, the young, friend-
less Salam, is taken under the wing of his paternal uncle Halyaré, the man
who should rightfully have become king rather than Salam's father. These
children are thus associated with figures occupying the margins of their societies: childhood is a space in which not only can they fool around but they
can also learn to question the values and attitudes of their elders. In this
sense, Ouédraogo's vision of childhood might, justifiably, be seen as slightly
sentimental or idealised. However, rather than treating such an appraisal as
the occasion to dismiss his work, it is much more useful as a springboard
from which to apprehend the precise 'register' of these films. If certain of his
films are, essentially, 'family films', is it not to be expected that they will shy
away from hard-edged realism?

The most important recurring feature of Ouédraogo's work is comedy: in
fact, it is difficult to think of another African director in whose films the characters spend so much time laughing. Ouédraogo's comedy is quite different
from the often biting satire of Sembene or the surreal comedy of Mambety.
He rarely, if ever, invites us to laugh at a character. Instead, he gleans laughter from the everyday pranks of children (*Yaaba, A Karim na Sala, Le Cri du
coeur, The Wrath of the Gods, 11/09/01 – September 11*), from jokes or
proverbs (*Tilaï, Kini and Adams*), from comic asides by passers-by on
marital disputes (*Yaaba, Tilaï*): in particular, he enjoys giving wives the
opportunity to bring their husbands down to size (see, for example, the
control that Bila's mother exerts over her husband in *Yaaba*; or the refusal
of the wives to sleep with the old husband in *Tilaï*). The fact that everyone
is supposed to get the joke – and to leave room for laughter in the audience –
is underlined by the repeated trope (mentioned above) of focusing on the
laughing face of a character. Even in his darker films (*Tilaï, The Wrath of the
Gods*), the director makes widespread use of humour: see, for example, the
mischievous younger sister Kuilga, in *Tilaï*, who answers back to her parents
and sides with the outlawed young lovers. Played by Roukiétou Barry,
Kuilga is in certain respects a reprise of the role of Nopoko, which she had
earlier played in *Yaaba*, but in this tragic context her mischievousness serves
mainly to lighten the tone of an otherwise grim situation.

Thus far, this section has focused on the light, comic, family-friendly elements of Ouédraogo's films but it is crucial at this point to try and sketch
out a more complex picture of his work. For if Ouédraogo's darker films

contain moments of light comedy, then it is also true that even his most 'family-friendly' films present a vision of Burkinabe society in which tragedy and conflict are rarely far away, a fact often overlooked by his critics.[6] The village in *Yaaba* is riven from the outset with tensions: a grain store burns down and the villagers disagree about the identity of the person responsible; the eventual decision to lay the blame at the feet of Yaaba is in many ways an attempt to displace these tensions on to a sacrificial 'outsider'. However, the tensions mount with conflicts erupting across the village: Noaga and his wife fight over his drinking; the mother of the troublesome boy who cuts Nopoko with the knife is thrown out of her home by her husband. Similarly, *Kini and Adams* begins as a light-hearted film about friendship between a married man (Kini) and his best friend, a single man and naive dreamer (Adams). However, their dreams of repairing an old car and driving away to the city are soon torn apart by the arrival of a mining company. They both get jobs but the smarter and more astute Kini is quickly promoted. His familial and professional responsibilities soon distance him from his friend, and the initial lively comedy of the film becomes drowned in the conflict created by their increasingly different expectations, responsibilities and trajectories.

Ouédraogo's darkest and most tragic film is perhaps *Tilaï*. (*Samba Traoré* and *The Wrath of the Gods* are also quite dark and claustrophobic narratives.) From its opening images, *Tilaï* presents a portrait of human beings caught up in a web of powerful forces and emotions. A man on a donkey crosses a barren landscape, moving towards a solitary tree, framed in the top left-hand corner of the screen: Abdullah Ibrahim's brooding African jazz score, accompanied by Youssou N'Dour's plaintive vocals, sets the tone for the events that follow. We soon learn that the man, Saga, is returning from two years away from the village (for reasons never specified), but it is immediately apparent that this is an unwanted homecoming, for Nogma, the girl promised to Saga, has now been married to his father. Only his brother, Kougri, advances to meet him, while the rest of the villagers remain behind the perimeter wall. Saga's refusal to accept his father's actions cause him to be banished, literally excluded from the space of the village, which Ouédraogo represents visually in extremely powerful fashion. In contrast to the open space of the savannah, where Saga finds a home and is able to transgress the rules of his community, the village is a place of segregation: repeatedly, Ouédraogo has his characters speak to each other from either side of low walls, their inability to communicate or tell the full truth represented visually by the barriers between them. The village is a dark, shadowy space, often filmed at night: rather than bringing people together as a community, it acts as a kind of prison with arbitrary rules and vicious punishment for those who step out of line: Saga is banished, then sentenced to death; while Nogma's father feels obliged to commit suicide when confronted with the 'shame' of his daughter's actions.

Thus, we can see that, although Ouédraogo's films are based on so-called 'human' stories, they present what is often an extremely complex portrait of social and gender relationships within his society. Although his style is markedly different to that of Sembene, Hondo or Cissé, and he rarely adopts a specific 'position' in his films, his work none the less echoes their progressive stance on questions such as authority, power and the status of women, and it is this combination of the progressive and the popular that will be examined in the final section of this chapter.

Valuing the popularity of African Cinema?

In his article 'Exiles on Main Stream: Valuing the Popularity of Postcolonial Literature', Chris Bongie begins with an anecdote about the reaction of the Antiguan-American author Jamaica Kincaid upon discovering that the US comedian Roseanne Barr had been invited to act as guest editor of a special women's issue of *The New Yorker* in 1995: 'Put me in a room with a great writer, I grovel. Put me in with Roseanne, I throw up' (2003a: 1). Bongie highlights the contrast between Kincaid's willingness to fawn upon a notional 'great writer' and her disgust at the 'vulgar' American comedian, in which he locates an unquestioned acceptance of the value of 'high' literary culture. For Bongie, this opposition between high culture and coarse, mass-produced or consumed culture has (ironically) been central to the development of postcolonial studies, and Kincaid's 'testy comments direct us towards the surprisingly uncharted territory in which postcolonial and cultural studies (don't yet) meet' (2003a: 1). This situation is ironic precisely because so much of the work carried out under the banner of postcolonial studies has been involved in demolishing such 'European constructs' as the divide between 'high' and 'low' art (2003a: 6). Frantz Fanon writes in *The Wretched of the Earth* of an authentic postcolonial culture being consumed by 'the people': why then has postcolonial studies not embraced the cultural 'democracy' of cultural studies?

Essentially, postcolonial studies emanated from English literature departments, and its primary (but far from exclusive) focus has, understandably, been on a textual, literary culture. Bongie traces these developments (via the work of Robert Young) back to Edward Said's reading of Michel Foucault, which concentrated on its textual aspects at the expense of consideration of wider social and cultural practices. Consequently, for Bongie, the two main strands of postcolonial theory replicate the modes of 'resistance' at the heart of literary modernism: the 'difficult' style of Homi Bhabha and Gayatri Spivak can be interpreted as an attempt to resist simplistic approaches to truth and knowledge, while politically engaged intellectuals such as Said, Benita Parry and Aijaz Ahmad use their work to engage in political debates about the relationship of high literature to (post)colonial questions; and neither approach seems to leave much room for analysis of mass-produced, 'lowbrow' culture. Elsewhere, Bongie persuasively writes of the need for postcolonial studies to engage in 'a transformative dialogue with cultural studies' (Bongie 2003b: 18), and the following pages will briefly explore the issues at stake in such a move.

To return to a question that has surfaced at various points in this volume, it is important to ask to what extent African cinema is an expression of popular culture, in whatever sense of that term we wish to choose. Is it a 'lowbrow' form of cultural expression, an inauthentically popular (i.e., commercial or mass-produced) and essentially 'bad' cinema aimed at the lowest common denominator? Is it, on the contrary, an authentic expression of African people's culture(s)? Or might it even be a politically radical, cinema? As has been argued above, Ouédraogo's films contain elements that might lead one to consider them 'popular' in all of these senses: they clearly engage with themes and forms that emerge from Burkinabe society, and they are acted in a syncretic fashion that merges elements of a (Western) naturalistic acting style and more exaggerated (African) performance styles. They contain elements of social (if not political) critique couched within their human stories, and they play to as wide a popular audience as possible in what is at times a rather mawkish and sentimental fashion.[7] Despite the presence of these diverse 'popular' elements, many critical appraisals of Ouédraogo's work have stressed his appeal to Western visions of Africa: his 'apolitical' style and his calls for a commercially viable African film industry have seen his films become the object of ferocious critiques by certain commentators and fellow African directors who have accused him of making films solely for Western audiences.[8] Even at the height of his international fame, critical appraisals of his work were often quite half-hearted and he seems to have inspired none of the critical fervour that has accompanied the work of Souleymane Cissé, alongside whose films Ouédraogo's have often been classified. A potential explanation for this critical scepticism may be found precisely in the 'popular' nature of much of Ouédraogo's work. For he is a director who seems continually to face in several directions at once: he wants to make films that will attract audiences both in Africa and beyond the continent, and he makes films that almost always bear traces of a popular African aesthetic, even when he is making supposedly 'art house' movies. However, is there a space within either African film criticism or indeed postcolonial studies in which one can attempt to value the popularity of African cinema?

In his brief assessment of *Yaaba*, Manthia Diawara argues that the film's message of tolerance – 'Don't judge others, for they have their reasons' – is a 'bourgeois humanist conception of tolerance, which is imported from the big city' (1992: 162). Diawara acknowledges the popularity of Ouédraogo's film in Burkina Faso and with certain critics, 'which forces one to respect him as an artist and to think that his simple style reveals more than is discussed here' (162). However, in his extremely brief discussion of *Yaaba*'s popularity in Burkina, Diawara proceeds only to compare the film (unfavourably) to Kaboré's *Wend Kuuni*, which is deemed a far superior film, as it presents a more complex picture of Burkinabe society. Diawara finds *Tilaï* to be Ouédraogo's best film because 'the director's poetic style is supported here with a complex story' (163); conversely, he is dismissive of the director's 'postmodernism', which allegedly leads Ouédraogo to reject the political engagement of his predecessors.

At the other end of the critical spectrum, Ukadike praises *Yaaba* as a 'deceptively simple parable, filmed in an unadorned, lucid style' (1994: 278). However, Ukadike's appraisal of the film's style contains a number of seemingly paradoxical elements, as he describes the film as both 'elitist' and 'popular'. It is 'elitist' in the sense that the director combines a range of styles – and oral narrative structures, in particular – in a complex fashion and also because it attempts to 'educate' its audience about the failings of tradition and superstition. At the same time, it has a clear desire to 'entertain' the audience:

> The 'new' African cinema interweaves elements of melodrama, satire, and comedy in a manner that attempts to satisfy the spectator's appetite for entertainment. *Yaaba* typifies this trend and its success and international acclaim exemplify the goals of the new crop of African filmmakers. (1994: 272)

In many ways, this is a compelling account of *Yaaba*, and it tallies with many of the arguments about Ouédraogo's cinema that have been expressed throughout this chapter. However, it is necessary to dwell for a moment on what exactly Ukadike means when he speaks of 'the spectator's appetite for entertainment'. Does he mean the Western spectator as is implied by the reference to 'international acclaim'? Or, given his positive comments about the film's engagement with elements of orality, is he implying that *Yaaba* primarily whets the appetite of African spectators? Or, to posit a third option, is it in some sense 'universally' popular?

This ambiguity as to the precise audience being addressed by *Yaaba* opens up a number of extremely important questions. Effectively, both Diawara and Ukadike, in very different ways, seem to prioritise *Yaaba*'s commercial and critical success in the West in attempting to define both its nature as a film and the audience that Ouédraogo is seeking to address. However, do commercial success in Africa and commercial success in the West necessarily mean the same thing? And what space does this leave for *Yaaba* as a popular African or Burkinabe movie?

As was argued in the final section of Chapter 5 on Souleymane Cissé, the expectations of a Western art house movie audience cannot be unproblematically assimilated with those of a 'popular' cinema audience in West Africa. *Yaaba* may have been very successful for an African film (roughly three hundred thousand spectators in France alone) but its success did not extend far beyond the art house market. Of course, the 'popular' and the 'art house' are clearly not watertight categories and there have been several high-profile, recent examples of non-Western films crossing over this divide – e.g., *Crouching Tiger, Hidden Dragon* and *City of God* – and attracting a wide audience beyond the relatively limited art house circuit. However, by and large, non-Western films are seen as art house movies, which creates a certain level of expectation as to their content and in particular to their style. (Kung

Fu and Bollywood movies occupy a rather different space as rare examples of non-Western popular film styles that have entered the Western popular consciousness, even if they have not attracted wide Western audiences.) If, as has been argued above, *Yaaba* contains many elements that belong to a popular Burkinabe aesthetic, why exactly did it win the Critics' Prize at Cannes, which is renowned as a festival that awards innovation, experimentation and 'high' artistic merit? Might it be argued that the award, at some level, was based on a cultural 'misunderstanding', which interpreted the mix of narrative styles and the simple, pared-down structure as a case of formal, high artistic experimentation? To return to the ideas explored in the introduction, is this is a case of the popular in Africa meeting up unexpectedly with the Western avant-garde?

The aim here is not to deny artistic 'credibility' to Ouédraogo: he is clearly a very talented director whose work has deployed range of styles and forms across his entire career, and the Grand Prix awarded to *Tilaï* at Cannes in 1990 was a highly deserved reward for a taut and haunting tragedy, which contains far more 'high' artistic innovation than *Yaaba*. However, the evidence suggests that he is a filmmaker for whom the desire to make accessible, popular films has always taken precedence over pure, artistic experimentation and innovation, and the most commercially and critically popular of his films have been those that have played well with his home audience. In this context, the failure of *Le Cri du coeur*, which has often been attributed to Ouédraogo's 'abandonment' of his Burkinabe context for France, might be better explained by the fact that it attempts to adopt certain aspects of French art house cinema (in particular, the very 'wordy' and 'poeticised' relationship between Mokhtar and the magician), while retaining many elements from the popular family comedies that he had made in Burkina Faso: the standard Ouédraogo trope of dwelling on his fellow pupils breaking into laughter as Mokhtar yawns when reading in class can only have seemed misplaced to those French viewers expecting a naturalistic evocation of African village life; while Burkinabe viewers would have been faced with a French art house aesthetic that would most likely have jarred with the expectations of a popular, West African audience. The recent commercial and critical success of Ang Lee and Fernando Meirelles has shown that non-Western directors can thrive within the Western film industry but this often entails the development of 'adaptive strategies' (e.g., making films that are 'generically comfortable' for Western audiences). Ouédraogo's brush with the international art house mainstream in *Le Cri du coeur* thus acts as something of a cautionary tale, and the lesson that he appears to have learned is that African directors must build up a home audience before attempting to conquer the fickle international market.

Ouédraogo is without doubt the African filmmaker who has pushed furthest the process of reflection upon the nature of African filmmaking and the audience to which it is addressed. Having passed through social realism, documentary, family films, tragedy and international co-productions, he is well placed to comment on the relationship between African cinema and its local audience:

> *Poko* was a period of youth, but also of intelligence because I was thinking that the cinema has a social and educational character. That is why I made *Poko*. But 85 percent of the population, the people who live in villages, do not have theatres for films. They don't have lights and electricity, so our films don't reach them. That means that the films that Africans make, even if they say they are for Africans, they aren't. In each of our countries, 85 percent of the population does not see our films. It is not for them that we make films. They are elitist films, made only for the cities, because only the cities have the means to watch them. I said to myself that films of social and educational purposes are good but in the cities people are used to seeing other films such as American, French and Indian fiction films. The African is also a curious being who can laugh and cry. That too is political. (Ukadike 2002: 153)

Ouédraogo seems set to continue to make 'popular' African films, which may or may not also be popular in the West. As Bongie indicates (in the conclusion to 'Exiles on Main Stream'), the recognition of the need to examine popular work does not entail the abandonment of any sense of distinction between 'high' and 'low' art: it is a case of attempting to understand more precisely the nature of the work under discussion rather than simply dismissing the popular for failing to meet the perceived standards of 'high' culture. The immediate goal for African film criticism, and for postcolonial studies more widely, is to learn how to 'value' the popularity of such work.

Notes

1 At just over 50 minutes long, *Obi* (1991) and *Afrique, mon Afrique* (1994) might better be described by the French term *moyen-métrage*.
2 For a very complete, if rather partisan, account of the development of a national cinema in Burkina Faso see Bachy (1982). A more nuanced account can be found in Diawara (1992: 73–6).
3 In this context, it seems easy to understand the affinity between Ouédraogo and Djibril Diop Mambety, the most renowned nonconformist of the first generation of African cinema, and a director who refused to adopt any specific political line in his work.
4 For a clear-headed assessment of the problems posed by 'national cinemas', including government interference see Diawara (1992: 76–83).
5 Elisabeth Lequeret claims that Ouédraogo is the first African director to place the exploration of individual emotions and desire at the heart of his work (2003: 36–7), although this neglects the work of pioneers such as Mambety and Ecaré, which was also highly concerned with such issues.
6 For example, Diawara claims that 'Ouédraogo has only been able to deal with simple surface stories' and 'there are no villains in *Yaaba*' (1992: 162).
7 In many ways, this portrait of Ouédraogo's style contains echoes of the description of African popular literature, which has been the object of very interesting scholarly work over the past decade (see Newell 2000).

8 A recent example of this is to be found in the comments of fellow Burkinabe director S. Pierre Yameogo, who claims that Ouédraogo has spent so much time
'looking towards the outside world' that he has cut himself off from his 'roots':
see Achour (2005). Curiously, Yameogo includes Sembene – a very different director from Ouédraogo – in his scattergun critique of 'alienated' African directors.

Filmography

Pourquoi (Why) (1981)
Poko (1981)
The Bowls (1983)
The Funeral of the Larle (1983)
Issa le tisserand (Issa the Weaver) (1984)
Ouagadougou, Ouaga deux roues (1984)
Tenga (1986)
Yam Daabo (The Choice) (1986)
Yaaba (1989)
A Karim na Sala (1990)
Tilaï (The Law) (1990)
Obi (1991)
Samba Traoré (1992)
Afrique, mon Afrique (Africa, My Africa) (1994)
Le Cri du coeur (Cry from the Heart) (1995)
Samba and Leuk-the-Hare (1996)
Kini and Adams (1997)
Les Parias du Cinéma (The Pariahs of Cinema) (1997)
*Le Gros et le maigre / La Boutique / Pour une fois (The Fat and the Lean / The Shop
/ For Once)* (1997)
Le Monde à l'endroit (The World Turned Upside Down) (2000)
Le Marché des deux roues à Ouagadougou (The Bicycle Market in Ouagadougou)
(2001)
11/09/01 – September 11 (2002; one of 11 contributions to a portmanteau film)
La Colère des dieux (The Wrath of the Gods) (2003)

Chapter 8

Moufida Tlatli

Introduction

At first glance, Moufida Tlatli's rapidly growing international reputation might seem to align her closely with Djibril Diop Mambety, since the widely acknowledged status of both is based on a very limited cinematic output: in Mambety's case, two feature films and a handful of shorts; in Tlatli's, just two feature films. The closeness is, however, more apparent than substantive; the similarity the result of very different circumstances. At its simplest, the lack of films in Mambety's case is attributable to the lengthy and inadequately explained period of silence and inactivity between his two major works, as well as to the frequently acknowledged problems for African directors to find sufficient funding for their projects; in Tlatli's, it has more to do with another recurrent difficulty – the belated emergence of women as cultural producers in the postcolonial context, something repeatedly borne witness to by women writers from Africa and elsewhere.

An important factor in this belatedness is the relegation of girls' and women's access to education to, at best, second place behind their male counterparts. A pressing problem in many formerly colonised countries, even in otherwise progressive milieux, it finds classic expression in Tsitsi Dangarembga's novel *Nervous Conditions*, where the central character, Tambu, achieves education only through a combination of her own strength of will and the unexpected death of her brother. A different facet of the problem is embodied in Tambu's aunt Maiguru, who, even though she has managed to achieve education to university level and is married to the (apparently) progressive Babamukuru, still has to occupy a quasi-traditional position of secondariness and subservience to men. Some elements of Maiguru's situation, as we shall see shortly, may be relevant to the particular shape of Tlatli's career.

In the case of Tunisia, postcolonial women's writing in French and women's filmmaking emerged at the same (belated) moment in the mid-1970s, some two decades after independence. From a certain traditional gender or cultural perspective, of course, the emergence should not have taken place at all, not even belatedly: 'The idea that a woman should express herself openly is seen not only as a transgression but also as a *fitna*, a threat to the structure of moral values and religious beliefs that underlie traditional society' (Brosseau and Ayari 2005: 281). Significantly, *fitna* is also the sexual power supposedly embodied in women and which threatens to create chaos if not properly controlled – which is one of the arguments put forward for the (necessary) veiling of women. The control of women's sexuality in North African culture is one of the difficult subjects which Tlatli's films address, something made all the more remarkable by the fact that, as Deniz Kandiyoti has suggested, with the exceptions of Fatima Mernissi and Nawal El Saadawi, there has been little discussion of sexuality by women in the Islamic world (Kandiyoti 1994: 14).

If it is difficult enough for a postcolonial woman to become a writer, how much more so to become a filmmaker, not least because of the additional male prejudice that, even if women might qualify for education, how could they cope with the artistic, technical and technological demands of directing a film? The combination of these gendered priorities, restrictive practices and sexist assumptions just outlined has resulted in women being repeatedly underrepresented in the field of African filmmaking. In that respect, Tunisia has, until recently, not been very different from most other postcolonial nations in terms of the slow emergence of women as directors, and Tlatli's own (slow) emergence made her, after Selma Baccar and Nejia Ben Mabrouk, only the third Tunisian woman director in forty years of independence. Even then, her debut came only after a distinguished career as a film editor lasting two decades. Since then, however, the process of emergence has speeded up somewhat, helped no doubt by the impressive international success of Tlatli's films, and there are now half a dozen women filmmakers from Tunisia, including younger ones such as Raja Amari and Nadia El Fani, both of whom released their first feature films in 2002. This leaves Tunisia in the slightly surprising – but also, as we shall see in the next section, understandable – position of having more women directors than the other North African countries.

Tlatli's interest in film is a long-standing one: she was born in 1947 in the village of Sidi Bou Said near Tunis, and her teenage passion for the cinema was noticed, and fostered, by the French schoolteacher who ran the *ciné club* where she encountered the work of Fellini, Bergman, Rossellini and other European directors. Partly as a result of her teacher's encouragement, Tlatli went to Paris in the 1960s and, like many other future filmmakers from North Africa, studied at IDHEC (Institut des Hautes Etudes Cinématographiques), in her case specialising in film editing. She subsequently worked in French television for several years, returning to Tunisia in 1972, since when she has collaborated on many Tunisian films, including ones from the 'Cinema Jedid' (New Cinema) movement: *Fatma 75* (Selma Baccar), *Traversées* (Mahmoud ben Mahmoud, 1984), *Les Baliseurs du désert* (Nacer Khemir, 1986), *La Trace* (Nejia ben Mabrouk, 1988) and *Halfaouine* (Ferid Boughedir, 1990), as well as working with directors from across the Arab world such as Michel Khleifi from Palestine (*La Mémoire fertile*, 1981; *La Cantique des pierres*, 1988), Fatima Benlyazid from Morocco (*Une Porte sur le ciel*, 1987) and

Merzak Allouache (*Omar Gatlato*, 1976) and Farouk Beloufa (*Nahla*, 1979) both from Algeria.

Tlatli's first film *Samt al-Qsur* (*The Silences of the Palace*) was released in 1994. The story of the illegitimate daughter of a servant growing up in a princely palace in Tunis in the final period of the French colonial regime, it won prizes at Cannes, San Francisco, Carthage, and Toronto film festivals, and was even – relatively speaking – a commercial success. It has gone on to be recognised, in the words of a recent major survey of North African film-making, as 'the finest of all Maghreb fictional films by a woman director (and a film of truly world class)' (Armes 2005: 73).

Tlatli's second film, *Mawsim al-Rijal* (*The Season of Men*, 2000) is a study of the lives of women in the Tunisian south whose husbands leave to work in the capital for eleven months a year, returning only for their brief 'season'. Armes feels, however, that it is altogether a less successful film, since it is 'markedly more uneven' and 'the overall tone is unremittingly bleak' (Armes 2005: 78). Leaving aside the possibility that overall (unremitting) uniformity of tone might have resulted in a film which was not 'markedly . . . uneven', the film, like its predecessor, contains moments of female solidarity, warmth and bawdy humour. In particular, the sequence where the women wash the henna from their hair in the sea, and sing, and joke, seems anything but bleak.

Tlatli's most recent project is a reworking of the story of Scheherazade from *The Thousand and One Nights*. Although Tlatli has not infrequently said that she is not a feminist, eschewing above all 'the stupid American variety of feminism, where women become as strong as men, live like men and work like men' (Tlatli 2001), it is hard to see her stated desire to show the Sultan undergoing the same suffering as women (whatever precise shape that takes) as anything other than a profoundly feminist statement. Whether the use of *The Thousand and One Nights* makes it more feminist (tampering with a classic text for political purposes), or less (it does not take place in the real world) is open to debate. What is less debatable is that Tlatli looks set to make another film which, like her first two, will be, at the very least, quietly controversial.

Commenting on her first film, Tlatli said: 'The heroine of my story is a woman, the type that in our countries is sometimes said to be "colonised by the colonised", a woman inferior by birth, a woman born to serve man' (Tlatli 1994: 8). This perspective on women's social subordination has interesting implications not only for her films but also for the shape her career took. As she said in another interview: 'My name in Arabic means "useful". I was therefore quite contented working beside a director. I did not think I would become a director myself' (Tlatli 2000b). Whether that contentment at playing second fiddle is a reflection of Tlatli's character, or of the internalised social expectations of women's appropriate career paths, or even of the fatalities of naming, is not clear. Although she does not subsequently mention any particular moment of personal revolt against this – relatively privileged but nevertheless still subordinate – role as handmaiden to the (important) man in the cinematic relationship, the question of the constraints imposed by female servitude and subordination, by the idea of 'a woman born to serve man', runs throughout the films that Tlatli has gone on to make in her own right, and is a topic to which we will return.[1]

Historical, social and cultural context

The recorded history of Tunisia stretches back over more than two millennia, and the rich sedimentation of its cultures has included Phoenician, Roman, Arab, Byzantine, Spanish and Turkish. The invasion of Tunisia in 1881 by the French, bringing to an end centuries of rule by the Ottoman Empire, was in one sense, therefore, simply the latest of many such incursions. It was also the last major French colonial intervention in North Africa in the nineteenth century, coming a full fifty years after the invasion of neighbouring Algeria. Having spent the following three-quarters of a century as a French protectorate, Tunisia, like Morocco, but unlike Algeria, achieved its freedom in 1956. This came at the end of an independence struggle which, though by no means bloodless, nevertheless paled into insignificance compared to the ferocity of what was happening at the time in Algeria. Although the fighters available to oppose the French were fewer in number than in Algeria, their level of organisation meant that they could be particularly effective in spite of this. That was partly due to the co-ordination made possible by the exceptionally high percentage who belonged both to the UGTT trades union and to the broad-based, and broadly socialist, Neo-Destour (Constitution Party), founded twenty years earlier by Habib Bourguiba, who was himself imprisoned numerous times by the French in the run-up to independence.

As Tunisia's new president, Bourguiba removed the hereditary head of state, the Bey (whose power had in fact been reduced to nominal status by the French colonial regime) and pursued policies which were modernising and frequently centralising, for instance in the radical replacement of structures of local government based on kinship or tribe with ones which were bureaucratised and centrally organised. Bourguiba's policies were also often independent of what was happening in other postcolonial, non-aligned states: for example, having fought the French, he was nevertheless in favour of maintaining substantial links with them, rather than going along with the rejectionism which characterised the approach of other newly liberated countries. Although he grew increasingly autocratic with advancing age, Bourguiba remained a moderniser and more consistently committed to a form of socialism (albeit a decidedly moderate variety) than many of his contemporaries elsewhere in Africa who claimed more radical or revolutionary stances. As a result, Tunisia benefited from a range of social and economic policies which were more progressive than the norm in Africa or the Muslim world as they attempted to negotiate accommodation between Islamic norms and contemporary secular aims. (Sometimes, it must be said, 'accommodation' was not very much in evidence, as for example when Bourguiba proposed do away with the month-long fast of Ramadan, on the grounds of its negative effect on the national economy.)

Among the principal beneficiaries of this postcolonial progress were the women of Tunisia. Under the Code of Personal Status of 1956, some very far-reaching changes were introduced. For instance, polygamy was made a criminal offence, and the traditional male privilege of getting rid of a wife by simply repudiating her was abolished and replaced by divorce as a right for both women and men. In addition, the legal minimum age for marriage was raised to eighteen for women, while the wedding ceremony could now be a civil one, rather than obligatorily religious. Enforced marriages, with power vested by Islam in the decision of the father or guardian, were banned: brides were now required to express voluntary consent for the marriage to be legal. Wearing the veil was discouraged (and subsequently banned in schools, universities and government offices). Women were also allowed to inherit appropriately, instead of being legally 'half-men', forced always to take second place at best. Access to education, to the professions, and – in a very literal way – to social mobility (being able to drive a car) now became a possibility. Most importantly, perhaps, women were given the vote.

At one level, these changes to the juridical and social condition of women created a context in which positive developments – such as the one which most concerns us here, the emergence of women filmmakers like Tlatli – became less of a surprise. At the same time, and in a way which is also unsurprising, these changes clashed head-on with deeply embedded and tenaciously maintained attitudes towards women, social liberalisation and equality, held by both men and women across the country. It is this kind of focus of postcolonial tension which Moufida Tlatli's films, particularly her most recent, explore in detail.

Filmmaking in Tunisia also benefited to a certain extent from the policies of the Bourguiba government, which aimed to control the import of foreign films, and, more usefully, to help in the production of Tunisian-based films. To that end, a state film production company (SATPEC) was set up, and a studio complex was established at Gammarth. Unfortunately, like many other postcolonial projects, neither of these was able fully to realise its potential, with the studio running at an almost permanent deficit, and SATPEC losing ground to independent producers and international co-productions from the 1980s onwards.

Filmmaking in Tunisia had, however, begun earlier, during the period of French rule: in 1922, Albert Samama, generally known as Chikly, made the short film *Zohra*, starring his daughter, and two years later went on to make the only North African feature film from the silent era, *The Girl from Carthage*. (Chikly had also been responsible for the first screenings of the Lumière brothers' classics such as *Arrival of a Train in La Ciotat* in Tunis in 1897.) After his pioneering efforts, however, little happened by way of Tunisian filmmaking (as opposed to French-directed films made in Tunisia) until after independence. In the post-independence period, Tunisia has produced films at a rate which might be characterised as slow-but-steady: better than the majority of sub-Saharan countries, but slower than Algeria, and even Morocco, among the North African nations, and certainly very far behind Egypt in terms of output. This is paralleled by the emergence of Tunisian filmmakers: although the country boasts internationally recognised and prize-winning directors such as Nouri Bouzid and Ferid Boughedir (and Moufida Tlatli), the rate of emergence is undeniably slow.

In addition, there have been the problems concerning the direction an independent and distinctively Tunisian cinema might take. 'When the Arab countries won their independence, their first instinct was to build a cinema that would be the exact opposite of the existing Egyptian industry, which they saw as escapist and stultifying' (Tlatli 1995: 19). The preoccupations of this 'Cinema Jedid' (New Cinema) – in many ways those of contemporary European *auteur* and art house films, and similarly open to criticisms of elitism, intellectualism and the like – proved to have only a limited attraction for Tunisian audiences accustomed to the mass-market appeal of Hollywood, Egypt and India. As a result, more recent filmmaking has produced generically hybrid works with wider appeal: 'I think our cinema went through a period of self-criticism, as a result of which something positive emerged. We are coming back to the melodrama, but in a much more nuanced manner. Nowadays our cinema is trying to reach a popular audience, and is branching out into love stories and comedies' (Tlatli 1995: 18). Part of this nuanced return to the melodrama is Tlatli herself, melodrama having constituted her earliest cinema viewing and now forming part of the range of styles on which she draws in different ways in her own work. Indeed, one could argue that there is rather more nuance than melodrama in Tlatli's films. While *The Silences of the Palace* has its moments of possible melodramatic excess, both involving Khedija (being raped and bleeding to death), these are far outweighed by the 'culture of the indirect', stemming from Arab poetry, which Tlalti identifies in her filmmaking, and which includes, for example, silences, looks and gestures, all of which require interpretation by the spectator. In her first film in particular, to the extent that the palace constitutes a realm of silence, the looks and gestures become all the more important as forms of expression or modes of communication.

Another theme which has a general relevance for Tunisian filmmaking, as well as being of obvious importance to Tlatli personally, is the question of women, and especially women's liberation, which represents 'a litmus test for Arab society' (Tlatli 1995: 18). However, despite her view that women's liberation has constituted the special theme of postcolonial Tunisian filmmaking, it remains the case that no one has approached it with quite the degree of courage or insight demonstrated by Tlatli herself.

Also, addressing the question of women's liberation has not necessarily been straightforward, particularly perhaps where women's own self-expression is concerned. Thus, the first film made by a Tunisian woman director, Selma

Baccar's *Fatma 75*, was originally commissioned, and then banned, by the Tunisian government. It was commissioned for the United Nations Women's Year, but banned because it contained scenes of sex education in school which were considered unacceptable. (Another version has it that the banning took place on the orders of Bouguiba himself, apparently because the film showed women's liberation as a process of self-emancipation, rather than something graciously bestowed on them by a far-sighted President Bourguiba.) Tunisia's second female-directed film, *La Trace* by Nejia ben Mabrouk, suffered in a similar, but ultimately less extreme, fashion: following problems with SATPEC, the state-run body overseeing film production, the release of the film was blocked, though it did eventually appear six years later.

Responding to an interviewer's question, 'What do you advocate: revolt or resistance?', Tlatli replied: 'To my mind, both are right; both are neces-sary! The film explores different paths without advocating any one' (Tlatli 2000a). Although it is not clear precisely what the interviewer means by the two terms, the fact that they are offered as potential opposites suggests that revolt may be construed as the more active alternative to passive resistance; what is clear, however, is that both are oppositional, and both have liber-atory aspirations, even if these are focused on the bodily and the domestic, and, in Tlatli's words, require to be achieved 'little by little'. In this, however, Tlalti's films, her female characters and their modes of resistance may be entirely of their time:

> While early Third-Worldist films documented alternative histories through archival footage, interviews, testimonials, and historical reconstructions, gen-erally limiting their attention to the public sphere, the films of the 1980s and 1990s use the camera less as revolutionary weapon than as monitor of the gen-dered and sexualised realms of the personal and the domestic, seen as integral but repressed aspects of collective history. They display a certain scepticism toward metanarratives of liberation, but do not necessarily abandon the notion that emancipation is worth fighting for. (Shohat 2003: 74)

Timely or not, the films face a battle with audiences at home in Tunisia, and in the wider Islamic world as a result of their representations of women in general and female sexuality in particular. As Tlatli commented, 'The slightest thing in the film will seem very risqué in Tunisia. When the woman gently says: "please caress me", it's a revolution in Djerba! The Djerban men are going to be mad at me! They will say: "our wives never say that to us!" But I know inside that it is like that' (Tlatli 2000a). The extent to which the films can constitute a threat to Arab male intellectuals as well as to the ordin-ary men of Djerba is indicated by Amy Taubin in *The Village Voice*: 'at a recent conference on Middle Eastern and North African film . . . a male Arab film scholar chastised me for reading *The Season of Men* as anything other than one neurotic woman's personal fiction. He told me that it's fine to enjoy the film, but not to extrapolate from it anything to do with the condition of women in Arab society' (Taubin 2001).

As Edward Said pointed out time and again, a central aspect of the politics of representation is the sets of preconceptions that structure and filter the interpretation of any given text. In relation to Tunisian filmmaking in general, Ahmed Attia notes how Eurocentric attitudes prevalent in French funding bodies mean that films which do not fit preconceived notions of what African or Tunisian films should be are quite likely not to receive any funding (Attia 2002). Different preconceptions, but similarly grounded in notions of truthful representation, can profoundly structure – and divide – audience reactions: 'I've had to defend *The Season of Men* a lot to the Tunisian community in France. Most of them just want to see a movie about Tunisia, and when they discover it's not what they expect, they claim what I'm showing isn't true. But I've also screened the film for hundreds of Muslim women in France and I was very moved when they said it wasn't just about Djerba but about their own situation' (Tlatli 2001: 24).

As Tlatli has remarked on many occasions, the battle to change attitudes is the one she continues to fight by means of her films, and in that sort of contest, as Said argued, it is not the 'truth' of representations which is important, but their power. To that extent at least, Tlalti's chances in the battle seem quite promising.

The films

Both *The Silences of the Palace* and *The Season of Men* are narratives of return and remembering. In the former, set in postcolonial Tunisia in the 1960s, Alia, now in her mid-twenties, returns to the palace where she grew up as the daughter of one of the women servants. Her memories retrace key moments from her life in the palace during her girlhood, culminating in the national liberation struggle, her mother's death from an abortion and her own simultaneous escape from the palace. In the second film, set in the present day, Aicha, her marriage crumbling and her young daughters' lives in turmoil, returns from Tunis to her husband's family home on the island of Djerba, where she spent the unhappy early years of her marriage. Her process of recollection details the difficulties and the costs involved in struggling to retain a degree of autonomy within the oppressive domestic regime.

Tlatli's films are clearly both, above all, women-centred texts – though this does not mean that they neglect the condition of men, or their impact on the predominantly female worlds which the films portray. They are studies of women's spaces, as well as of women's bodies in those spaces. Although the principal spaces are in many ways very different in period and location – a royal palace in Tunis in the dying days of French colonial rule; and a family home on the island of Djerba, in the relatively underdeveloped south of the country, in the 1970s and 1990s – there are, nevertheless, significant parallels both in the spaces themselves and in the women's lives they contain.

The palace in *The Silences of the Palace* belongs to one of the branches of the family of the Bey of Tunis, hereditary ruler of the country under the Ottoman empire and retained as useful figurehead by the French. As an Islamic palace, it also occupies a particular position in the Orientalist imaginary as the location of the harem, the focus of centuries of lurid, if not racist and sexist, speculation by Europeans about Islamic culture. Indeed, in an early nineteenth-century epistolary novel, whose title, *The Lustful Turk*, is better known than its contents, one of the principal sites for the erotic action is the harem of the palace of the Bey of Tunis. (And the recycling of the image continues: in a book published in the same year as *The Silences of the Palace* was released, the author argues: 'The Turkish harem was not the figment of some overheated Victorian pornographer's imagination. It really existed for almost five hundred years, from 1453 forward. The basic setup: one Ottoman sultan with three hundred or more beautiful half-naked virgins at his beck and call' (Schick 1999: 86). No overheated imagination there, then . . .) It is precisely this endlessly repeated image of the harem as locus of sensuality – if not worse – which Tlatli's film comprehensively demystifies, constructing as it does something like an anti-harem, where women's bodies labour and suffer rather than lazing indolently, smoking *nargileh* pipes; where they are not necessarily good-looking, and certainly not half-naked, but where they are nevertheless prey to the abusive, coercive sexual power of men. In the 1950s Tunisia of *The Silences of the Palace*, even if the princes are apparently 'normal' or modern in only having one wife – and no sign whatsoever of the hundreds of virgins – they still expect to exercise their *droit de seigneur* in having sex with any of the female servants who take their fancy, even if it means raping them. Being more attractive than the average, as is the case with Khedija, mother of the central character Alia, means taking the fancy of more than one of the princes, and suffering accordingly.

Just as in the classic version of the harem, though without the ubiquitous eunuchs on guard, this is a constricting and confining space for women, all the more so for the nature of the lives they lead within its walls. None of them ever leaves the palace, but even inside it they are subject to further restriction, a confinement within confinement, since the palace gardens are usually forbidden territory for them, and the kitchen where they work and the rooms where they sleep constitute the spatial limits of their world.

Since none of the women leaves the palace, the very little they learn of the outside world comes either via Houssein, the son of Khalti Hadda, doyenne of the servants, or via the radio. Through these two media they – and we the audience – discover that the anticolonial struggle is in full swing. The news of the fight for national liberation prompts an unprecedented outburst from one of the women in a parallel fantasy of self-liberation: 'I don't belong to myself. I want to go out into the streets, to run unhindered, naked and barefoot, and scream and shout out loud. Only their bullets can silence me as they run through me, turning my body into a sieve.' The range of freedoms or transgressions here: to get out of the palace, to move freely, to be naked, not to be silent any longer, to resist the state, constitute such a powerful combination in their bodily overturning of the order of things that it would indeed require the force of a bullet to stop their momentum.

The fact that we see this servant do no more than shout her defiance and desire is none the less already something akin to an emergence, in Gayatri Spivak's terms, from a condition of subalternity. Spivak's much-debated conclusion to her article 'Can the Subaltern Speak?' was that the gendered subaltern subject could not, at least in so far as 'speaking' implied escaping from the overarching discourses of colonial or indigenous patriarchal males, and the relevance of the silencing of the subaltern female to this film hardly needs to be stated. One kind of 'speaking', one mode of escape, might then be an insurgent discourse like that of the unnamed servant, and in an interview Spivak subsequently offered a more optimistic assessment: 'If the subaltern can speak, then, thank God, the subaltern is not a subaltern any more' (Spivak 1990: 158). However, even the act of insurgency is not in itself a guarantee as far as Spivak is concerned: 'So, to repeat what I have said before, subaltern insurgency . . . *is* an effort to involve oneself in representation, *not* according to the lines laid down by the official institutional structures of representation. Most often it does not "catch". That is the moment that I am calling "not speaking"' (Spivak 1996: 306). Beyond this, one mode of 'the undoing of subaltern space' is 'the subaltern's insertion into citizenship, whatever that might mean' (Spivak 1996: 307). While this is not (yet) available to the servant and those like her, it is, of course, the aim of that other ongoing insurgent dream, the national liberation struggle.

The dreams of colonised servant and nation are combined in the central character Alia.[2] She too dreams of escaping from the palace: after the rape of her mother by Si Bechir, she imagines herself running, screaming, towards one of the gates, which closes in her face. The fact that her scream is soundless emphasises another of the brutal silencings which the palace enforces on the bodies of its oppressed women. It is all the more significant, then, that Alia's un-silencing of herself by singing the forbidden nationalist song 'Green Tunisia' should take place within the space of the bitter enemies of that song, the princes, in the palace's upper rooms. Along with the struggling nation, Alia does break free into the space of independence and non-subaltern citizenship; that this does not offer her the full liberation she hoped for is, for Tlatli, one of the fundamental contradictions of her postcolonial country.

Part of the importance of Alia's action is that the palace is a space of silence, or more precisely of a range of enforced silences. As Khalti Hadda says to Alia towards the end of the film, 'They taught us one rule in the palace: silence.' The first area of silence concerns Alia herself: the silence surrounding the identity of her father. The second concerns all the women servants: the silence preventing any complaint or verbalised resistance to the forms of oppression and exploitation they suffer. The third silence concerns the outside world, the daily life of the city and the nation, from which they are (almost) entirely cut off. However, while her singing might be seen as an intervention from the space of the second silence which simultaneously invokes the world silenced by the third, it still does nothing to bring her closer to ending the one silence she most wants to break, the first.

The space of the palace is also clearly hierarchised, especially in terms of class, and the upper realm of the masters presents a strong visual contrast in its decorative opulence with the bare walls of the lower depths where the servants work. The spatial separation is also strongly marked in visual terms by the steep, narrow staircase which leads from one to the other, and which the masters almost never 'lower' themselves to descend. The servants' area thus represents in Kristevan terms an 'abject' space: 'that which is rejected from which one does not part' – in other words, although the princes may despise and largely ignore the space, its inhabitants and what they do, their way of life could not survive without them.[3]

Moving from a richly decorated space (reminiscent of the upper levels of the palace) to a simpler, barer one (with echoes of the servants' quarters) and also thereby from the present to the past, is what Aicha, the main character in *The Season of Men*, does, as she leaves the expensive family home in Tunis to return to Djerba and the large old house where she spent the early years of her marriage. This, while not straightforwardly a subaltern space, was certainly a space of constraint and confinement for Aicha, and as such has strong affinities with the palace. In the absence of her husband Said, and the other men who go to work for eleven months of the year in Tunis, returning only for their one-month 'season', the house is run by Said's mother Ommi, whose matriarchal regime, if it lacks the official patriarchal power of the princes', makes up for it in bitterness and ferocity. Part of what Aicha does, therefore, through her return to the old house in the diegetic present of the film is to come to terms with that past and to reclaim this space of domestic and familial oppression. Significantly, there is a space of possible escape or respite within the overall confinement, and that is the room where Aicha weaves her carpets for Said to sell in Tunis. That this is lit more softly and coloured more warmly by Tlatli marks it as the space of potential healing for Aicha, and, most importantly, after the return it fulfils that function for her autistic son Aziz.

The parallels just outlined in terms of spatial configurations and bodily confinement are typical of the careful structuring of Tlatli's films, in a manner which, following the analogy of the carpet weaving, one could see as a patterning. The different modes of patterning include the formal, visual, aural, temporal and moral aspects of the films.

Formal patterning here involves, for instance, elements such as repetition (with a difference) in the narrative, parallels such as those just indicated, and circularity. The latter might typically involve returning to where you started, but now being in a better place or condition as a result of the experiences en route. Both of the central characters, Alia in *The Silences of the Palace* and Aicha in *The Season of Men*, end up back where they started, though differently – Aicha back where she began her difficult married life; Alia back where she was before the visit to the palace – but each has now reached some understanding and, through that, actual or potential healing, as a consequence of the revisiting and coming to terms with the past.

Relevant elements of visual patterning include the speed and length of sequences, and repetition of shots. Tlatli has commented on the way in which, in *The Season of Men* for instance, she has used her experience of editing to create different rhythms which embody at the same time different individuals and different generations. In contrast to the extreme slowness of the lives of the women of Djerba, which she says is 'no longer tolerated in the context of world cinema' (but which she nevertheless portrays at length), 'I followed Emna's [Aicha's younger daughter] rhythm . . . she rebels, goes fast, dances, breaks things off very fast, speaks on the phone, against her mother's will, grabs her things, and rushes off' (Tlatli 2000a). Repetition which complements the formal patterning can be seen, for example, in the opening and closing sequences of *The Silences of the Palace*, which begins with a close-up of the adult Alia's face, looking at the audience as she prepares to sing, and closes with a freeze-frame of her face as she contemplates an uncertain and difficult future. Among the repetitions in *The Season of Men* are the semi-close-ups and medium shots of Aicha's loom, and those shots looking through the threads of the loom towards Aicha, Zeineb or Aziz are particularly visually striking.

The aural patterning in Tlatli's work is examined in a recent article by Florence Martin (Martin 2004) which discusses the films as movements in a carefully organised 'cinematic suite' of silences and screams, structured in ways analogous to music. Music, as Tlatli has commented, is part of everyday reality in *The Silences of the Palace* and also has a symbolic dimension. Different types of music relate to the different spaces of the palace: communal and popular for the women below stairs, formal and classical for Sidi Ali's lute playing above stairs, and the indeterminacy of Alia's position is indicated by the way she moves between the two. A different type of symbolism can be seen in the song Alia sings at the beginning of the film – 'Amal hayati' (Hope of my heart) by the greatest of Arab women singers, Oum Khaltoum – this being, in many ways, a film about hope – deferred, disappointed and reborn.

One of the important aspects in the temporal patterning of Tlatli's films is generational continuity. This appears, for example, in the usually positively construed process of handing on tradition, seen as essential for the survival of culture. Equally, however, it can take the altogether less useful form of perpetuating taboos and constraints, not least in relation to women and their bodies. A key contradiction here for Tlatli is that it is the victims who are principally responsible for perpetuating from one generation to the next the system which victimises them. Thus, for example, it is Khalti Hadda in *The Silences of the Palace* who, as the head servant, oversees the continuation of the regime of silencing which so oppresses the women, while in *The Season of Men* it is Ommi, as mother of the male head of the household, who holds power while the men are away, and who subjects the other women to a tyrannical and arbitrary rule. As Tlatli commented, 'What I wanted to convey is that the women are very much responsible for this heritage in spite of themselves. They hand it on from daughter to daughter and if they don't decide to stop it one day, it will never end' (Tlatli 2000a). A significant phrase here is 'in spite of themselves': the image of succeeding generations of women caught up in an institution, a set of practices and an ideology to whose reproduction they contribute almost willy-nilly, is a perfect example of the efficient functioning of an Ideological State Apparatus as theorised by Althusser, to which we return in the main section of this chapter.[4]

Another aspect of the temporal patterning is the interaction and alternation of the present and the past which both films share, and which is one of the most important of their organisational principles. *The Silences of the Palace* begins in the diegetic present with death (the death of Sidi Ali, which means for Alia the final death of childhood, and the disappearance of any possibility of discovering who her father was), and ends with the affirmation of life in the face of possible death; meanwhile, the past narrative has moved towards its double climax of life and death (death for Khedija; entry into a new life for Alia), though in fact this moment is perhaps more properly seen as a double stillbirth, even if the audience are not yet aware of that.

In the area of the moral patterning (if that is quite the term) of the films, we encounter in particular a process of desire and (non-) fulfilment, along the lines of 'You get what you ask for, but it isn't necessarily what you want'. In *The Silences of the Palace*, for example, Alia leaves the palace for a new life of freedom with Lotfi, but this produces very little of what she had imagined. As she says, 'I thought that Lotfi would save me. I have not been saved.' In *The Season of Men*, year after year Aicha longs to escape from Djerba and go to Tunis with Said; eventually, she achieves this, but once again the reality does not match her imagination and desire. Said's condition for allowing Aicha to move to Tunis is that she should provide him with a son, their first two children having been daughters, and Said eventually gets his son, but Aziz turns out to be autistic, and thus totally unfitted for the designated role of firstborn son and heir. The women of Djerba long for the return of their men from Tunis, and prepare for it in an atmosphere of mounting excitement, mutual grooming and bawdy jokes. For none of them, however, does the return provide the desired fulfilment and satisfaction.

Importantly, however, there is occasionally a process of reversal here, too: something like a negation of the negation, as something positive is able to emerge from the negative. Thus, in *The Season of Men* Aziz, whose autism is the reason for his mother's return to the potentially difficult space of the Djerba house, is, if not necessarily healed (though that is what his mother hopes for), at least calmed and improved by his absorption in weaving, which is of course traditionally women's work. In *The Silences of the Palace*, Alia is healed or enabled to face the difficulties of the future through her acceptance of her pregnancy and her determination not to have an abortion. These bodily resolutions to problems which may or may not also be problems of the body is typical of Tlatli, and is something on which we will now focus more closely.

'The problems of the body and liberty of the body'

The apparent absence of any moment of conscious or intellectual revolt on Tlatli's part against her secondary position as editor rather than director, which was mentioned in the introductory section, becomes clearer in the light of a comment she made in an interview: 'I stopped being an editor the day I felt the visceral need to make my films. I've never wanted to go looking for a film, I wanted it to come to me, and that there should be some kind of urgency' (Tlatli, in Levieux 2000). The crucial, not to be gainsaid, impact of 'the visceral need', the predominance of the corporeal agenda rather than the cerebral one, makes perfect sense in the light of the films which this need subsequently produced: ones in which bodies – women's bodies above all – are the focus. As well as the originary motivation being physical, the very act of filming has its bodily, even sensual, aspect for Tlatli:

> The film is inherent in me, it's my way of feeling things . . . With the camera, we united our heartbeats and we approached things in the same way, with the same slowness as the women . . . I sense the camera in a very carnal way. For me, it is really the rhythm of these women . . . These women take time too, because they put all their sensuality into it. (Tlatli 2000a)

This is categorically not to suggest, however, that, as a woman director addressing issues pertinent to women's bodies, Tlatli is somehow operating at a less intellectual level, in the way that the classic sexist stereotype – woman = body/emotion; man = mind/rationality – would have it. For Tlatli, far from expressing some essentialist truth about the natural concerns of the sexes, her focus on bodies is an approach to some of the pressing social issues with which postcolonial Tunisia has not yet adequately come to terms: 'As a society we have not moved on in this area . . . the problems of the body and liberty of the body' (Tlatli 2001).

There is also an important quality of immediacy in the way in which the real-life 'problems of the body' – of Tlatli's daughters, her mother, and even of Tlatli herself – influence the films. Thus, for example, although there is clearly no one-to-one relationship of representation involved, *The Silences of the Palace* is in one sense born from the physical withdrawal, particularly into silence, of Tlatli's mother. In a similar-but-different way, issues around her daughters' safety, particularly in the context of sexuality, was a powerful motivation in the making of *The Season of Men*. Finally, and very courageously, Tlatli has talked about her own problems in a way which, without either film being named, seem to relate particularly to *The Season of Men*: 'After I married I had so many difficulties with sex: I was in love with my husband, but I was ashamed. Slowly I changed, but it took years' (Tlatli, in Said 2001). While this highlighting of (bodily) immediacy might seem to have problematic overtones of the way in which second-wave feminism argued for women's closer, more intimate relation to lived experience (as opposed to the distancing produced by male analysis of that experience), its personally grounded approach does not mean that it necessarily falls into the essentialising which bedevilled the earlier feminist position.

> A discourse which is 'purely' feminist or 'purely' nationalist, we have tried to argue, cannot apprehend the layered, dissonant identities of diasporic or post-independence feminist subjects. The diasporic and post-Third-Worldist films of the 1980s and 1990s, in this sense, do not so much reject the 'nation' as interrogate its repressions and limits, passing nationalist discourse through the grids of class, gender, sexuality and diasporic identities. While often embedded in the autobiographical, they are not always narrated in the first person, nor are they 'merely' personal. (Shohat 2003: 74)

Against the possible over-generalising of the body to which a number of theories are prone, Spivak argues:

> The body, like all other things, cannot be thought as such. I take the extreme ecological view that the body as such has no possible outline. As body it is a repetition of nature. It is in the rupture with Nature when it is a signifier of immediacy for the staging of the self. As a text, the inside of the body (imbricated with the outside) is mysterious and unreadable except by way of thinking of the systematicity of the body, value coding of the body. It is through the *significance* of my body and others' bodies that cultures become gendered, economicopolitic, selved, substantive. (Spivak 1993: 20)

Any possibility of a generalised, abstract 'body as such' disappears in Tlatli's films in the face of the multitude of ways in which bodies are lived, constituted and ascribed meaning and value. Thus, to take only a few examples, we see bodies hierarchised by class, gender and generation; bodies neglected (by their owners or by others) and abjected; bodies exploited either economically or, above all, sexually; bodies circumscribed and constrained; labouring bodies; performative and performing bodies; bodies present and absent; bodies silent, speaking, singing and screaming; desiring bodies; suffering bodies; bodies striving for liberation.

In the context of Tlatli's films, one of the most important spheres in which to observe the operations of these processes of the constituting and controlling of bodies is 'the machine for the socialisation of the female body through affective coding' (Spivak 1993: 82) – the family. The family is also one of the central examples, in Althusser's terms, of the Ideological State Apparatuses (ISAs), whose role is to secure the reproduction of society – here, at the bodily level (through the creation of children) as well as at the level of the economic relations of production. As their name suggests, the ISAs function principally via the medium of ideology, but the latter, far from being anything immaterial, is embodied in the materiality of institutions, and the repetition of their practices as modes of behaviour. The ISAs create subject positions, which individuals are invited or called ('interpellated', in

Althusser's terms) to occupy. In the case of the family these include, for example, loving parent, obedient child, dutiful wife, all-providing husband, etc. Answering the call is expected – if not enforced – and sets in motion a three-stage process, whereby the subject, as notionally autonomous individual, accepts their subjection to the greater Subject (the family, the state, God); this in turn generates recognition by the Subject that they are indeed a good parent, a responsible citizen, etc., and finally the guarantee that, as long as they continue to be this, then everything will be all right. Conversely, any failure to answer the call or to occupy the appropriate position(s) marks the individual out as a 'bad subject', liable to censure, rejection, social ostracism or even the full punishment of the law.

Both films detail the extensive efforts which go into the production of good subjects in the context of the family and quasi-familial situations. 'Good' here means, among other things, appropriately gendered and embodied, and, in Althusser's phrase, 'working all by themselves' – in other words, producing the correct forms of behaviour while giving the appearance of autonomy. *The Season of Men* also traces the emergence, or the construction, of Aicha as bad subject: wilful, disobedient and disrespectful daughter-in-law, bad mother, a wife who brings dishonour on her husband and the rest of the family – or so she is told.

Discussing the generational transmission of patterns of subjection within the family in an interview, Tlatli expressed the idea that the matriarch Ommi behaves as she does 'against her will'. This is apparently very strange: firstly because Ommi gives no visible sign of reluctance; and secondly because of the 'obvious' response: Why should she behave so badly if she doesn't want to? In fact, to the extent that Tlatli is correct, Ommi offers a classic illustration of the subjection of the subject to the ISA: working for the greater good, ensuring, to the best of her ability, that others conform to the ideological requirements of the family system, even if this means behaving cruelly, obliges her to repress that part of herself whose potential gentleness, or female solidarity, would obstruct the efficient reproduction of the apparatus. In doing so, she is confirmed as a 'good' mother or mother-in-law in the terms of the ISA. Interestingly, when Aicha goes to see her mother to complain about the manner in which Ommi treats her, her mother explains that Ommi suffered in a similar way with her own mother-in-law, and says to Aicha, 'But one day you will be a respected and feared mother-in-law, like Ommi.' The assumption of the unproblematic naturalness of the reproduction of the role and its embodied behaviours, regardless of questions of individual will or choice, is striking. Aicha, however, refuses to be interpellated by the proffered position, confirming yet again that, in the context of the ideology of the family structure, she is very much a bad subject. The fact that she has her own preferred ways of being a good mother, however, does nothing whatsoever to redeem her in the eyes of the guardians of the ideology.

The problem here for Tlatli is the gap between formal progress at the juridical level in terms of women's emancipation and any changes in the embodied ideologies of family and femininity. She does, however, believe that the gap can be closed: 'Time will sort things out because it is not about laws, it is about changing mentalities. Things will not change in men's or women's minds with a wave of a magic wand and laws. I show the combat from within. I know that women are emancipated. They are beginning to ask themselves questions, but it isn't so for everyone' (Tlatli 2000a).

If the problem for Aicha is that the family and its coercive norms are all too present, the problem for Alia is precisely the absence of anything in her life which resembles a normal family. When Khalti Hadda says that Sidi Ali felt that Alia had renounced the family by leaving the palace, Alia's reply – not for the first time – is, 'Family? What family?' In the world of the palace, 'the family' refers only to the princely Beys, since, in a manner which recalls slaves in the Caribbean sugar plantations, no one else is allowed ordinary family relations – with the exception of giving birth to illegitimate children fathered by the Beys. In the face of Alia's search for her impossible family, Khedija says, 'Don't feel lost any more. I am your father and your mother' – which in a sense she is forced to be, since she refuses to tell Alia who her father is. Khedija, Khalti Hadda and the others may indeed provide a nurturing and protective environment for Alia, but the strain it imposes only accentuates the absence of the family for which it is a substitute.

Even if Khedija is unable to provide a family for her daughter, however, she nevertheless works hard to instil in her a series of regulatory maxims governing her sexuality. An entire conversation consists of: 'You are grown up. Be careful. Don't let anyone come near you. If a man touches you, run away. If anything happens to you, you're lost. No one can save you afterwards.' 'Not even Sidi Ali?', asks Alia, in a touching display of faith in the redemptive power of a (possible) father. In *Woman's Body, Woman's Word*, Fedwa Malti-Douglas argues that, unlike the Christian worldview, the Islamic one does not involve any obsession with virginity. While this non-obsessive attitude towards virginity may be true at some hypothetical level, it scarcely matches the lived experience of women in Tlatli's films, or indeed that of Tlatli herself. Apart from Khedija's increasing, and increasingly well founded, fears regarding Alia and sex, *The Silences of the Palace* offers one of the oldest traditions regarding virginity: the display of the bloodstained sheets from the wedding night, confirming the bride's virgin status. The fact that this bloody display coincides with the onset of her own first menstruation is one of the many things that renders sexuality problematic for Alia. In *The Season of Men*, when the young Meriem is the victim of a (failed) sexual attack, instead of receiving any sympathy or comfort, she is subjected to a further sexual assault as her grandmother proceeds, brutally and without explanation, to examine her to see whether she is still a virgin or not. Ironically, as a result of this, the adult Meriem, now a married woman, remains a virgin. Even Tlatli, faced with the prospect of one of her daughters going to France to study, found herself reduced to repeating Khedija's warning 'Be careful!' when the subject of sex before marriage was raised.

For Tlatli, sexuality is 'the very basis for being a balanced person. To emancipate women without liberating them sexually was, for me, only doing half the job. That is why I had the courage, and the audacity . . . to speak certain truths about Tunisian society' (Tlatli, in Levieux 2000). The formal freedoms of the Bourguiba era were insufficient in that regard, and work – including the making of films which address these issues – remains to be done to bring about the changes in attitude which will allow a fuller form of liberation.

Of all the many forms of female embodiment in the films, one of the more persistent, and more unfortunate, is that of the suffering body. This is so much the case that Tlatli's preferred – if ultimately unusable – title for *The Season of Men* was *My Whole Body Hurts*, and the phrase recurs throughout the film, uttered by different characters in differing circumstances, but pointing to a shared condition of pain. Perhaps unsurprisingly, men and sexuality are the cause of much of this pain, through either their absence or their presence (either undesired or inappropriately desired). Thus we see Fatima take to her bed, declaring that her whole body hurts, because her husband will not be returning with the other men (and, following the experience of Zeineb, there is always the fear that a temporary absence will prove permanent). Zeineb, too, experiences physical absence as pain, and in her case this is heightened by the impossibility, as an abandoned wife, of doing anything to relieve the situation. The scene where, having also taken to her bed declaring that her whole body hurts, she is examined by a male doctor is uncomfortable to watch, as Zeineb transforms her pain into near-orgasmic sensations as the doctor's hands search her abdomen for signs of disease. For the young Meriem, on the other hand, it is the undesired presence of a man which is the problem, a problem compounded when, as mentioned, the sexual attack is followed by the brutal verification of her virginity by her grandmother, and it is this combination of assaults which produces the pain she feels.

A related but different form of the bodily expression of suffering in other areas of life can be seen in the adult Meriem and the adult Alia. Both suffer from debilitating headaches, which seem to have their origin in the sexual problems each has: Meriem's childhood sexual trauma leaves her unable to consummate her marriage; Alia, fertile like her mother, repeatedly falls pregnant, and is pressured into having an abortion by her partner. 'Each abortion is painful. I am losing a part of me', she declares. Both of these situations ultimately derive from male sexuality and its accompanying attitudes, rather than from any inherent problems in the female body: on the one hand, male sexuality in its predatory mode; on the other, the regulatory patriarchal norms for sexuality, which will not allow Lotfi to marry Alia because she has no family and no name, thereby condemning her either to raise illegitimate children or to have abortions. In both cases, however, the final scenes of the film witness a possible end to this particular suffering, as Meriem and her husband are at last able to make love, while Alia decides to refuse to have the abortion and keep her child.

Along with the problems of the body, the other area mentioned by Tlatli in the heading to this final section as one with which postcolonial Tunisia has yet to deal adequately was the liberty of the body. Certainly, in the lives of the women in her films, bodily freedom – especially, but not only, sexual freedom – is conspicuous by its absence. For Alia, the gradual development of her body and her bodily consciousness is also a consciousness of limitation. This ranges from spatial limitation to the limitation of possibilities. Although she enjoys slightly more freedom than the women servants – freedom, for example, to move around the garden – that is limited both in duration (confined to snatched moments), and in extent (the palace gates are closed in her face by one of the male servants in case she should go out). The limitation is emphasised by the fact that when she sees Sidi Ali going into her mother's room, obviously to have sex with her, and she wants to run away, she is reduced to running round in circles until she collapses.

For most of the women in both films, such bodily freedom as there is consists of what they can carve out for themselves in the face of variously restrictive regimes. In particular, and in another echo of African slaves on the plantations, song and music constitute the special, and almost only, spaces of their freedom. Usually, these are joyous communal moments, sometimes celebrating a welcome event such as a birth, but just as likely to be a spontaneous expression of collective high spirits. Sometimes, however, as with Zeineb in *The Season of Men*, song can provide the space in which to express freely an otherwise inarticulable personal sadness.

Against this background, Alia's singing at Sarra's engagement party both expresses and aims for a very different kind of freedom. Although artistic or creative activity – singing, playing the lute, weaving carpets – can be a form of cultural transmission or the continuity of tradition, it can also provide the opportunity for something like individualist self-assertion, resistance to tradition and a claim for freedom. Alia's cry early in the film, 'I hate pots and pans. I want to play the lute', is a first step along this road, especially in terms of freeing her body from the life of drudgery which is the lot of the female servants. In a parallel first step, Aicha takes up weaving for reasons other than the highly suspect, non-traditional, self-indulgent ones her mother-in-law attributes to her, but, having begun, her love of improvising in the design of her carpets means that she does indeed break with tradition, and simultaneously expresses herself. (The fact that, on her own admission, Tlatli likes to improvise in her filmmaking is clearly not coincidental.)

Beyond this, these cultural practices have transformative power, affecting the body, the mind, and more besides: weaving provides release and keeps Aicha sane; ultimately, it calms Aziz, thereby offering an otherwise unattainable freedom to his mother; music in the shape of Sarra's lute playing releases Alia from her traumatised state after her mother's rape; song, as Alia sings to the party guests, is the life of the soul, but above all it has power. Having told them, Alia proceeds to demonstrate it, singing the forbidden 'Green Tunisia', disrupting the party and catapulting herself into her longed-for space of bodily freedom and independence, beyond the palace walls and in the company of Lotfi. To that extent, she is emerging from the space of subalternity-as-silencing which is the condition of the women servants and from which she tried to encourage her mother to free herself: 'Just for once, say "no". No, I won't wait on you! No, I don't belong to you!' That her mother is unable to enact this resistance, and remains sexually subservient to the Beys, is the source of Alia's frustration and anger towards Khedija. Although, as already mentioned, Alia's own hard-won space of freedom proves not to deliver what she was promised, it does nevertheless provide her the space or distance from which to understand her mother, to no longer condemn her, and to decide on a future course of action requiring the sort of courage which at least matches that which her mother demonstrated. It is something which women of all kinds will require to secure and sustain appropriate forms of 'liberty of the body'.

Notes

1 In the meantime, to avoid any oversimplification, it needs to be made clear that Tlatli has of course worked with women directors from Tunisia (Selma Baccar, Nejia Ben Mabrouk), and Morocco (Fatima Benlyazid).
2 This connection between personal and national liberation is the one best analysed in the relatively few substantial studies of Tlatli's work, and therefore one which will not be dealt with at great length here. On woman and nation see for example: Naaman 2000, Hochberg 2000.
3 For a useful discussion of abjection in the colonial context see McClintock 1995.
4 In case this should seem like the untimely reappearance of another tired old masculine theory in an inappropriate context, it is worth pointing out that feminists such as Spivak and Butler continue to make use of Althusser's insights.

Filmography

Samt al-Qsur (*The Silences of the Palace*) (1994)
Mawsim al-Rijal (*The Season of Men*) (2000)

Chapter 9

Jean-Pierre Bekolo

Introduction

Jean-Pierre Bekolo is at the forefront of a wave of innovative and dynamic young African filmmakers who have emerged since the early 1990s. Openly embracing the values and forms of urban African youth culture, Bekolo has created a cinema that exists at the interface between a global youth aesthetic (fast-paced editing, fashion-conscious characters, a fascination with celebrity culture) and an experimental narrative approach that blurs both identities and genres. Born in Cameroon in 1966, Bekolo trained in Paris as a television film editor at the Institut National Audiovisuel (INA) – studying under the celebrated film theorist Christian Metz – before returning to Cameroon to work for Cameroon Radio and Television. In the late 1980s, he began to make short films – *Boyo* (1988), *Un Pauvre Blanc* (1989) and *Mohawk People* (1990), none of which has been screened widely – but his major breakthrough came with the release of his first feature-length film, *Quartier Mozart* (1992), which was very well received at Cannes (winning the Prix Afrique en Création). The film combines the brusque energy of the pop video aesthetic – Bekolo has made music videos for the French band *Les Têtes brûlées* as well as his Cameroonian compatriot Manu Dibango – with a radical experimentation at the level of narrative, form and subject matter.

The sheer energy and innovation of *Quartier Mozart* saw Bekolo heralded as the leading figure in a new wave of African filmmaking. He was also aligned with 'independent' US film directors, such as Spike Lee and Jim Jarmusch who were at that time beginning to achieve 'cross-over' success. For Melissa Thackway, Bekolo's work reflects the 'cultural synthesis' of urban life on the continent, and she describes *Quartier Mozart* as a film in which 'snappy, urban youth culture cohabits with traditional supernatural beliefs in a fast, quirky style' (2003: 12). The film also sets out the broad template that one finds in all of Bekolo's films: a blend of fantasy and farce with a highly distinctive visual style, involving bold colours, fast-paced editing and striking shot composition (which reveals a particular taste for the bizarre and the comically grotesque). *Quartier Mozart* also breaks new ground in terms of its transgressive narrative – a teenage girl makes a pact with a 'witch' and is temporarily transformed into a boy – which deals with sex, power, identity and magic: Clyde Taylor refers to the film's 'code violations' in relation to previous African films (2000: 140). Bekolo and other young directors who emerged in the 1990s were increasingly concerned with personal issues, many of which, such as sexuality and in particular homosexuality, had previously been seen as taboo subjects for African filmmakers. (Nouri Bouzid's *Bezness* (1995), Mohamed Camara's *Dakan* (1997) and *Karmen Gei* (2001) by the Senegalese director Joseph Rokhaya Geye are recent explorations of homosexuality, which still remains a very controversial subject.)

From the beginning of his career, many critics identified Bekolo as the cinematic heir to Djibril Diop Mambety, sub-Saharan Africa's other leading maverick filmmaker: for instance, the prominent African film critic Frank Ukadike describes *Quartier Mozart* as 'a work of unparalleled imagination and stylistic and aesthetic virtuosity unknown in African cinema since the release of Djibril Diop Mambety's *Touki-Bouki* in 1973' (2002: 218). At the time of their respective releases, both films appeared as bolts out of the blue in the African film landscape, announcing the arrival of singular and daring young talents. The two men were in their mid-twenties when they made their first feature films and both eschew the dominant social realism of their fellow African directors in favour of a far more eclectic approach (combining farce, fantasy, sensuality or sexuality), in which the exploration of cinematic form takes precedence over content. Their experimentalism and desire to explore marginal, 'queer' identities has, at various moments, seen both directors cast as 'postmodern', which is often (but not always) shorthand for defining their work as entirely Western-influenced. Although Bekolo is uncomfortable with the label of 'African filmmaker', he has always maintained his admiration for Mambety, whom he views as the only African filmmaker to have attempted to create a new film 'language', and he is often quite dismissive of other pioneering figures such as Sembene whose work he characterises as 'formulaic' and entirely derivative of Western film codes (Ukadike 2002: 218–20), even if he concedes that 'Sembene is doing great work' (225). Indeed, Bekolo's next film – *Grandmother's Grammar* (1996) was a documentary devoted to an analysis of cinematic innovation in Mambety's work. Bekolo clearly sees in Mambety a kindred spirit for whom cinema is primarily a mode of expression, and not a tool for educating the masses, a view that runs against the dominant African vision of cinema that has been explored in this volume. The desire on the part of Bekolo to forge his own specific lineage within African cinema is a subject that will be examined in greater depth in the final section of this chapter, for (as was argued in the introduction to this volume) it underlines the importance of tracing multiple strands within African cinema, and developing more complex genealogies of African filmmaking practice.

Bekolo's second feature film, *Aristotle's Plot* (1997), which was commissioned by the British Film Institute (BFI) as the African contribution to a series of documentary films marking the centenary of cinema (in 1995), was equally inventive and allowed Bekolo to further this meditation on the cinema in Africa. Unlike the other illustrious names called upon to make films in the series, such as Martin Scorsese, Bernardo Bertolucci and Stephen Frears, who made interesting, but (ultimately) relatively conventional documentaries, Bekolo made an extremely innovative 'film essay', which reflects on the nature of both filmmaking and film consumption in Africa. This critical 'reflection' is conveyed in typically comic fashion: set in Zimbabwe, the film pits a rather earnest African film director, who purports to know exactly what African film audiences want, against a gang of African youths devoted to the violent Hollywood and Kung Fu movies that form the staple diet of many African filmgoers.

Bekolo's latest film, *Les Saignantes* (2005), explores similar terrain to *Quartier Mozart*, using sexuality as a means of exploring the power relations governing Cameroonian society. Set in the Cameroon of 2025, the film follows the adventures of two sensuous young women who use their beauty to attract the attentions of powerful, older men. Shot mostly in the garish light of a dank and decaying urban nightscape, the film uses farce and fantasy to explore the corruption that stalks Cameroonian society.[1] This foray into science fiction underlines Bekolo's desire to use the full range of cinematic expression. An extremely opinionated and forthright figure, who has taught film in a number of top US universities, he has consistently bemoaned the timidity of African filmmakers and has called on them to develop their own unique film language. As he argues in an interview with Ukadike: 'In the African circle, we never talk about aesthetics, and that is what made me enter this business of filmmaking' (2002: 221). This is a long way from the rallying calls of the pioneers of postcolonial African cinema in the 1960s and 1970s with their demands for a radical cinema that would counter the political and cultural hegemony of the West, and critics are divided as to whether this is a positive or a negative development. However, whatever critics think of Bekolo's films, it seems undeniable that his work has at the very least helped to give cinematic style and technique a more prominent place within discussion of African cinema than it has hitherto enjoyed.

Social, cultural and political contexts

Postcolonial Cameroon has produced many important writers, directors and musicians, although, given the harsh political, social and economic climate, many of them have been forced to live in exile. Since independence, Cameroon has effectively been subjected to one-party rule with only two presidents having governed the country for over 40 years: Ahmadou Ahidjo (1960–82) and Paul Biya (1982 to the present). The discovery of oil and other natural resources has given Cameroon an impressive GNP but it has also led to massive corruption: in fact, Cameroon is regularly ranked towards the bottom of the global corruption index of over 150 countries by

Transparency International, usually placing it amongst the likes of war-torn countries such as Sierra Leone and Liberia, or its oil-rich neighbour Nigeria (in 1998, Cameroon received the unwanted recognition of being classified as the world's most corrupt nation).

One of the major fault lines in Cameroonian politics is the sense of isolation and lack of belonging felt by the Anglophone minority in the north of the country. This situation can be traced directly to Cameroon's complex colonial history: originally colonised by Germany in the late nineteenth century, Cameroon was later divided between French and British 'mandates' after Germany was forced to cede control of its colonies at the end of the First World War. The British were awarded only one-fifth of the territory of German *Kamerun*, and, although they administered the territory as part of their Nigerian colony, it remained for them a marginal region that received minimal funding and remained relatively underdeveloped in terms of infrastructure compared to the French-controlled south. In the aftermath of the Second World War, there were growing calls both for the 'reunification' of Cameroon and for independence from France. In the mid-1950s, this led to an attempt at violent revolt, which was quickly and brutally suppressed by the French.

Like the rest of France's sub-Saharan African colonies, Cameroon gained its independence in 1960 with Ahidjo as its first leader. Following a UN plebiscite, the southern part of British Cameroon opted to 'reunite' with the former French colony, while the northern section opted to join Nigeria. The reunification of the country proved extremely problematic, and violent confrontations with northern rebels continued into the early 1970s until Ahidjo's troops finally brought the revolt to an end and executed the rebel leaders. As happened in many other African countries at this time, Ahidjo sought to control opposition by drawing the fragmented opposition within a single, umbrella national party. This meant that, by the mid-1970s, Cameroon was relatively stable, although not exactly democratic, and tensions continued to simmer, particularly in the Anglophone north. The discovery of oil deposits in the 1970s strengthened Ahidjo's hand even further, as it seemed to herald a new era of peace and prosperity. However, the huge wealth to be made from oil unleashed a wave of political and economic corruption that continues to disrupt Cameroon's development. Then, in the early 1980s, the country went through a period of major political turmoil. In 1982, Ahidjo stepped down from the presidency on grounds of ill-health, passing over the reins of power to his Prime Minister, Paul Biya. What was originally seen as a model transfer of power (at that time Biya enjoyed a reputation for competence and integrity) soon turned sour: the following year, Biya ousted his political rivals in his own party over an alleged plot; then, in 1984, there were pitched battles in the streets of Yaoundé, as troops loyal to Ahidjo attempted to carry out a coup. They were defeated by Biya's army, and a period of brutal repression followed, during which Biya consolidated his hold on power and rejected calls for a move towards multi-party democracy. However, as the economic situation deteriorated in the late 1980s, a widespread social movement emerged, which called for Biya to allow the formation of opposition political parties (a phenomenon that was sweeping through Africa during this period). Although the marginalised Anglophone north of the country was at the heart of this movement, it attracted support from all regions. Despite initial attempts to suppress the fledgling democratic movement, Biya was eventually forced to make concessions and, in 1992, he sanctioned multi-party legislative and presidential elections. Although he and his party won, the elections were classified by international observers as blatantly rigged ballots. Since the early 1990s, Biya has exploited the fragmented nature of the opposition to maintain his quarter-century grip on power.

Like his African cinematic 'father' Mambety, Bekolo is not an explicitly 'political' filmmaker in the manner of pioneers such as Sembene and Hondo or the likes of certain of his contemporaries such as Cheick Oumar Sissoko: essentially, Bekolo has no specific political answers or critiques to offer in his work. However, as with Mambety, it can just as easily be argued that Bekolo makes films in which the socio-political climate of his country is explored in startling and highly imaginative ways that allow the spectator a unique perspective on Cameroonian society. For example, the chaotic but vibrant nature of Cameroonian urban life is brilliantly captured by Bekolo in *Quartier Mozart*: the urban youth culture of hip hop, MTV, teen magazines offering romance, the playful banter between teenage boys and girls that masks often highly charged sexual power struggles. This latter aspect of the film is used by Bekolo as a means of exploring not only relations between the sexes but also the very nature of power and authority in contemporary Cameroon. 'Mad Dog', the aptly named police chief, is both dim-witted and brutish (as is the policeman in *Aristotle's Plot*): his contempt for women is presented as an extension of his general conception of the authority conferred on him by his position as a police inspector.

The excessive, non-naturalistic acting style, with actors explicitly playing out exaggerated 'types' that are well known from contemporary African popular culture, is characteristic of the shift away from social realism or naturalism that has marked certain strands of African filmmaking since the early 1990s. (As will be argued at length in the next section of this chapter, this approach represents an intriguing mix of the popular and the experimental.) For instance, one can make strong comparisons between Mad Dog and the buffoonish but tyrannical male authority figures in the short films of Balufu Bakupu-Kanyinda, *Le Damier* (1997) and *Article 15 bis* (1999), which explore the interface between popular street culture and a repressive state structure in the former Belgian Congo (perhaps unsurprisingly, Mad Dog's appearance also contains echoes of the rotund policemen in Mambety's *Badou Boy* and *Touki Bouki*). Jean-Marie Téno's outstanding documentary film, *Chef!* (1999), arrives at a similar view of Cameroonian society to Bekolo but via the opposite route, its general reflection on power and authority leading the filmmaker to explore how the rigidly hierarchical and patriarchal society that he describes might be seen to stem from the relations between the sexes.

Bekolo's comic vision is highly iconoclastic and he uses social satire as a means of exploring issues that might be seen as taboo if dealt with in naturalistic fashion. For example, in *Quartier Mozart*, his satirical sideswipes take in both the police and the Catholic Church, two extremely powerful forces within Cameroonian society. As was mentioned above, Mad Dog is a tyrannical figure who brutalises his wives and his children, and who looks down upon the 'riff-raff' who populate Quartier Mozart. Elsewhere in the film, in the sequence at the police station, we hear the screams of a prisoner being tortured offscreen while the characters onscreen continue about their business as though nothing untoward is happening; when the policeman-torturer leaves the prisoner momentarily to come and speak to the receptionist, he speaks light-heartedly of the recalcitrance of journalists. As for the Church, it is presented as a force that is in league with the political establishment: the priest is a jovial character who instantly forgives Mad Dog for taking a second wife, and agrees – for the right price, cash in hand, of course – to bless his house in order to ward off 'evil spirits'. (Bekolo's approach to witchcraft – which is a major and extremely complex social issue in Cameroon – will be examined in the next section of this chapter.)

In many ways, the comic dimension of Bekolo's work can be seen as a continuation of the tradition of filmmaking that had developed in Cameroon during the 1970s and 1980s (although in terms of its experimentalism, it also constitutes something of a rupture with that tradition). More than most other Francophone African national cinemas, Cameroon had developed a brand of popular comic films, which were part-funded by the government. Two of the best-known directors were Daniel Kamwa – who made *Boubou cravate* (1972), *Pousse-Pousse* (1975) and *Notre fille* (1980) – and Jean-Pierre Dikongue-Pipa – director of *Muna Moto* (1975) and *Le Prix de la liberté* (1978). Although critics have generally been kinder to Dikongue-Pipa than to Kamwa, there has been an overwhelming critical consensus that their films are primarily escapist comic melodramas that act as 'opium to the masses', neglecting the political radicalism deemed 'necessary' to African cinema.[2] For example, Manthia Diawara states that Kamwa's film *Pousse-Pousse*, a broad social comedy about marriage and dowries in contemporary Cameroon, 'is considered by many African directors as naïve and iconoclastic toward African traditions and less critical toward French cultural imperialism in Cameroon. The film is also loosely edited, which makes it unartistically repetitious' (1992: 31). Essentially, Kamwa is damned as an artistically and politically naive filmmaker, whose very popularity is viewed with suspicion by critics. Bekolo's work might thus be a seen as an attempt to revisit the popular comic tradition of Cameroon and to imbue it with an artistic and representational sophistication that it did not previously enjoy. As will be argued at length in the next two sections, it is this tension between the popular and the experimental that characterises all of his work.

The films

Although Bekolo's work has engaged with a relatively wide range of filmmaking styles in just three feature films – supernatural fantasy (*Quartier
Mozart*), film essay (*Aristotle's Plot*), science-fiction (*Les Saignantes*) – they
all display a common sensibility, which revolves primarily around the use of
an exaggerated physical, verbal and situation comedy. For comedy and satire
are essential to Bekolo's conception of African storytelling:

> I bought 'how-to' books on how to write screenplays. In the beginning of one
> of those books, the author quoted Aristotle as saying that a good story should
> inspire pity and fear. I had a problem with that . . . I am from Cameroon, and
> I think humour and satire are basic elements of culture. As I was reading *The
> Poetics*, I realised that something was missing – comedy. That is why I became
> paranoid, as the title *Aristotle's Plot* seems to indicate. So, the 'plot' is not just
> the plot in storytelling, but also the subplot. (Ukadike 2002: 229)

The pun on the double meaning of 'plot' illustrates Bekolo's firm belief that
film is dominated by Western narrative structures, which have little to do
with African forms of storytelling. If African filmmakers wish to break with
Western cinematic conventions, then they need to rethink not only the
subject matter of their films but also the ways in which they construct their
narratives. Such ideas might lead one to view Bekolo as quite a cerebral
director of complex, experimental movies, and, indeed, his films are often
quite 'difficult' in terms of their narrative construction and their challenging
of received social and cinematic norms. However, his films are in fact,
extremely hybrid in form, and his work might best be situated within the
same type of filmmaking practice as that of independent US directors such
as Spike Lee and Quentin Tarantino, whose work is deeply influenced by art
house film culture, as well as being steeped in references to popular film and
culture more generally (although Bekolo's willingness to embrace narrative
opacity goes far beyond the self-imposed limits placed on the narratives of
Lee and Tarantino). In particular, Bekolo's consistent use of comedy, including broad slapstick and farce, situates important aspects of his work quite
clearly within a popular African comic tradition. Despite the serious and
often quite tragic nature of his subject matter, his films are resolutely played
out as satirical farces in which the actors play the part of heavily exaggerated 'types' who often seem almost cartoonish in their behaviour. In this
sense, his films readily tap into the popular theatrical traditions common in
much of sub-Saharan Africa: as was mentioned above, Bekolo is the first
African director since Mambety so clearly to eschew any element of naturalism in his approach. (Equally, Bekolo's films walk the same fine line
between the farcical and the surreal that one finds in Mambety's work.)

This section will focus primarily on Bekolo's first feature film, *Quartier
Mozart*, although some comparisons will be drawn with his approach in
Aristotle's Plot. (The final section of this chapter will provide an in-depth

analysis of the 'theoretical' questions raised by *Aristotle's Plot*.) The comic and exaggerated world of *Quartier Mozart* is made evident from the opening sequence. After the hip-hop-inflected Afropop, which plays over the opening credits (the excellent original music by Philip Kikwé contributes hugely to the vibrant rhythm of the film), seven of the main characters introduce themselves to the audience, speaking directly to camera and revealing their nicknames, which are keys to understanding their personalities (the fact that all of the main characters have nicknames rather than 'real' names adds to the cartoonish nature of the film's world): Chef de quartier is a brash, teenage girl who defiantly stakes out her position within the neighbourhood and refuses a cloistered existence within the home;[3] Atango, the ageing tailor, preens himself like a proud cockerel as he claims to have a diploma from the Sorbonne and swaggeringly describes himself as 'young ladies' candy'; the handsome but mysterious Myguy paces back and forth as he claims intriguingly that a boy died on the day he was born and wonders aloud if he is really a man (as we later discover, he is in fact the teenage girl Chef de quartier, a 'fact' wilfully conveyed in oblique narrative fashion by Bekolo); Special Messenger, a teenage boy, stands hands on hips, boldly stating that he has a 'special file' on the entire neighbourhood; his older sister, the glamorous Saturday nonchalantly proclaims her preference for doing over thinking; Good for the Dead is the macho shopkeeper who bemoans being taken for granted by customers looking for credit; finally, the menacing figure of Mad Dog – father of Special Messenger and Saturday – glowers at the camera and refers to his nickname as his 'combat name', before putting the ever-present walkie-talkie to his ear.

This must rank as one of the most bravura openings in African film history, especially for a young director making his first feature film. The swagger and self-confidence of the characters, the fast-paced editing, the use of contemporary pop music are all clearly designed to announce Bekolo's arrival on the film scene, and his desire to break with the dominant narrative and cinematic conventions within African cinema. Although this sequence is clearly influenced by the dynamism of the pop video aesthetic, it should not be dismissed as a triumph of style over content, as some critics, such as Clyde Taylor, have suggested: 'A critical inertia postpones the finding that the contribution of *Quartier Mozart* to the evolution of African culture is slight, beyond its engaging novelty as an internationally hipper type of crowd-pleaser than *La Vie est belle* or *Bal Poussière*' (2000: 144). On the contrary, style is inextricably tied to content in Bekolo's work: as each character is introduced to the audience, the camera pans in from either left or right towards a head-on medium shot before panning away once again (the one exception is Special Messenger, in whose case the camera zooms in head on to a medium close-up, perhaps indicating his central position as a 'go-between' in the narrative); in essence, Bekolo refuses to allow any one character's perspective to dominate, and the remainder of the film is an exploration of the world as viewed from their differing perspectives. The film can thus be read, in part, as a celebration of the complex and multiple identities to be found in the contemporary African city.

Despite the disturbing nature of certain aspects of the narrative, they are all systematically played out as comedy, no matter how dark this comedy might be. The narrator's reference to witchcraft on the voiceover gives rise to a scene of a wife mourning her husband who died in suspicious circumstances, dropping dead at the wheel of his car. However, the conclusion to the scene is played out as burlesque physical comedy as we see a passer-by open the car door and the inert body of the husband collapses into the street. When Mad Dog brings home a second wife, he announces this in a matter-of-fact way to his daughter, Saturday. The impact of this development is then illustrated in powerfully understated comic detail when we see a photograph of the new wife added to the shelf alongside those of Mad Dog and his first wife, Sytsalla, as a particularly jaunty version of the Wedding March plays on the soundtrack. The three older women who gather at the public water pump to exchange gossip find no subject too grim for humour: they laugh raucously when they hear that Good for the Dead has had his penis shrunk by a stranger; Saturday's liaison with Myguy is the subject of further mirth; and Mad Dog's decision to throw Sytsalla, his wife and the mother of his children, out of the house leaves them in hysterics.

In essence, the film creates a dark, but cartoon-like world in which there are no genuinely damaging consequences to people's actions, for everything is played out as comedy: for instance, when Myguy is beaten up near the start of the film, we see the men line up to aim punches at him but we do not see any of these blows connect with him, and the exaggerated crashing noises on the soundtrack allow us to view this sequence as harmless cartoon violence; after Sytsalla is kicked out of the family home, she quickly recovers and sets up her own market stall where men fall over themselves to express their love for her; Panka has been beating his wife but the situation is played solely for laughs, as the spectator is invited to revel in Panka's discomfort when his boss, Mad Dog, inexplicably sides with the former's wife. (Equally, *Aristotle's Plot* derives great humour from the violent 'deaths' of its main characters.)

As well as this strong visual and situation comedy, Bekolo also extracts great humour from the dialogue. His characters speak the extremely rich, popular French of the streets of Douala: the French-produced DVD of the film (released in 2005) provides a lexis of Cameroonian terms such as 'bangala', 'gombo' but also 'normal' French words such as 'chose', 'homme' and 'pointure', all of which are given new meanings in their urban African context. (Previous generations of African directors derived great humour and drama from the deployment of proverbs with their often rich and incisive use of language.) Men and women engage in verbal battles about their respective virility or chastity. One the richest veins of verbal comedy stems from Atango's use of elaborate football metaphors – 'the game could be tight', 'penalising errors', 'scoring penalties' – in order to 'educate' the naive

Myguy in the 'art' of getting women into bed. One of the funniest sequences in the film takes place in the grocer's shop where Atango, Capo and Good for the Dead engage in a knowing and highly ironic conversation about the differences between Africans and African-Americans (their one conversation that does not revolve solely around sex, although Atango does finally drag their discussion back to this most favoured of topics). Atango and Capo immediately poke fun at the slightly dim-witted Good for the Dead who has never heard the expression 'African-Americans', which leads to the following exchange:

Capo: You, you read the papers?
Good for the Dead: *Paris-Match* every week.
Capo: Right. Then, tell us when Caroline of Monaco last menstruated.

The conversation then turns to American misconceptions about Africa and the stereotype that all Africans are poor and hungry. Good for the Dead claims that no one has ever died of hunger in Quartier Mozart, leading Capo to wind him up even further: 'There's starvation here. I almost starved. I didn't have a dime and came to you; you denied me. You let a black brother starve.' (The passage works better in the original French as Capo's final comment 'Tu as laissé mourir un frère *noir* du Quartier *Mozart*' accentuates his mockery of Good for the Dead through its exaggerated rhyme on 'noir'/'Mozart'.) Bekolo is here making an extremely telling comic point not only regarding Western preconceptions about Africa but also regarding pre-conceptions about African cinema and its style and content matter. The verbal jousting between characters is an integral part of Bekolo's exploration of youth culture, which is accepted, and generally celebrated, for what it is rather than deployed in order to make a moral, social or political point (just as the proverbial 'jousting' that one finds in a film such as *Mandabi* tapped the linguistic verve of oral culture). As was argued above, for Bekolo, cinema is expression rather than education. (Similarly, as will be shown below, *Aristotle's Plot* derives much of its humour from the verbal clashes between Cineaste and the gang.)

The heart of the story revolves around sexuality and gender identity but it is witchcraft that supplies the plot device that allows the brash teenager Chef de quartier to experience life as a man (Myguy) and to gain access to parts of her neighbourhood that would normally be forbidden to a woman. She is initiated into the ways of the world by the mysterious figure of Mama Thécla, who claims to have regularly travelled the country in the shape of a man. In a country where witchcraft is widely present but can often be the subject of official sanctions (see Fisiy and Geschiere 1996), Bekolo places his representation firmly within the comic register of the rest of the film. Mama Thécla is a comic rather than a threatening character: even in her male guise as the fausse-naive Panka, her use of her powers to shrink Good for the Dead's penis just by shaking his hand is played out as exuberant visual comedy. When Mad Dog questions Panka about his actions and forces him to shake his hand to see if his penis will shrink also, any tension in the situation is soon dissipated by Mad Dog's decision to hire Panka to guard his house. Witchcraft is, quite simply, a 'reality' of life in Bekolo's quirky fictional world.

Throughout the film, various conceptions of masculinity are subjected to sustained mockery, which is mostly gentle but can, at times, be quite vicious. Bekolo gleefully uses the plot device of Chef de quartier's transformation into a man as a means of exploring masculine identity, as Atango and the other men of the neighbourhood attempt to 'educate' the naive Myguy in the ways of manhood. As was mentioned above, Myguy's 'initiation' is often cast in terms of sporting, and especially footballing, metaphors. When he is first discovered by the people of the neighbourhood, they think that he is a 'mercenary' and he is subjected to a test of his 'masculinity', which involves him standing between the goalposts and failing to save a series of shots on goal. Later in the film, when Myguy is on his date with Saturday, the two protagonists stand framed at either end of the goalposts, as this trainee man attempts to 'score' on his first date as advised by his macho friends. It is highly significant that Myguy is pushed by his new male friends into arranging this 'hot date' with Saturday as a forfeit because of his failure to beat Capo in a game of draughts (checkers), the form of competitive recreation that punctuates life for (young and old) men in so many African cities. As in the magnificent short film *Le Damier* by the Congolese director Balufu Bakupu-Kanyinda, board games provide a forum in which young men compete in bouts of both mental and verbal dexterity: successfully taunting one's opponent is as important as beating him in the game itself.

Atango leads his young apprentice on a journey into manhood that primarily involves duplicity and vulgarity. Charm is something to be used solely as bait with which to lure women into bed: Atango and Myguy nonchalantly urinate on the wall of Mad Dog's compound and then spit simultaneously as they close their flies; Atango lures women into his bed with fine words and a promise to make them fine clothes but, as he announces in his introduction at the start of the film, he is in reality simply carrying out a sexual 'inventory' of the women of the neighbourhood; however, when one of his conquests falls pregnant by him, he slaps her and attempts to buy her off with a token sum of money. Equally disrespectful attitudes towards women are found in virtually all of the male characters: Capo beds a woman, then pretends to go to the toilet in order to allow Good for the Dead to come in and take his 'turn' to the dismay of the woman (both men find it hilarious when she flees in terror). The most excessive display of masculinity is associated with Mad Dog: he does not bother with the niceties and fine words used by his male counterparts, and acts callously towards both his wives and his children, resorting to violence whenever he feels his authority threatened. He is a grotesque caricature of the male authority figure: the number plate of his car reads 'SN Boss'; and, throughout the film, he preeningly holds his (phallic) walkie-talkie to his ear in order to speak in a rasping, authoritative voice to other policemen with equally macho monickers (Viper, Hot Sauce). As a representative of the repressive state system, Mad Dog's excessive masculinity produces perhaps the darkest humour in the film.

However, within this comic world, such machismo is destined to fail. It is not that the film sets up a binary between 'nasty' men and 'virtuous' women: on the contrary, Bekolo seeks to explore the comic nature of the relationships between men and women in his community, which involves mockery of both sides. Women are on occasions bitter rivals for the affections of even the most vicious men: Mad Dog's second wife is, at first, delighted to have seen off the first wife; Saturday's girlfriend runs to tell Mad Dog about the former's supposed sexual encounter with Myguy out of pure jealousy; while the women at the water pump do not let a sense of female solidarity get in the way of some juicy gossip. None the less, it is undeniable that the film's plot is centred on the female exploration (and critique) of masculinity through the adventures of the man-woman, Myguy/Chef de quartier, and Bekolo gives the greatest complexity of character to two of his female characters – Saturday and Myguy/Chef de quartier. Both are assertive young women who refuse to remain 'locked up at home' (as Chef de quartier exclaims at the start of the film) and demand equality with men. They invariably give as good as they get in verbal exchanges with men, thereby laying claim to allegedly 'masculine' traits, and they refuse to give up their virginity to just any passing man. (They know that men who sleep around are jack-the-lads while women who do the same are cast as 'whores'.) This is comically illustrated by Bekolo when Saturday goes on her first date with Myguy wearing multiple pairs of knickers (an early precursor of Bridget Jones's 'Granny Knickers'). Equally, just as male sexuality is mocked as an extension of competitive sport, Bekolo playfully casts feminine romance as a dreamy *roman-photo*, the clichéd romances, featuring black-and-white photos and inane speech bubbles, which enjoyed such popularity in the 1970s and 1980s (featuring comments such as 'does she like me?' in bubbles above the characters' heads).

The comment by the offscreen narrator (played by Bekolo himself), moments prior to her 'transformation', that Chef de quartier is 'arrogant as only a girl who has never known a man can be', is somewhat intriguing. Is he suggesting that her boldness would not survive her first sexual encounter with a man who would thereby 'tame' her? Or is he simply suggesting that her naivety is what allows her to challenge the status quo? It is difficult to pin down the film's stance on this question, for, ultimately, its comic, exaggerated vision creates a fictional world in which all sorts of transgressions are permitted, even if only temporarily. In this context, it is highly significant that Saturday falls for a man who is really a woman on the inside. As a woman, Myguy eventually disregards the advice of his male friends and offers Saturday the love and respect that she desires. Ferid Boughedir's claim that the film conveys a primarily 'conservative' message of 'be who you are, do not pretend to be someone you are not' simply does not hold water

(2000: 117): its open ending (in which Myguy is transformed back into Chef de quartier) does not convey any such readily digestible message, and, besides, the film as a whole is far too playful in its narrative style to be pinned down to an explicit 'message'.

Essentially, Bekolo imagines a highly exaggerated, comic world in which anything can happen (including Mad Dog mysteriously inviting Myguy to sleep with Saturday in his own home). Although 'normality' returns in the film's final sequence, in which Chef de quartier turns back into a teenage girl, the experience of the preceding comic fantasy has offered both Chef de quartier and the spectator the opportunity to imagine the world differently. For Bekolo, it is this ability to imagine the world differently that lies at the heart of the filmmaker's craft.

Aristotle's Plot: Beyond African cinema?

As has been argued throughout this chapter, Jean-Pierre Bekolo is a director who refuses easy categorisation and who has been particularly reluctant to view his work as part of something that might be called 'African cinema'. However, despite his distinctive cinematic vision, Bekolo has also consistently signalled his attachment to Africa, as well as his profound belief in the necessity for African filmmakers to make greater efforts to develop their own unique film language. A striking example of the tensions between these individual (artistic) and communal (African) identities can be found in the following quotation from a 1998 interview in which he lambasts FESPACO, the biennial African film festival that takes place in Ouagadougou:

> FESPACO is an institution. It is a very conservative institution that is dragging along all the things we need to get rid of to move on. It is dragging colonialism; it is dragging all the weight Africa has to get rid of. Even if we can admire all the work people do around the institution, this institution is still too old for Africa, the new millennium and for whatever we have to do. Definitely, the festival has become a giant dinosaur, but it is not just a dinosaur in terms of the festival itself, but also in terms of the people in charge. It is not just a matter of creating a generational war. No. That is not the point. The problem may be because many African filmmakers are rooted in this tradition of respecting the elders, some of whom I really respect and like; but at the same time you cannot respect an elder who is keeping you down or preventing you from moving with the times. You cannot respect a corrupt father who is selling your future. (Ukadike 2002: 235)

These comments about both FESPACO and older generations of African filmmakers reveal a huge amount of anger and frustration. For Bekolo, it is not simply a case of younger artists situating themselves in opposition to their elders. He believes that the elders are actively preventing the likes of him from making an artistic breakthrough. Effectively, he is being thwarted in terms of his individual (as an artist) and his collective (as an African) identities, for older directors are presenting an image of Africa that is outdated.

These are harsh and rather exaggerated claims but Bekolo's complex film-essay *Aristotle's Plot* offers a fascinating and much more measured analysis of the situation of film in Africa. (Bekolo frequently emerges as a rather fiery interviewee whose excessive pronouncements seem designed to provoke reaction.) In yet another bravura opening, two men confront each other at a railway crossing – held at arm's length from one another by the mediating presence of the policeman – one announcing himself as a 'Cineaste', the other claiming to be called 'Cinema'. (Cinema and his gang later mock Cineaste by deforming this name and referring to him as 'silly ass'.) Their quick-fire exchange once again underlines Bekolo's talent for verbal comedy:

Cinema: They call me 'Cinema' because I've watched 10,000 films.
Cineaste: Oh yeah. How many of them were African?
Cinema: Very few . . . because they're shit!
Cineaste: If they are shit then you are shit because you're African!

Bekolo thus establishes from the beginning of his film a tension between the African filmmaker and the African audience. Which of them can be said genuinely to represent the state of cinema in Africa? Is it the director whose work is deemed 'shit' by 'Cinema' and his gang? Or is it the gang, who are interested only in Hollywood-style action movies and Kung Fu films, as is indicated by their names: Nikita, Van Damme, Bruce Lee, Schwarzenegger? After the verbal confrontation with Cineaste, Cinema is asked to produce his ID by the policeman, and, seemingly to his own bemusement (given the look on his face), he presents a series of ID cards that feature his photograph and the names of several of the most fêted African film directors: Mambety, Kaboré, Sembene, Hondo, Gerima, Cissé. Is Bekolo suggesting, as Cineaste says, that African films are part of Cinema's identity whether he likes it or not? Or, more prosaically, are these the names of the 'very few' African filmmakers whose names are, most definitely, not 'shit'? The film offers no easy answers to any of these questions but, in its exploration of the tensions between the expectations of director and audience, it provides an important reflection on the future of the seventh art on the continent and, as ever with Bekolo, it is a process of reflection that is expressed in comic and exaggerated fashion. In many ways, the tone for the film is set by Bekolo's impish voiceover, which acts both as an ironic commentary on the unfolding plot and as a comic reflection on the very nature of the film he is making, and the BFI's reasons for inviting him to make it. As Cinema produces his ID cards, the narrator asks: 'Then I started wondering "why me"? Was it Christian charity or political correctness? Was I accepting a challenge from someone already standing on the finish line?' Is African cinema inherently cast as a 'belated gesture', vainly attempting to catch up with the rest of the world, destined only to copy rather than to innovate?

In the same manner as *Quartier Mozart*, Bekolo creates an exaggerated fantasy world in which ideas and identities are pushed to ever more absurd limits. Cineaste is extremely earnest and believes that his vision presents

the real Africa. However, he is also a faintly ridiculous character who pushes
his movie reels around the city in a shopping trolley. The narrator refers
to him as an artist *maudit* who learned his trade in Paris and has been
hounded by the police since his return to Africa. His real name is Essomba
Tourneur, which Bekolo mischievously abbreviates as 'ET', for in many
ways Cineaste's cinematic obsession makes him something of an 'alien' to a
largely uninterested public. The spectator is also forced to ask whether his
outsider status and dissenting voice are purely in his head, as, throughout
the film, the authorities – in the form of the dim-witted policeman (described by the narrator as a 'keystone cop') – consistently side with him.
(Perhaps a sarcastic sideswipe at what Bekolo views as the institutionalisa-
tion of a certain type of 'oppositional' cinema in Africa, which consistently
overstates its radical intent and impact?) Cineaste forges a decree from the
Ministry of Culture demanding that the police shut down the local cinema,
'Cinema Africa', because the action movies screened there are a malign,
corrupting influence. 'Cinema' and his gang (referred to as *tsotsis*, or hoodlums) are thus evicted from their regular haunt, and 'Cinema Africa' is
(ironically) renamed 'Heritage Cinema', where only African films are
screened.

The subsequent attack on the cinema by the gang is portrayed by the
narrator-filmmaker as his attempt to provide a sense of Aristotelian 'pity and
fear' but the actual depiction of the raid is, in fact, a hybrid mixture of dramatic tension and burlesque comedy. The gang slit the projectionist's throat
and gun down the sole member of the audience in a stylised execution scene,
filmed in silhouette through a white curtain, which gradually turns red.
However, the sequence also works as an extremely sarcastic commentary on
African filmmaking. The decision to screen only African movies has resulted
in a dramatic decline in audiences: when the gang enter the cinema, there is
just one paying customer in the audience, and he is an African-American
there to look for his roots. Once again Bekolo endlessly plays with notions
of authenticity through the questions posed by the characters but also in
terms of his style. He claims that his film is 'Aristotelian' but the dramatic
violence is balanced by a comedic approach, which – as was illustrated above
– Bekolo views as integral to African narrative traditions and sensibilities.
The narrator's claim that 'the decision to invite me to celebrate the centenary
of cinema could only be a subplot twenty-three centuries old, Aristotle's Plot'
proves to be a deliberately misleading one, for the evidence of the film is that
it is possible to create a hybrid cinematic form in which 'Aristotle's plot' is
adapted to African narrative demands.

This idea is reinforced when the gang seek refuge in the countryside and
build their own makeshift cinema – the walls are cobbled together from
scrap metal and pieces of cloth – called 'New Africa', where they screen the
stolen prints. To the disgust of all but one of the gang, the stolen prints are
African movies, but, to their amazement, the rural audience love them. As
they finish work on the movie theatre, Cinema stands back and declares that

this is the 'real Africa' for it combines the new and the old. Is this Bekolo's conception of African cinema: the hybrid marriage of urban and rural, old and new, modern and traditional? Intriguingly, there is an ox's skull attached to the sign over the entrance in what may be a visual reference to the skull attached to the handlebars of Mory's motorbike in Mambety's *Touki Bouki* (see Chapter 4). As Bekolo's African cinematic 'father', Mambety might be seen to offer a model of hybridity that allows a way out of the impasse constituted by the strict opposition between a 'heritage Africa' and a simplistic imitation of the West (in the closing credits, Mambety is thanked for his 'participation' in the film).

Bekolo's account of African audience expectations – namely, that African films are popular solely with rural audiences – is a highly contentious one but the verisimilitude of the situations he depicts is not what matters in this cinematic hall of mirrors; Bekolo seeks instead to undermine the certainties of both parties in order to explore the relationship between fiction and reality. The gang discover that the world depicted by African filmmakers can be popular and they call for directors to make 'African movies that kick ass' ('not that fucking Jean-Pierre Bekolo though!'), while Cineaste is transformed into a character from the type of film that he despises: after the theft of the film prints, he abandons his high ideals and becomes a leather-clad avenger on a motorbike. The confrontation between Cineaste and the gang is first played out as classic Hollywood action movie – in which all of the main characters are killed – but the narrator is dissatisfied with the end product and decides to tear up the Aristotelian rulebook: he brings the characters back from the dead and the final sequences of the film are played out as surreal farce in which the confusion between fiction and reality becomes ever more blurred. Death has been banished as the rules of the fictional world come to dominate: no one dies, for all is just cinematic illusion. This sense of comic playfulness, which takes pleasure from using cinema to transgress the rules of reality, while refusing to succumb to cinematic conventions (good guy versus bad guy), has marked all of Bekolo's work.

By tracing his own lineage within African cinema, and aligning his work with the maverick talents of Djibril Diop Mambety, Bekolo underlines the existence of different styles and approaches within the category of African cinema. As was argued in the introduction to this volume, it is necessary to chart a far more complex genealogy of African cinema than has often been assumed by critics. The didactic, realist strand of postcolonial African filmmaking may have begun with *Borom Sarret* in 1962 but African cinema, north and south of the Sahara, cannot be limited to this approach. Rather than positing a monolithic vision of African cinema, it is vital to trace the series of distinct but intertwining paths that have been followed. *Aristotle's Plot* is a very useful starting point for such a critical reflection, for it rejects any simplistic definition of African cinema and instead illustrates the range of storytelling possibilities open to African directors.

Notes

1 As this film had not yet been released in the UK at the time of writing in mid-2006, it will not be possible to include analysis of it here. However, Bekolo's blog for the film gives a strong sense of its striking visual style: http://quartiermozart.blogspot. com/2005/07/lessaignantes-pictures.html (last accessed on 30 August 2006).
2 There has often been a similarly dismissive approach to popular comedies from the Ivory Coast, perhaps most notably the work of Henri Duparc, director of the hugely popular *Bal Poussière* (1988).
3 The Americanised English subtitles refer to this character as 'Queen of the Hood', an extremely liberal translation that evokes very different connotations to the original French 'Chef de quartier'. The neighbourhood known as Quartier Mozart may be rough-and-ready but it cannot in any meaningful way be described as a 'hood' in the US sense of a deprived urban ghetto.

Filmography

Boyo (1988)
Un Pauvre Blanc (A Poor White Man) (1989)
Mohawk People (1990)
Quartier Mozart (1992)
Grandmother's Grammar (1996)
Aristotle's Plot (1997)
Original Sin Toronto (1998)
Les Saignantes (The Bloody Ones) (2005)

Chapter 10

Darrell James Roodt

Introduction

Even within the contradictory conditions of film making in South Africa (for more on which see the following section), Darrell Roodt is a contradictory figure. Categorised by the country's foremost film producer (and his long-time collaborator) Anant Singh as one of the very best filmmakers in South Africa, director of some of the most important and memorable films made there in the last twenty years, he is nevertheless also responsible for what many critics would regard as some of the worst and most instantly forgettable offerings from the same period. One commentator even went so far as to suggest that Roodt might be suffering from multiple personality disorder: that while one Darrell Roodt was engaged in making serious 'art' films about social problems in South Africa, his alter ego was furiously churning out would-be blockbusters in the United States. Humorous or not, there is something to be said for the image, and one of the aims of this chapter will therefore be to explore and attempt to understand some of the contradictions which Roodt and his films embody.

If there is any substance to a recent claim that Roodt is 'the self-defined bad boy of South African Cinema' (Beittel 2003: 80), then one – slightly generous, perhaps – way of understanding the extreme variability of his cinematic output might be in terms of pushing the boundaries of the acceptable in different directions. Thus, for example, at the political boundary, his first major film, *Place of Weeping* (1986), was also the first South African anti-apartheid feature film, and was shot entirely in South Africa while keeping one step ahead of the security police; also, his next important film, the controversial anti-war, anti-apartheid piece *The Stick* (1987) was banned until the 1990s. At the other extreme, Roodt's 'popular' films, especially those made in Hollywood, such as *Second Skin* (2000), *Witness to a Kill* (2001), *Pavement* (2002) and *Dracula 3000* (2004), push relentlessly in the direction of mass populist appeal across genres including action, thriller and horror. As Roodt has readily acknowledged, these films have not been his best by any means, yet he continues to make them. In this contradictory division, Roodt may, however, be doing no more than embodying powerful tendencies within the South African film industry in general, where opinion is deeply divided over whether the future should look more like Hollywood or take on a more distinctively national caste.

Another 'powerful tendency' which Roodt could be seen as embodying is the (unsurprising) white dominance of the film industry in South Africa, which will be examined at greater length in the following section, and which – the demise of apartheid, the advent of democracy, the inauguration of a new era for the country notwithstanding – continues to constitute an obstacle to the democratisation of the industry itself. However, given his propensity to champion black people and their causes in his films, the extent to which Roodt actually embodies white dominance is, at the very least, open to question.

The championing of black people is one of the important aspects of Roodt's 'independent' status – part of the independent (i.e. non-state-funded) film-making sector, but also independent in terms of being independent-minded, oppositional, different in his approach to the making of films. Having failed to gain admission to drama school at the University of Witwatersrand, Roodt quickly turned to filmmaking and directed his first film, the horror/murder mystery *City of Blood*, in 1983 at the age of twenty-one. Although, like his later Hollywood-based returns to the genre, this lacked anything resembling critical acclaim, either at the time or subsequently, it nevertheless contains traces of the racial politics which mark so much of his later work. Within three years, however, he had teamed up with producer Anant Singh, and organised the funding which allowed him to make the altogether different *Place of Weeping*. This alternation in style and genre has also operated on a larger scale, as a group of five South Africa-based films, culminating in Roodt's major international breakthrough *Sarafina!* (1992), was followed by twice as many thrillers and horror films, the majority shot in Hollywood, and interspersed only with *Cry, the Beloved Country* (1995). This 'independent' approach brought mixed results: films distributed abroad, but not shown at home (especially during the period of apartheid); films critically acclaimed but commercially unsuccessful (*Sarafina!* is a rare example of a work which achieved both); 'popular' films which failed to be popular . . . Nevertheless, Roodt's work has included a number of significant firsts: *Place of Weeping*, as mentioned, was the first anti-apartheid feature film made in the country; *Cry, the Beloved Country* was the first major film of the post-apartheid era; and *Yesterday* (2004) was the first South African feature film about AIDS, the first feature film in isiZulu, and the first South African film to be nominated for an Oscar. There is, however, an unavoidable irony in the fact that, after two decades establishing himself as the only South African director with a truly international reputation, Roodt is still not treated particularly well in his own country: despite the fact that *Yesterday* attracted attention world-wide, won prizes at the most prestigious film festivals and was endorsed by politicians from Nelson Mandela to Hillary Clinton, it ran for only a very few weeks in South African cinemas. For Roodt, much of the blame lay in the fact that Hollywood films occupy over 90 per cent of screen time in South African cinemas, leaving everyone else fighting over the remaining scraps, but, as a *Washington Post* article pointed out, there is a strange, and contradictory, culture of indifference in South Africa:

> There is much discussion in Cape Town film circles about how to foster a more vibrant industry of home-grown film. Yet the head of the Cape Film Commission, Martin Cuff, said he had not seen *Yesterday*. He is not alone. Two of Cape Town's biggest producers, David Wicht and Philip Key, also said they hadn't seen it. Nor had South Africa's Minister of arts and culture, Z. Pallo Jordan, nor President Thabo Mbeki. (Timberg 2005: 16)

Despite these setbacks, Roodt continues on his independent path, and has followed up *Yesterday* not, as many people anticipated, with a glossier, bigger-budget attempt to secure his position in the global cinema market-place, but with something very like its antithesis. The recently released *Faith's Corner* (2006) has caught critics off guard: made extremely quickly and cheaply (estimates suggest it was done in less than two weeks, and for something like R1 million – a small fraction of the time and cost of *Yesterday*); shot on out-of-date film stock giving it a bleached tonal palette, and using a hand-cranked camera which produces occasional jerks; replacing dialogue with the kind of title cards used in silent films; its soundtrack dominated by a Philip Glass score; the film is experimental, pared-down, even minimalist, deliberately anachronistic, and disconcerting for a number of viewers. The subject matter represents yet another pressing social problem – racialised urban poverty, homelessness and unemployment – which, while it may lack the somewhat apocalyptic dimensions of the AIDS pandemic, nevertheless requires addressing urgently. It is tempting to see Roodt's approach to the question as quintessentially Brechtian: like the city dwellers who fail to see Faith and her children begging on the street corner, cinema audiences are all too likely not to 'see' the problem – to examine it, understand it, respond to it appropriately – because we all know about urban poverty, we have heard about it so many times . . . and a sharp course of defamiliarisation – formal, visual and aural, at the very least – may go some way to rectifying that kind of unhelpful automatic response.

Historical, social and cultural context

As mentioned in the previous section, the history and current circumstances of film production, and cinema more generally, in South Africa are paradoxical and contradictory. For instance, there is the country's status as both first and last: on the one hand, the very first film screenings on the African continent were in South Africa in 1895, and, on the other, there is the fact that, in the opinion of critics such as Lindiwe Dovey, it is only a hundred years later that South Africa can be considered as a maker of truly 'African' films. In addition, although this entry into the production of properly African films is a result of the advent of democratic government and a

notionally unified nation, the film industry itself remains divided and fragmented. A further contradiction resides in the fact that this is the most tech-
nologically advanced film industry in Africa, yet it lacks a level of filmic
output to match its level of technological development. (The fact that there
was a dramatic decline in production, from approximately 170 feature films
per year in the late 1980s to fewer than ten in 1994, no doubt reflects a
certain level of investor uncertainty in the declining years of the apartheid
system, as well as, perhaps, the recognition that the historical moment represented the end of the line for a particular kind of white filmmaking.) In
addition, the strikingly beautiful country of South Africa markets itself to
the global film industry as anywhere but itself, with different parts of the
country appearing in films as location doubles for anywhere from Britain to
the Swiss Alps to Hong Kong.

Some of these contradictions are certainly explicable in terms both of the
exigencies of the contemporary economics of filmmaking in South Africa
and of the complexities of its cinematic history. That history has – unsurprisingly, in view of the colonialism and racism which have been the
country's lot for the past four centuries – been one of white dominance,
though there have been some significant black interventions. One of the earliest and most important of these was by the remarkable Solomon T. 'Sol'
Plaatje, one of the founders of what became the ANC, journalist, author of
the important political study *Native Life in South Africa* (1917) and the even
more important *Mhudi*, the first novel in English by a black African (written
1917–20 but not published until 1930). Plaatje was also part of the New
African Movement, inspired by the post-emancipation New Negroes in the
United States, and similarly concerned that black people should have an
important role in modernity and social progress. Part of his clear-sighted
approach to modernity was an awareness of the possibilities represented by
cinema. In the mid-1920s, Plaatje travelled the country, showing a range of
films, both informational and entertaining, relating particularly to the
achievements of black people in the United States, to audiences which were
largely though not exclusively black. Despite the success of his 'bioscope'
tours – acknowledged in the short film *Come See the Bioscope* made by
Lance Grewer and Zaharia Rapola in 1994 – Plaatje's project ran directly
counter to prevailing white ideology which held that black people were fundamentally unsuited to film: culturally distanced from it, intellectually incapable of appreciating it, temperamentally likely to be corrupted by it. As
such, there was a struggle to be waged over the screening of films for
Africans. Bhekizizwe Petersen, for example, argues that:

> the basis for the subsequent spread and popularity of cinematic screenings
> among Africans can be traced back to the early 1920s, and in many respects it
> was due to the efforts of Phillips and AMB [American Missionary Board]. Even
> before the opening of the BMSC [Bantu Men's Social Club], Phillips and
> Bridgman were publicly acknowledged as 'the pioneers of the pictorial educa-
> tion of the Native'. (Petersen 2003: 38)

Is important to note, however, that the supposedly benevolent paternalistic efforts of the American missionaries were precisely premised on the undermining of schemes such as Plaatje's:

> Plaatje's project of introducing some of the fundamental principles and achievements of modernity to Africans through film was perhaps destined to failure because of the activities of the American Missionary Board. Through its leading ideologues, Dr F.B. Bridgman and the Reverend Ray Phillips, the organisation was already introducing films in the mining compounds of Johannesburg – films meant as entertainment but also as an instrument of white superiority and a means of controlling the morals of Africans. (Masilela 2003: 20)

The fact that these films were also heavily censored, particularly to remove negative representations of white people (as criminals, drunkards or prostitutes, for example), further indicates the ideology driving the particularly circumscribed introduction of film for black South Africans.

For the next three-quarters of a century, and despite the continuing interest of important black intellectuals such as Herbert Dhlomo in the 1940s, and the likes of Can Themba, Bloke Modisane and Lewis Nkosi associated with *Drum* magazine in the 1950s, the 'whiteness' – in a variety of ways – of South African cinema constituted its dominant characteristic. The whiteness, of course, was there from the very start: the original screening in 1895 was for a very restricted white audience; the first filming carried out in South Africa was of the 'white' Anglo-Boer War; while the first significant film made in the country, *De Voortrekkers* (1916), glorifies the qualities of the Boers, culminating in their slaughter of three thousand Zulus at the Battle of Blood River in 1838, their historical triumph over black adversaries (supposedly) constituting the retrospective grounds for their contemporary oppression and dispossession of the descendants of those adversaries.

Following the coming to power of the Afrikaner National Party in 1948 and formalisation of apartheid as a system, the imbrication of whiteness in dominance through the combination of the in-country production of films which offered sanitised, laudatory representations of Afrikaners and the censoring of films, especially those to be screened to non-white audiences, intensified. In 1963, the Minister of the Interior offered arguments in support of censorship which would not be out of place a century or two earlier in their simple racist dismissiveness:

> [we] know what sort of film it would be to show to a race that has not yet reached the level of civilisation that we have reached . . . things which they cannot understand should not be shown to them, and . . . there are some films which can be exhibited more safely to a white child of fourteen years than to an adult Bantu. (Quoted in Tomaselli 1989: 22)

The system of the state subsidy of films introduced in the 1950s further supported the position of the white minority, as Martin Botha argues:

> Since 1956 and the introduction of a regulated subsidy system, government and big business have collaborated to manipulate cinema in South Africa. Ideology

and capital came together to create a national cinema that would reflect South Africa during the Verwoerdian regime. However, it was initially a cinema for whites only, and predominantly Afrikaans. Of the 60 films made between 1956 and 1962, 43 were in Afrikaans. Four were bilingual and the remaining 13 were in English. (Botha 1995)

No one would expect the apartheid regime to promote films for, about – or, still less, made by – black Africans, and that was by and large the case. Nevertheless, in line with the racialised divisions instituted by apartheid, and as a counterpart to the cosy myths of cuddly Afrikanerdom peddled by the dominant cinema, the government in the 1970s inaugurated a separate 'Bantu' subsection of the film industry, with mainly white directors making substandard and appropriately sanitised films to be shown to black audiences. Given the absence of proper cinemas for black people – Soweto, for example, had a mere two cinemas for a population of some three million – these films were screened in schools, community centres and churches. Even when films were, for a time, made for the majority population in South Africa, the racist bias of the state system meant that prior to 1977 a 'white' film could earn an unlimited amount by way of subsidy, while a 'black' film was restricted to a meagre R45,000, and, even when a limit for 'white' films was later introduced, it was 15 times as much as for black films. (As with all race-related categorisation in apartheid South Africa, the colour-coding of films was not straightforward, and white directors could find their work labelled as 'black', with all the negative financial implications which that entailed.)

During the period of apartheid, little happened – or was allowed to happen – to disturb the status quo embodied in the film industry, or the social status quo as represented in the industry's products. Even *u-Deliwe* (1975), the first film to be made in Zulu, by Simon Sabela, the first black South African director, a work which might therefore potentially disturb ideological assumptions or challenge norms of filmmaking, proved so ideologically assimilable that it qualified for state subsidy. Work critical of apartheid tended either to be made clandestinely or to come from the small independent sector, which received no state subsidy and was therefore not manipulable in the same way as the industry at large. Notable examples of the former include *Come Back, Africa* (1959) directed by the American Lionel Rogosin, *Mapantsula* (1988) by Oliver Schmidt and Darrell Roodt's *Place of Weeping* (1986). *Come Back, Africa*, for which Rogosin obtained permission with the promise that he was making a pro-apartheid musical, and which then had to wait 30 years before it could be shown publicly in South Africa, is a landmark film in a number of ways. Not the least of these is the fact that it portrays the increasing urbanisation of black life in South Africa – while still a struggle – as more than a simple, inevitable process of decline and degradation (the problematic perspective of, for example, Alan Paton's *Cry, the Beloved Country* to which we will return later in the chapter). In particular, the fact that black urban life, instantiated here by the

Sophiatown district of Johannesburg, possessed a cultural and intellectual richness ignored – if not summarily dismissed – by the regime and its followers is one of the film's major oppositional statements. As part of the demonstration of that fact, Sophiatown intellectuals Can Themba, Bloke Modisane and Lewis Nkosi were involved in writing the script, and, in a striking interpolation of the 'real' into the fictional narrative of the central character Zachariah, appear in the film, discussing, among other things, the failings of white liberal culture, epitomised by Alan Paton and *Cry, the Beloved Country*.

As far as the achievements of the independent sector are concerned, a number of films critical of apartheid were made in the 1970s representing different constituencies: Afrikaans, white Anglophone and black. Among the best of the first group is Jans Rautenbach's *Jannie Totsiens* (*Goodbye Johnny*) (1970), an allegory of the condition of the nation set in a mental institution, and which, like all the best allegories, managed to evade the attentions of the state censor. Typical of the second group are the collaborative films made by director Ross Devenish and playwright Athol Fugard, *Boesman and Lena* (1973), *The Guest* (1977) and *Marigolds in August* (1980). Although Fugard can be seen as embodying the problems and contradictions of liberalism, which will be examined in the final section of this chapter in relation to Roodt, and which typically consist of not going far enough in terms of socio-political critique, he found himself under attack by the producer Emil Nofal, who worked with Rautenbach, precisely for going too far in 'siding with the underdog', which Nofal, remarkably, considered to be the easy option. In the area of black filmmaking, the playwright Gibson Kente adapted the stage musical *How Long (Must We Suffer)?* (1976), which, politically far removed from Sabela's *u-Deliwe*, resulted in the arrest of Kente and the banning of the film.

Regarding the next decade, Martin Botha notes that while almost a thousand feature films were made in South Africa between 1979 and 1991, most of these were at best mediocre, and the 20 to 30 'remarkable indigenous local feature films' which appeared in those years were almost entirely the work of independent filmmakers. The fact that Botha's very short list includes three of Darrell Roodt's films (*Place of Weeping, The Stick* and *Jobman*) – which Botha actually categorises as a trilogy – signals a level of critical regard not always in evidence where Roodt's films are concerned. For Botha, the work of these independent directors constitutes the beginning of a new cinema able to generate a critique of society and to form the potential nucleus of a properly national cinema in the post-apartheid era.

Certainly, the issue of a national cinema remains a vexed one in the contemporary South African context. Questions debated include whether such a thing as a national cinema is possible or desirable, and, if so, what its formal, aesthetic, cultural and political components might be. Although he more than most people has been involved in the long struggle to create a national film industry, Anant Singh – surprisingly, no doubt – does not believe that such a thing yet exists. For Martin Botha, it is the historical process of the fragmentation of the industry – its division along racial lines, the inequality of its funding, its flight into mediocrity – which means that there is still nothing which might be appropriately identified as South African cinema. From a rather different position, Jacqueline Maingard also rejects the idea of a national cinema:

> There is no national cinema in South Africa, even though some cinema might seem – or seek – to represent or evoke a sense of 'the national': recent examples are *Mandela* (1995), *Cry, the Beloved Country* (1995), and *Fools* (1997). In proposing this topic, therefore, the underlying question is: Why frame South African film and television as national? The easy answer is that democracy is being made in South Africa and it is mediated through the images presented in film and on television. (Maingard 2003: 115)

This rather begs the question of whether a more fully achieved democratic dispensation will allow for, or even create, a fully national cinema, but for many the implication would no doubt be that it could or should.

The arguments concerning the future of the film industry in South Africa replay, perhaps inevitably, some of the debates over the future of African cinema in general, and one of the issues frequently raised centres on 'political' or socially conscious cinema versus cinema of entertainment. According to an article in *SA Film*, South African filmmakers continually 'fail' their audiences by choosing to make films which are insufficiently entertaining. The occasion for the author's attack is the release of Darrell Roodt's *Yesterday*:

> *Yesterday* doesn't contain any elements that would get a majority of the cinema-going audience excited. It does, however, contain elements that would rather make them stay at home. The synopsis reads like a high school maths textbook, and it immediately sounds preachy. It's too didactic and too concerned in getting a 'message' across. And, in my opinion, this is where the majority, if not all of South African post-Apartheid cinema fails. (Oberholzer 2004)

Oberholzer's recipe for success in the midst of all this filmmaking failure is to copy imported comedy-dramas, though he neglects to say what kind of comedy about AIDS would 'get a majority of the cinema-going audience excited'.

It is, perhaps, just conceivable that if Oberholzer is correct, and all that audiences want from a film is escapism, then a comedy about AIDS might indeed be a success, though so far no one has shown any signs of wanting to make one – indeed, apart from Roodt and Tsitsi Dangarembga from Zimbabwe, no one in southern Africa, it seems, wants to make a film about AIDS at all. While the pandemic is obviously a regional, continental and global problem, it is also inescapably a national one for South Africa. More than 70 per cent of the approximately 40 million people globally who are now infected live in sub-Saharan Africa, there are over 13 million AIDS orphans and in South Africa an estimated 20 per cent of the adult population have HIV/AIDS, making it the country with the highest number of HIV carriers in the world. Faced with the daily disaster which this represents, cultural producers of all kinds have been remarkably slow to respond appropriately. Roodt, however, is in no doubt about the scale of the problem which AIDS represents for his country. For both Roodt and the producer Anant Singh, AIDS has replaced apartheid – which they spent so many years opposing in the films they made – as the fundamental destructive force threatening the people of South Africa.

Interestingly, in spite of the criticisms made by Oberholzer, producing a 'message' film is what Roodt most emphatically denies he has done in *Yesterday*. 'But this is not a message movie by any stretch of the imagination. This hasn't got any answers in it. This is just a story about a simple person in a very difficult environment, and how she has to deal with it. So it's not a message movie. It's very important to understand that, because movies can't solve the problems of the world' (Roodt 2006). While 'the problems of the world' may be a little too much to tackle, *Yesterday*'s potential to help in the fight against AIDS is marked by plans on the part of Nelson Mandela's AIDS foundation, which helped in the film's financing, to tour the film countrywide, particularly in rural areas, screening it for free – a useful and timely reminder of the social and political effects of cultural products, whatever the avowed intentions of their authors may be.

The films

The overwhelming historical and political presence in the development of filmmaking in South Africa is the apartheid state, but no other South African director has responded to that fact in the same way or to the same extent as Darrell Roodt. Arguably, the best of his films prior to *Yesterday* – *Cry, the Beloved Country*, *Sarafina!*, *Place of Weeping*, *The Stick*, *Jobman* – are all in their different ways attacks on the regime and its system of 'colonialism of a special type': oppressive, divisive, racist, murderous. The theory of 'colonialism of a special type' has a particular history in the context of the alliance between the ANC and the SACP (South African Communist Party), and is not uncontested as an analytical concept, but it remains a useful reminder of the differential forms of colonialism. In the words of the ANC:

> The South African National Liberation Movement, the ANC and its allies, characterise the South African social formation as a system of 'internal colonialism' or 'colonialism of a special type'. What is 'special' or different about the colonial system as it obtains in South Africa is that there is no spatial separation between the colonising power (the white minority state) and the colonised black people. But in every respect, the features of classic colonialism are the hallmark of the relations that obtain between the black majority and white minority. (http://www.anc.org.za/ancdocs/history/special.html)

Roodt's anti-apartheid films clearly belong in the tradition of African films of anticolonial struggle, but could be seen as simultaneously constituting a 'special type' within that tradition as they work towards the belated emergence of a South African postcolonialism (of a special type, no doubt, since the defining feature of its difference – the spatial non-separation – has not, unlike in so many other countries, changed with the moment of decolonisation). One of the things to note is the variety of forms in which Roodt has articulated his opposition to apartheid: *Place of Weeping* is a straightforward realist narrative in a broadly thriller/adventure genre; *Sarafina!* is an adaptation of a successful musical, which crosses generic boundaries as it mixes the light-hearted and 'stagy' aspects with the grimly realist ones; like *City of Blood*, though here in the context of border wars rather than urban crime, *The Stick* dissolves the real and the (African) supernatural in its thriller/horror format; finally, *Cry, the Beloved Country* adapts the most successful South African novel of all time, and is in dialogue with the famous 1951 Korda film version.

In a similar way, the forms and effects of apartheid, as well as the methods used to resist them, vary in the different films. *Place of Weeping*, for example, centres on an individual murder which focuses and epitomises the brutal collusions on which the system thrives. Beating to death a black former employee found stealing chickens would not have presented a problem for the farmer van Rensburg, had he used the police and judiciary to cover his tracks rather than merely ignoring the event, but with the (unrelated) arrival of an investigative journalist, things begin to unravel. In the end, breaking the silence which surrounds the killing occurs through the efforts of one courageous black individual, but it is a collective, and armed, response which brings about the final retribution.

At the other extreme from *Place of Weeping*, both generically and spatially, is *Sarafina!*. In spatial terms, the remote rural setting is replaced by the streets and alleys of the Soweto township, the farm by the schoolroom. It is the generic shifts, however, which have caused critics the greatest problems with *Sarafina!*, and they remain fundamentally divided over whether the format of the musical offers an image of resistance to apartheid which has its appropriately joyous and celebratory side, or whether having song and dance sequences in the style of *Fame* simply trivialises the experiences of the people of Soweto at the time of the uprising, while not even presenting an accurate picture of culture, especially musical culture, in the township in the mid-1970s. Oppression and resistance are both, appropriately for the historical circumstances, collective, rather than individual as in *Place of Weeping*, and in the front ranks of the resistance are the schoolchildren of Soweto, of whom Sarafina is one. Her subsequent arrest and torture are shocking, though whether this is because or in spite of the shift in genre and mood from the light-hearted sequences of singing and dancing remains a matter of debate.

One of the things which *Sarafina!* and *Place of Weeping* have in common, as well as sharing with films such as *Yesterday* and *Faith's Corner*, is the presence of a strong black woman as the central character (and in what risks looking like favouritism or typecasting – or perhaps just playing to your strengths – three of the four are played by the remarkable Leleti Khumalo). To that extent, they offer some diminishment of the overriding whiteness of South Africa cinema, and mark a significant improvement on films such as *Cry Freedom, A Dry White Season* and *A World Apart*; which were the ones articulating South African experience to a global cinema audience in the late 1980s. Although neither *Yesterday* nor *Faith's Corner* deals with apartheid, they both, as indicated in previous sections, tackle extremely difficult contemporary problems, and in each case the central female character's fortitude is called upon in response to poverty and hunger, torture, terminal illness and death.

Gracie in *Place of Weeping* wages a one-woman struggle against the oppressions of apartheid. Lonely, threatened, misunderstood even by her own people, she nevertheless persists in her efforts both to expose the system for what it is and to encourage others to stand up for themselves in similar ways. Her approach – quiet, non-violent, law-abiding, to that extent coded as 'female' in the terms of the film – is contrasted with that of Lucky, leader of the armed guerrilla group hiding in the hills and personification of the 'male' approach. Although it is Gracie's approach that the film seems to lend weight to, and although when she and Lucky argue over tactics it appears that Lucky's stance of (badly) armed rebellion is probably futile, if not suicidal, nevertheless it is he and his men who exact retribution for the murder, while Gracie is last seen hiding in a disused building with the black woman servant she has persuaded to give evidence against the farmer, as the boots of the Afrikaner thugs hunting them down draw ever nearer. (Whether we are meant to infer that they are discovered and killed is not clear, and this narrative ellipsis is foremost among the film's 'arty' moments, along with non-diegetic shots of landscapes, buildings and sunsets.) However, if Gracie's approach is coded female, what might we call that of the white clergyman, Father Egan? He also resists apartheid by sheltering and giving rudimentary medical treatment to wounded guerrillas, but time and again delays taking any action to bring the killer to justice, and to that extent is even more passive than her.

Sarafina! also offers models of 'female' resistance, especially in the shape of Mary Masembuko, the inspirational history teacher at Sarafina's school. While Sarafina's nascent political consciousness results in her becoming involved in the group killing of Sabela, the local black policeman who symbolises betrayal of the community and its aspirations, Mary adopts an ethically more complex position: strongly opposed to violence, but prepared to fight because she will not tolerate anyone giving their life for her, she nevertheless also refuses to kill as part of the struggle. After Mary's death in custody, and her own arrest and torture, Sarafina is reconciled with her mother, whom she now recognises as 'a hero' because of her inner strength and ability to survive.

Like Sarafina's mother's, *Yesterday's* resistance is not to any political system: it is quite simply a case of not allowing herself to be defeated by all that life throws at her. Daily existence is already hard, with no money and a husband absent for long periods working in the mines. That, combined with debilitating illness, subsequently diagnosed as HIV, would be too much for many people to bear, but there is more: Yesterday's husband savagely beats her when she confronts him with the fact of her illness, yet he returns to be nursed by her when his own condition becomes critical; when the nature of his illness becomes known to the village, he and Yesterday are ostracised by their ignorant and fearful community; and the 'hospital' Yesterday builds for her dying husband fails to do what hospitals are supposed to do, and provide a cure. Through all this, Yesterday is sustained by her own quiet tenacity and, above all, by the desire to see her daughter Beauty begin the education she herself never had.

In the ANC document quoted at the beginning of this section, the defining characteristic of colonialism in South Africa was cited as being 'the lack of spatial separation' between the coloniser and colonised. That is simultaneously quite correct and something of an oversimplification. The definition is correct in so far as two antagonistic populations coexist within the boundaries of the nation state, and to that extent are not spatially separated; however, it oversimplifies because one of the central strategies of apartheid was obviously to maximise separation between black and white in every conceivable way, and above all, perhaps, in the realm of the spatial. In the manner classically analysed by Fanon, colonialism is particularly concerned to control the land as fully as possible, which involves dispossessing and removing the native people – including, in the case of South Africa, ignoring legal documents guaranteeing black ownership of land. The production of 'good' space (ordered and inhabited by whites) and 'bad' black space, as separate from the former as possible, is also part of this process.

> For a colonised people the most essential value, because the most concrete, is first and foremost the land: the land which will bring them bread and, above all, dignity. But this dignity has nothing to do with the dignity of the human individual: for that human individual has never heard tell of it. All that the native has seen in his country is that they can freely arrest him, beat him, starve him: and no professor of ethics, no priest has ever come to be beaten in his place, nor to share their bread with him. (Fanon 1967: 34)

Aesthetically at least, the land is clearly of great importance to Roodt: his South African films typically start with some evocation – frequently in very long takes – of the landscape, most often of the beauty of Kwa Zulu Natal, though sometimes, as in *Jobman*, of the more arid and challenging Karoo. However, as one might expect by now in relation to Roodt, opinion is divided over this aspect of his work: some critics find the use of the landscape powerful or inspirational; in the journal *Africultures*, Olivier Barlet, on the other hand, can talk dismissively about 'décors de carte postale' (Barlet 2002).

Ideologically, too, the land is enormously significant, especially in a film like *Cry, the Beloved Country*. What we see rather less of is the political importance of the land, at least in terms of its importance to the colonised people in the sense outlined by Fanon. *Place of Weeping* is the principal exception here, and part of what drives Lucky and his men to armed rebellion is a desire to recover the land of which they have been robbed. Conversely, what we do see is how important the land is to the white usurpers, the racist assumptions which underpin their control of it, and the brutal lengths to which they are prepared to go to retain that control. Part of the problem which Jobman represents is his refusal, in Fanon's terms, to 'know his place', and his necessarily unspoken – he is deaf and dumb – though potentially revolutionary demand for freer access to the land threatens the very bases of the system.

Overcoming the contradictions of liberalism? – *Cry, the Beloved Country*

The year 1995 saw the release of the first major film of the post-apartheid or postcolonial period (*Cry, the Beloved Country*) which just happened to be an adaptation of – in the words of South Africa's first Nobel laureate for literature, Nadine Gordimer – 'the most influential South African novel ever written', and the powerful combination of the iconic novel and the iconic moment – the inauguration of post-apartheid South Africa – make this a film which demands scrutiny. The novel, however, already had a long history of dividing, if not completely polarising, opinion, which Roodt's adaptation continued, albeit in sometimes different ways, and, before turning to an analysis of the film, it is worth briefly outlining some of the ideological contradictions and limitations, both in the novel and in the wider discourse of liberalism, which constitute the material with which Roodt is working, and from which he constructs his own (variously contradictory) text.

Written two years before the National Party victory of 1948 and published in that year, the novel predates the formal introduction of apartheid but is nevertheless a product of a world in which racial hierarchisation, segregation and oppression were the norm. The fact that it was an international publishing success of remarkable proportions – millions of copies were sold during its author Alan Paton's lifetime – gave it an unrivalled status in forming world opinion about conditions of existence in South Africa. As a result, the ideology embodied in the novel, as well as in the two film adaptations, is a matter of particular interest. The novel tells the story of two men from rural Kwa Zulu Natal, one black, one white, neighbours but not acquaintances. Stephen Kumalo is an Anglican minister, John Jarvis a wealthy farmer; each of their sons dies a violent death in Johannesburg: Arthur Jarvis is shot by Absalom Kumalo during a failed robbery attempt; Absalom is tried and hanged for the murder. In the space between the two deaths, the fathers meet and achieve a level of mutual understanding and reconciliation.

The novel's ideological stance is overtly both Christian and liberal, reflecting the core beliefs of the author, and it is the combined effects and implications of these which have polarised opinion. Although the Liberal Party set up by Paton was made illegal by apartheid legislation in the 1960s, liberalism obviously continues as an often-criticised discourse in public life. For some, in the South African context, the kind of liberalism enshrined in the novel appeared as the sensible, rational middle ground between extremes of increasing black and white intransigence. However, as mentioned earlier in the chapter, for black intellectuals in the years following its publication, its significance was altogether different:

> they tended to approach *Cry, the Beloved Country* as a negative forebear, a book that clarified their sense of where it was they were not coming from. Modisane, Nkosi, Themba, Nakasa and Mphahlele all inveighed against Paton for demonising city life, and adopted his leading man, Rev. Stephen Kumalo, as an anti-hero who incarnated the unctuous religiosity, the deference, and the urban incompetence that were antithetical to all they professed. (Nixon 1994: 27)

Perhaps the most famous, and most trenchant, attack on liberalism was launched by Steve Biko in 'Black Consciousness and the Quest for a True Humanity', which also includes a reference to Paton: 'Thus after years of silence we are able hear the familiar voice of Alan Paton saying . . . "Perhaps apartheid is worth a try." "At whose expense, Dr Paton?" asks an intelligent black journalist' (Biko 1979: 89).

Such divisions of opinion could be seen as reflecting the contradictory, internally self-divided nature of liberalism itself. For instance, liberalism has historically been suspicious of traditional forms of authority, progressive, modernising, reformist and even, in its own way, on the side of the 'little people'. At the same time, however, many of the seemingly positive claims made in the name of justice and legality, individual rights and freedoms, civil society and economic progress, were problematically abstract, inherently limited or ultimately conservative in their impact. As Stuart Hall comments, 'The liberal commitment to individualism has always been hard to reconcile with the idea of a mass democracy . . . This is yet another tension in liberalism – between its universalistic claims on behalf of all citizens and its alignment with the interests of particular sections of society' (Hall 1986: 43). In the case of the novel, the fundamental liberal scepticism towards authority is overridden by a combination of deep respect for the authority enshrined in the law, as well as a sense of obedience (in many ways anti-liberal) derived from Christianity.

Roodt is certainly aware of both the novel and the 1951 adaptation as texts which present various problems and challenges. In answer to questions regarding the 'colonialism' of earlier versions, he replied, 'I kind of agree with that . . . but we're now allowed to approach the book with a Nineties perspective. The original film was colonial, the characters one-dimensional, divided between good old British upper-class guys and noble peasants, a bit too rah-rah. I'm making it more human' (Pretorius 1994: 34). The desire to humanise is an important indication that Roodt is perhaps doing more with his choice of film than simply aiming to reinstate liberalism as valorised perspective for the postcolonial period. It is a position that finds favour even with the radicals: Haile Gerima, for example, in a recent attack on the enduring whiteness of South African cinema, offers 'the human perspective' as the way forward for all filmmakers, black and white (Gerima 2003). Having said that, however, much depends on the ability to differentiate 'humanising' from the excessive focus on the individual which is central to liberalism, and even then, there remain powerful echoes of earlier forms of liberalism such as that of E. M. Forster, who famously argued that the British Empire in India would govern better if its administrators and officers were simply more (humanly) polite to those whom they ruled. The (apparently) liberal idea of white trusteeship – politely and respectfully expressed – of the kind that the novel espouses is bluntly rejected by Nadine Gordimer:

> It's not uncommon, now, to see quoted as 'liberal' white utterances the sort of white-leadership-with-justice statements that any South African recognises immediately as coming from people who are not and never have been liberals, but are good United Party members. To advocate a pat on the head instead of the *sjambok* [whip] on the back is not to be liberal. (Gordimer 1988: 100)

One of the most intractable problems for liberalism in the South African context (and one of its central contradictions) is the question of violence – starting perhaps with 'the *sjambok* on the back'. For Paton, accepting violence – however attractive or necessary it might appear – automatically excluded you from the ranks of the liberals. Whether such a position was formulated because of, or in spite of, the violence in South Africa is not clear, but it certainly put Paton and his Liberal Party at odds with the ANC, particularly after the latter accepted the need for violent struggle in 1961. At the same time, and despite this intransigent rejection of violence, Paton was able to speak in defence of Mandela and the others at the Rivonia treason trials in 1964, where he argued that the only two choices facing the defendants were 'to bow their heads and submit, or to resist by force' – though he did not go on to make clear which of the two he felt was the appropriate choice.

In *Cry, the Beloved Country*, Absalom's act of violence – unpremeditated murder – is (at least in the state's view) appropriately followed by its own act of fully premeditated judicial killing. While this reciprocity of violence might seem normal, or at least officially sanctioned, a more radical analysis of reciprocal forms of violence is offered by Arthur Jarvis's final article. Here, in a manner which anticipates, though it does not go as far as, Fanon's discussion in *The Wretched of the Earth* a few years later, the way in which white violence calls forth black violence is set out, and this is among those revelatory passages whose content shocks John Jarvis out of his white supremacist complacency, a fact which Roodt carefully emphasises through Richard Harris's almost incredulous repetition of key phrases. It is also one of the moments where the liberal position enters into contradiction. On the one hand, liberalism is premised on individual agency and responsibility: Absalom is deemed responsible for his violent actions and must be punished accordingly. On the other hand, the systemic critique of racially grounded state violence sketched out here by a white liberal provides a form of knowledge which renders classic liberal positions untenable, as well as opening on to something more like a postcolonial understanding of the functioning of violence. In emphasising its institutionalised nature, Roodt is moving beyond the liberal view of individual moral failure as causation.

Arthur Jarvis's assessment is backed up by a small but crucial interpolation by Roodt. In the multi-layered scene which is Arthur's funeral, where the principal action is John Jarvis's refusal to shake the hand of a black man, the soundtrack gives us a reading of perhaps the most famous passage from the novel, including the phrase which forms the title, but Roodt also intercuts a reportage-style sequence showing white police attacking and savagely beating black people. This is important, because it is one of the relatively rare occasions on which Roodt can be seen as transcending positions laid out by liberalism and its inappropriate individualism, but also because it provides an unexpected mode of justification for one particular individual in the narrative. In his trial, Absalom's defence is reduced again and again to the phrase 'I was afraid'. This appears weak, unbelievable, and an unacceptable excuse for carrying and using a loaded revolver, despite the recurrence, in the voiceover at the funeral for example, of portentous but unspecific phrases such as 'There is fear in the land, and fear in the hearts of all who live there'. What Roodt's brief interpolation offers, however, is a graphic explanation of exactly why there is fear in the land, and why a young black man might go in fear of his life, to the extent of carrying a loaded gun.

One of the phrases to which commentators frequently return is spoken by the young Reverend Msimangu: 'I have this great fear in my heart that one day, when the white man turns to loving, he will find that we have turned to hating.' This image of white moral progress juxtaposed to black regression is ideologically very powerful, and altogether negative. It is also contradicted by the lessons learned by Sarafina. After her arrest and torture she says: 'They called it "teaching us a lesson" . . . What was their lesson? To be like them? To torture and kill? To hate them more than they hate us?' As far as there is black hatred and violence – seen, for example, in the communal killing of the black policeman Sabela – it is, she realises, something in which they have been carefully and brutally schooled by the whites.

The land is another area of contradiction for Paton and, consequently, Roodt. For Paton, the countryside operates as the spatial and moral antithesis of Johannesburg which has swallowed up and corrupted three members of Kumalo's family. The land, and not the city, therefore, is the proper place for black people to live, and one of Kumalo's final hopes is a project of rural regeneration. Unfortunately, on the one hand, the land was becoming less and less a 'proper' place to live in the 1940s in worsening conditions of drought and rural decline, and, on the other, the idea that black people belonged in the countryside, not in cities, was one of the central tenets of apartheid. Although much of Roodt's film takes place in the city, the scenes of the Ixopo mountains are among his most beautifully shot. In addition, perhaps as a narrative counterpart to this aestheticising of the landscape, Roodt removes any mention of the difficult conditions facing those living on the land. Whether his idyllic landscape reproduces the novel's dominant pastoralism or not, Roodt certainly compounds Paton's antagonism towards black people in the cities and the mass political movements generated from their oppressed circumstances. The character who combines and embodies this is Kumalo's brother John: bad in the novel, worse in the film; betrayer of his brother and, particularly, of his nephew Absalom; a rabble-rousing politician and empty orator.

Given what we have already noted of his other films, Roodt's apparent wariness towards politics here looks surprising – even contradictory. It could, however, be seen as the product of a number of factors. Firstly, there is the constraining effect of Paton's ideological antipathies embodied in the novel. Secondly, there is his own tendency to focus, and focalise, political issues through individuals rather than collectivities (which has its own particular liberal inflection), the only significant exception to this being the students of Soweto in *Sarafina!*. Thirdly, there is his conviction that the era of a certain kind of cultural politics has ended; as he said in an interview, 'Confrontational protest films are over. *Friends* was the last nail in the coffin of that kind of cinema. Finish! Finish! Enough now' (Pretorius 1994). There is also the suggestion – a position shared with other postcolonial African filmmakers, as we have already seen – that politics can be done differently in the contemporary moment; indeed, for Roodt, what he defines as 'social' questions, rather than political – such as the AIDS pandemic – are the ones now requiring attention.

For Roodt, Paton's novel is 'the one definitive classic about contemporary South Africa, and still surprisingly relevant' – a relevance which embraces past, present and future: 'Things have changed. Some people argue not, but there is a cultural shift. People want to examine their history, their roots, to look at where they are now. It's very important to make films to do this' (Pretorius 1994). The urgent re-examination of history is obviously one element which connects Roodt to many other postcolonial filmmakers, but his handling of it in *Cry, the Beloved Country* may not be as successful as he might wish. In one of the extremely rare academic discussions of Roodt,[1] in the context of the two film adaptations of the novel Mark Beittel examines what he sees as the problematic distance between Roodt's desire for a positive re-historicising and what the film actually delivers.

> The intention to historicise Paton's parable of good versus evil is made clear early in the film with the caption: 'Natal, South Africa – 1946' and by the fact that Jarvis's metamorphosis is centred on such key words as 'memorials' and 'tributes' . . . Noting that Arthur's thinking is reduced to a preoccupation with memorials and his life is translated into a tribute to his father, we see clearly that this film is dominated by a conception of history that is monumental – it freezes

the process of the present continuous reinterpretation of the past into a series
of neatly connected 'facts' and magnified, isolated 'events' . . . Monumental
history involves a remembering of the past that reduces and eliminates even as
it magnifies and invents, in order to create a consistent – ultimately, a black and
white – tale. (Beittel 2003: 84–5)

This is an interesting and in many ways persuasive argument, but it is also
possible to read what Roodt is doing here in a way which indicates a more
complex politics and historiography. Part of the problem in Beittel's critique
stems from what one could call a 'monumentalising' of language, taking
terms like 'memorial' and 'tribute' in rather too static a way. Arthur Jarvis's
question 'What sort of memorial do we want?' points not to the calm con-
templation of the future monument, but – as the question which follows,
'What sort of memorial do we deserve?' makes clear – to the anguished uncertainty surrounding its nature, even its very existence. The manner in which
white rule will be remembered has yet to be determined, and it is a process of
(re-) construction in which both black and white have a role to play. Arthur
Jarvis's own assessment is thoroughly pessimistic: 'when posterity comes to
judge us, it will consign us to the sewers of history'. Although the challenge
to white rule in 1946 may appear somewhat tenuous, nevertheless the growth
of organised black resistance visible in the working-class meetings and the
bus boycott is sufficient to make someone like Arthur Jarvis foresee the possible end of racial dominance; for him, white rule is certainly not a matter of
a thousand-year Reich. His questions have even more force in 1995, however,
on the threshold of the postcolonial era, with apartheid dismantled and an
unparalleled process of national remembering about to begin.

Two points remain to be made briefly in connection with this argument,
firstly in relation to 'Arthur's thinking is reduced to a preoccupation with
memorials and his life is translated into a tribute to his father'. Arthur's
querying how whites will be remembered is obviously not the same as 'a preoccupation with memorials', even if his father does rather focus on that. In
the same way, Arthur's life constitutes an altogether contradictory 'tribute'
to his father, since it was based on concepts of human equality which go
beyond basic liberal notions, and was utterly removed from those precepts
according to which his father lives. Secondly, Beittel argues that James Jarvis
literally buys his son's memorial by asking that a stone in his memory be
placed in Kumalo's church, whose restoration he is paying for. Another way
of reading this, however, this would be to weigh the ideological significance
of the fact that the only memorial to the son of a prominent wealthy white
father will be located in a humble, isolated, rural black church, as a possible
intimation of a modest, united future for the people of the country.

The novel of *Cry, the Beloved Country* is the product of the last moment
when such a modest united future might have been possible, before the arrival
of half a century of apartheid divisions and brutal oppressions; the 1995 film,
read optimistically, is the image of a new moment of possibility, epitomised
for many in the Truth and Reconciliation Commission (the 'unparalleled

process of national remembering' mentioned above) set up in the same year. Reconciliation, embodied above all in the two fathers, John Jarvis and Stephen Kumalo, is clearly central to the novel's ideology; it is also quintessentially liberal in its individualism. The reconciliation to which the film looks forward is national in its scope, a process which in many ways transcends the limits and the contradictions of liberalism – even if it does, contradictorily, reinscribe them in others. On the ending of the film, Mark Beittel has this to say:

> The final evidence of Roodt's failure to 'retell history' is that his film, just like Korda's, ends by projecting on the screen the last two sentences of the novel, which read like an epigraph on a memorial: 'For it is the dawn that has come, as it has for a thousand centuries, never failing. But when the dawn will come, of our emancipation, from the fear of bondage and the bondage of fear, why, that is a secret.' (Beittel 2003: 87)

A secret, perhaps, in 1946; in 1995, however, the newly emancipated audience know that the (historical) dawn has arrived – whatever the day that follows may bring.

Note

1 Lindiwe Dovey's illuminating PhD thesis (Dovey 2005) and forthcoming book on cinematic adaptation of literature in Africa contain a chapter offering another of the rare academic analyses of Roodt's film.

Filmography

City of Blood (1983)
Place of Weeping (1986)
10th of a Second (1987)
The Stick (1987)
Jobman (1990)
Sarafina! (1992)
To the Death (1993)
Father Hood (1993)
Cry, the Beloved Country (1995)
Dangerous Ground (1997)
Second Skin (2000)
Witness to a Kill (2001)
Pavement (2002)
Sumuru (2003)
Dracula 3000 (2004)
Yesterday (2004)
Number 10 (2006)
Faith's Corner (2006)
Prey (2007)

Bibliography

Achebe, Chinua. (1988) *Hopes and Impediments: Selected Essays 1965–87*, London, Heinemann.

Achour, Bernard. (2005) 'La Chasse aux sorciers', *Téléobs*, 17–23 décembre.

Ahmida, Ali Abdullatif. (2000) *Beyond Colonialism and Nationalism in the Maghreb: History, Culture and Politics*, London, Palgrave.

Allen, Richard. (1995) *Projecting Illusion: Film Spectatorship and the Impression of Reality*, Cambridge: Cambridge University Press.

Althusser, Louis. (1984) 'Ideology and Ideological State Apparatuses', in *Essays on Ideology*, London, Verso.

Anderson, Benedict. (1983) *Imagined Communities: Reflections on the Origin and Spread of Nationalism*, London, Verso.

Andrew, Dudley. (1995) 'Falaises sacrées et espaces communs', *iris*, 18, pp. 113–24.

Appiah, Kwame Anthony. (1992) *In My Father's House: Africa in the Philosophy of Culture*, New York and Oxford, Oxford University Press.

Armatage, Kay. (1994) '*Les Silences du palais*', *Cinéaction*, 39 (Winter), pp. 24–7.

Armes, Roy. (2006) *African Filmmaking: North and South of the Sahara*, Edinburgh, Edinburgh University Press.

Armes, Roy. (2005) *Postcolonial Images: Studies in North African Film*, Bloomington, Indiana University Press.

Armes, Roy. (1996) *Dictionnaire des cinéastes du Maghreb*, Paris, ATM.

Armes, Roy. (1987) *Third World Filmmaking and the West*, Berkeley, University of California Press.

Ashcroft, Bill, Gareth Griffiths and Helen Tiffin. (1989) *The Empire Writes Back: Theory and Practice in Postcolonial Literatures*, London and New York, Routledge.

Attia, Ahmed. (2002) Interview with Olivier Barlet, *Africultures*, 22 October, www.africultures.com.

Bachy, Victor. (1982) *La Haute Volta et le cinéma*, Brussels, Cinémédia.

Bakari, Imruh, and Mbye Cham, eds. (1996) *African Experiences of Cinema*, London, BFI.

Bakhtin, Mikhail. (1986) *Speech Genres and Other Late Essays*, Austin, University of Texas Press.

Balseiro, Isabel, and Ntongela Masilela, eds. (2003) *To Change Reels: Film and Film Culture in South Africa*, Detroit, Wayne State University Press.

Barber, Karin. (1997) 'Introduction', in Karin Barber, John Collins and Alain Ricard, *West African Popular Theatre*, Oxford, James Currey, pp. vii–xix.

Barber, Karin. (1987) 'Popular Arts in Africa', *The African Studies Review*, 30.3, pp. 1–78.

Barlet, Olivier. (2002) 'Pleure, O pays bien-aimé', *Africultures*, 22 January, www.africultures.com.

Barlet, Olivier. (2000) *African Cinemas: Decolonising the Gaze*, London, Zed Books.

Barrot, Pierre, ed. (2005) *Nollywood: Le phénomène vidéo au Nigeria*, Paris, L'Harmattan.

Beittel, Mark. (2003) '"What sort of memorial?" *Cry, the Beloved Country* on Film', in Balseiro and Masilela, eds, *To Change Reels*, pp. 219–54.

Benabdessadok, Cherifa. (2003) '*Nha fala*', www.alterites.com.

Benjamin, Walter. (1982) 'The Work of Art in the Age of Mechanical Reproduction', in *Illuminations*, London, Fontana/Collins, pp. 70–87.

Bhabha, Homik. (1994) *The Location of Culture*, London, Routledge.

Biko, Steve. (1979) *I Write What I Like*, London, Heinemann.

Bongie, Chris. (2003a) 'Exiles on Main Stream: Valuing the Popularity of Postcolonial Literature', *Postmodern Culture*, 14.1, www.iath.virginia.edu/pmc.

Bongie, Chris. (2003b) 'Belated Liaisons: Writing between the Margins of Literary and Cultural Studies', *Francophone Postcolonial Studies*, 1.2, pp. 11–24.

Botha, Martin. (1995) 'The South African Film Industry: Fragmentation, Identity Crisis and Unification', *Kinema*, www.kinema.uwaterloo.ca.

Boughedir, Ferid. (2000) 'African Cinema and Ideology: Tendencies and Evolution', in Givanni, ed., *Symbolic Narratives/African Cinema*, pp. 109–21.

Brennan, Timothy. (1997) *At Home in the World: Cosmopolitanism Now*, Cambridge, MA, and London, Harvard University Press.

Brosseau, Marc, and Leila Ayari. (2005) 'Writing Place and Gender in Novels by Tunisian Women', in Falah and Nagel, eds, *Geographies of Muslim Women: Gender, Religion and Space*.

Buck-Morss, Susan. (2003) *Thinking Past Terror*, London, Verso.

Burns, J. M. (2002) *Flickering Shadows: Cinema and Identity in Colonial Zimbabwe*, Athens, Ohio University Press.

Cabral, Amilcar. (1980) *Unity and Struggle: Speeches and Writings*, London, Heinemann.

Cabral, Amilcar. (1976) *Return to the Source: Selected Speeches*, New York, Monthly Review Press.

Cabral, Amilcar. (1969) *Revolution in Guinea: Selected Texts*, New York, Monthly Review Press.

Cameron, Keith M. (1994) *Africa on Film: Beyond Black and White*, New York, Continuum.

Campbell, Jan. (2005) *Film and Cinema Spectatorship*. Cambridge, Polity.

Chabal, Patrick, with David Birmingham, Joshua Forrest, Malya Newitt, Gerhard Seibert and Elsa Silva Andrade. (2003) *A History of Postcolonial Lusophone Africa*, London, Hurst.

Chahine, Youssef. (2006) Interview, *Qantara*, www.qantara.de.

Chahine, Youssef. (2004) Interview, *L'Humanité*, 7 July: www.humanite.presse.fr.

Chahine, Youssef. (2001) Interview, *Vacarme*, www.vacarme.eu.org.

Chahine, Youssef. (1997) Interview, *L'Humanité*, 15 October, www.humanite.presse.fr.

Chahine, Youssef. (1996) 'Le Spectacle et la vie: entretien avec Youssef Chahine', *Cahiers du Cinéma*, October, p. 9.

Cham, Mbye. (1996) 'Introduction', in Bakari and Cham, eds, *African Experiences of Cinema*, pp. 1–15.

Cham, Mbye Boubacar. (1982) 'Ousmane Sembene and the Aesthetics of African Oral Traditions', *Africana Journal*, 13.1–4, pp. 24–40.

Charrad, Mounira. (2001) *States and Women's Rights*, Berkeley, University of California Press.

Childs, Peter, and Patrick Williams. (1996) *Introduction to Post-Colonial Theory*, London, Prentice Hall/Pearson.

Chinweizu, Onwuchekwa Jemie and Ikechukwu Madubuike. (1980) *Toward the Decolonization of African Literature*, London, Kegan Paul.

Cinquante ans de cinéma africain: Hommage à Paulin Soumanou Vieyra. (2005) Special issue of *Présence Africaine*, 170.

Cousins, Mark. (2006) 'Widescreen', *Prospect*, 118, January, p. 62.

Daney, Serge. (1979) '*Ceddo* (O. Sembene)', *Cahiers du Cinéma*, 304, October, pp. 51–3.

Davidson, Basil. (1994) *The Search for Africa: A History in the Making*, London, James Currey.

Davidson, Basil. (1992) *The Black Man's Burden: Africa and the Curse of the Nation-State*, London, James Currey.

Deleuze, Gilles, and Félix Guattari. (1975) *Kafka: Pour une littérature mineure*, Paris, Editions de Minuit.

De Rochebrune, Renaud. (2005) 'Idrissa Ouédraogo: "Le nouveau cinéma africain sera numérique"', *Jeune Afrique*, 2307, 27 March–2 April, pp. 58–9.

Diawara, Manthia. (1996) 'Popular Culture and Oral Traditions in African Film', in Bakari and Cham, eds, *African Experiences of Cinema*, pp. 209–18.

Diawara, Manthia. (1992) *African Cinema: Politics and Culture*, Bloomington, Indiana University Press.

Diawara, Manthia. (1988) 'Souleymane Cissé's Light on Africa', *Black Film Review*, 4.4, pp. 13–15

Diop, Buuba Babacar. (1984) 'Malaise autour de *Ceddo*', *Revue Africaine de Communication*, 7, pp. 45–52.

Dovey, Lindiwe. (2005) *Mimesis and the Critique of Violence: African Film Adaptation of Literature*, PhD thesis, University of Cambridge.

Downing, John D. H. ed. (1987) *Film and Politics in the Third World*, New York: Autonomedia.

Echenberg, Myron J. (1978) 'Tragedy at Thiaroye: The Senegalese Soldiers' Uprising of 1944', in Peter C. W. Gutkind, et al., *African Labor History*, Beverly Hills and London, Sage, pp. 109–28.

Falah, Ghazi-Walid, and Caroline Nagel, eds. (2005) *Geographies of Muslim Women: Gender, Religion and Space*, New York, Guilford Press.

Fanon, Frantz. (1989) *Studies in a Dying Colonialism*, London, Earthscan.

Fanon, Frantz. (1986) *Black Skin, White Masks*, London, Pluto.

Fanon, Frantz. (1970) *Toward the African Revolution*, Harmondsworth, Penguin.

Fanon, Frantz. (1967) *The Wretched of the Earth*, Harmondsworth, Penguin.

Fawal, Ibrahim. (2001) *Youssef Chahine*, London, BFI.

FEPACI. (1995) *Africa and the Centenary of Cinema/L'Afrique et le centenaire du cinéma*, Paris, Présence Africaine.

Fisiy, Cyprien, and Peter Geschiere. (1996) 'Witchcraft, Violence and Identity: Different Trajectories in Postcolonial Cameroon', in Richard Werbner and Terence Ranger, eds, *Postcolonial Identities in Africa*, London, Zed Books, pp. 193–221.

Forrest, Joshua. (2003) 'Guinea-Bissau', in Chabal, et al. (2003) *A History of Postcolonial Lusophone Africa*.

Gabriel, Teshome H. (1989) 'Towards a Critical Theory of Third World Films', in Pines and Willemen, eds, *Questions of Third Cinema*, pp. 30–52.

Gabriel, Teshome H. (1982) *Third Cinema in the Third World: The Aesthetics of Liberation*, London, Bowker.

Gadjigo, Samba, Ralph H. Falkingham, Thomas Cassirer and Reinhard Sander, eds. (1993) *Ousmane Sembene: Dialogues with Critics and Writers*, Amherst, University of Massachusetts Press.

Gardies, André. (1989) *Cinéma d'Afrique noire francophone: l'espace miroir*, Paris, L'Harmattan.

Gentile, Philip. (1995) 'In the Midst of Secrets: Souleymane Cissé's *Yeelen*', *iris*, 18, pp. 125–35.

Gerima, Haile. (2003) 'Afterword', in Balseiro and Masilela, eds, *To Change Reels*, pp. 201–27.

Gilroy, Paul. (1989) 'Cruciality and the Frog's Perspective: An Agenda of Difficulties for the Black Arts Movement in Britain', *Third Text*, 5, pp. 33–44.

Gilroy, Paul. (1993) *The Black Atlantic*, London, Verso.

Givanni, June, ed. (2000) *Symbolic Narratives/African Cinema: Audiences, Theory and the Moving Image*, London, BFI.

Gomes, Flora. (2004) Interview with Olivier Barlet, *Africultures*, 25 February (online version), www.africultures.com.

Gomes, Flora. (2003) Interview, *Africatime*, 23 September (online version), www.africultures.com.

Gomes, Flora. (2002a) Interview with Olivier Barlet, *Africultures*, 21 October (online version), www.africultures.com.

Gomes, Flora. (2002b) Interview with Catherine Ruelle, *Africultures*, 4 October (online version), www.africultures.com.

Gomes, Flora. (2002c) Interview with Olivier Barlet and Serge Zeitoun, *Africultures*, 3 September (online version), www.africultures.com.

Gordimer, Nadine. (1988) *The Essential Gesture: Writing, Politics and Places*, London, Jonathan Cape.

Gugler, Josef. (2003) *African Film: Re-imagining a Continent*, Oxford, James Currey.

Gugler, Josef, and Oumar Chérif Diop. (1998) 'Ousmane Sembène's *Xala*: The Novel, the Film and Their Audiences', *Research in African Literatures*, 29.2, pp. 147–58.

Guneratne, Anthony R., and Wimal Dissanayake, eds. (2003) *Rethinking Third Cinema*, London, Routledge.

Haffner, Pierre. (1978) *Essai sur les fondements du cinéma africain*, Abidjan and Dakar: Les Nouvelles Editions Africaines.

Hall, Stuart. (1986) 'Variants of Liberalism', in James Donald and Stuart Hall, eds, *Politics and Ideology*, Milton Keynes, Open University Press, pp. 34–69.

Haroun, Mahamat-Saleh. (2004) 'Du militantisme à la schizophrénie', www.african-geopolitics.org/articles.

Harrison, Nicholas. (2003) *Postcolonial Criticism: History, Theory and the Work of Fiction*, Cambridge, Polity.

Harrow, Kenneth W. ed. (1999a) *African Cinema: Post-Colonial and Feminist Readings*, Trenton, NJ, Africa World Press.

Harrow, Kenneth W. (1999b) 'Introduction', in Harrow, ed., *African Cinema*, pp. ix–xxiv.

Harrow, Kenneth W. (1995) '*Camp de Thiaroye*: Who's That Hiding in Those Tanks and How Come We Can't See Their Faces?', *iris*, 18, pp. 147–52.

Haynes, Jonathan. ed. (2000) *Nigerian Video Films*, Athens, Ohio University Centre for International Studies.

Hochberg, Gil. (2000) 'National Allegories and the Emergence of Female Voice in Moufida Tlatli's *Les Silences du palais*', *Third Text*, 50, pp. 33–44.

Hondo, Med. (2002) Interview with Olivier Barlet, *Africultures*, 2 September, ww.africultures.com.

Hondo, Med. (1988a) Interview with James Leahy, 31st London Film Festival, unpublished typescript.

Hondo, Med. (1988b) Interview with James Leahy, *Monthly Film Bulletin*, 55, 648, pp. 9–10.

Hondo, Med. (1987) 'The Cinema of Exile', in Downing, ed., *Film and Politics in the Third World*, pp. 69–76.

Hondo, Med. (1979) in A. Martin, 'Four West African Film-makers', *Framework*, 11, pp. 16–21.

Hondo, Med. (1978) 'African Dossier: Hondo, Gerima, Sembene', *Framework*, 7/8, pp. 20–39.

Huggan, Graham. (2001) *The Postcolonial Exotic: Marketing the Margins*, London and New York, Routledge.

Irele, Abiola. (1981) *The African Experience in Literature and Ideology*, London, Heinemann.

Jameson, Fredric. (1986) 'Third-World Literature in the Era of Multinational Capitalism', *Social Text*, 15, pp. 65–88.

Jancovich, Mark, Lucy Faire with Sarah Stubbings. (2003) *The Place of the Audience: Cultural Geographies of Film Consumption*, London, BFI.

Kandiyoti, Deniz, ed. (1994) *Gendering the Middle East: Emerging Perspectives*, Syracuse, NY, Syracuse University Press.

Kane, Cheikh Hamidou. (1972 [1961]) *Ambiguous Adventure*, trans. by Katherine Woods, London, Heinemann.

Lapsley, Robert, and Michael Westlake. (1988) *Film Theory: An Introduction*, Manchester, Manchester University Press.

Lazarus, Neil. (1999) *Nationalism and Cultural Practice in the Postcolonial World*, Cambridge, Cambridge University Press.

Lequeret, Elisabeth. (2003) *Le Cinéma africain: un continent à la recherche de son propre regard*, Paris, Les Editions Cahiers du Cinéma.

Levieux, Michèle. (2000) 'La Sexualité est le fondement même de l'équilibre humain', *L'Humanité*, 27 December, www.humanite.presse.fr.

Lott, Tommy. (1997) 'Aesthetics and Politics in Contemporary Black Film Theory', in Richard Allen and Murray Smith, eds, *Film Theory and Philosophy: Essays in the Analytical Tradition*, Oxford, Clarendon Press, pp. 282–302.

MacCannell, Dean. (1976) *The Tourist: A New Theory of the Leisure Class*, Basingstoke, Macmillan.

McClintock, Anne. (1995) *Imperial Leather: Race Gender and Sexuality in the Colonial Contest*, London, Routledge.

McLeod, John. (2000) *Beginning Postcolonialism*, Manchester, Manchester University Press.

Maingard, Jacqueline. (2003) 'Framing South African National Cinema and Television', in Balseiro and Masilela, eds, *To Change Reels*, pp. 115–31.

Malkmus, Lizbeth, and Roy Armes. (1991) *Arab and African Filmmaking*, London, Zed Books.

Malti-Douglas, Fedwa. (1991) *Woman's Body, Woman's Word*, Princeton, NJ, Princeton University Press.

Martin, Florence. (2004) 'Silence and Scream: Moufida Tlatli's Cinematic Suite', *Studies in French Cinema*, 4.3, pp. 175–85.

Masilela, Ntongela. (2003) 'The New African Movement and the Beginnings of Film Culture', in Balseiro and Masilela, eds, *To Change Reels*, pp. 15–30.

Massad, Joseph. (1999) 'Art and Politics in the Cinema of Youssef Chahine', *Journal of Palestine Studies*, 28.2, pp. 79–93.

Mayne, Judith. (1993) *Cinema and Spectatorship*, London and New York, Routledge.

Mercer, Kobena. (1994) *Welcome to the Jungle*, London, Routledge.

Mishra, Vijay, and Bob Hodge. (1993) 'What is Post(-)Colonialism?', in Williams and Chrisman, eds, *Colonial Discourse and Post-Colonial Theory*, pp. 276–90.

Moore-Gilbert, Bart. (1997) *Postcolonial Theory*, London, Verso.

Mulvey, Laura. (1993) '*Xala*, Ousmane Sembene 1976: The Carapace that Failed', in Williams and Chrisman, eds, *Colonial Discourse and Post-Colonial Theory*, pp. 517–34.

Murphy, David. (2007) 'Where Does World Music Come From? Globalisation, Afropop and Cultural Identity', in Vanessa Knights and Ian Biddle, eds, *Music, National Identity and the Politics of Location: Between the Local and the Global*, Aldershot, Ashgate, pp. 39–61.

Murphy, David. (2000a) *Sembene: Imagining Alternatives in Film and Fiction*, London, James Currey; Trenton, NJ, Africa World Press.

Murphy, David. (2000b) 'Africans Filming Africa: Questioning Theories of an Authentic African Cinema', *Journal of African Cultural Studies*, 13.2, pp. 239–49.

Murphy, David. (2000c) 'Alternative Media/Alternative Genres in Sembene's Novel and Film *Xala*', *ASCALF Yearbook*, 4, pp. 89–99.

Naaman, Dorit. (2000) 'Woman/Nation: A Postcolonial Look at Female Subjectivity', *Quarterly Review of Film and Video*, 17.4, pp. 333–42.

Needham, Gary, and I-Fen Wu. (2006) 'Film Authorship and Taiwanese Cinema', in Dimitris Eleftheriotis and Gary Needham, eds, *Asian Cinemas: A Reader and Guide*, Edinburgh: Edinburgh University Press, pp. 359–68.

Newell, Stephanie. (2000) *Ghanaian Popular Fiction: 'Thrilling Discoveries in Conjugal Life' and Other Tales*, Oxford: James Currey.

Ngugi wa Thiong'o. (1993) *Moving the Centre*, London, James Currey/Heinemann.

Niang, Sada, ed. (1996) *Littérature et cinéma en Afrique francophone: Ousmane Sembène et Assia Djebar*, Paris, L'Harmattan.

Nixon, Rob. (1994) *Homelands, Harlem and Hollywood*, London, Routledge.

Notcutt, L. A. and G. C. Latham. (1937) *The African and the Cinema*, London, Edinburgh House Press.

Oberholzer, Christo. (2004) 'Content versus Entertainment', *SA Film*, www.safilm.org.za.

Parry, Benita. (2002) 'Directions and Dead Ends in Postcolonial Studies', in David Theo Goldberg and Ato Quayson, eds, *Relocating Postcolonialism*, Oxford, Blackwell, pp. 66–81.

Petersen, Bhekizizwe. (2003) 'The Politics of Leisure during the Early Days of South African Cinema', in Balseiro and Masilela, eds, *To Change Reels*, pp. 31–48.

Petty, Sheila, ed. (1996) *A Call to Arms: The Films of Ousmane Sembene*, Trowbridge, Flicks Books.

Pfaff, Françoise, ed. (2004) *Focus on African Films*, Bloomington, Indiana University Press.

Pfaff, Françoise. (1988) *Twenty-Five Black African Filmmakers*, Westport, CT, Greenwood Press.

Pfaff, Françoise. (1986), 'Films of Med Hondo', *Jump Cut*, 31, pp. 44–6.

Pfaff, Françoise. (1984) *The Cinema of Ousmane Sembene: A Pioneer of African Film*, Westport, CT, Greenwood Press.

Pines, Jim, and Paul Willemen, eds. (1989) *Questions of Third Cinema*, London, BFI.

Pretorius, William. (1994) 'New Life for an Old Classic', *Weekly Mail and Guardian*, 9–14 December, p. 33.

Roodt, Darrell James. (2006) 'Interview', www.HBO.com/films/yesterday/interviews.

Rosen, Philip. (1991) 'Making a Nation in Sembene's *Ceddo*', *Quarterly Review of Film and Video*, 13.1–3, pp. 147–72.

Ruelle, Catherine, ed. (2005) *Afriques 50: Singularités d'un cinéma pluriel*, Paris, L'Harmattan.

Said, Edward W. (1999) *Out of Place*, London, Granta.

Said, Edward W. (1993) *Culture and Imperialism*, London, Chatto.

Said, Edward W. (1984) *The World, the Text and the Critic*, London, Faber.

Said, Edward W. (1978) *Orientalism*, London, Routledge and Kegan Paul.

Said, S. F. (2001) 'Island of Silences', *Sight and Sound*, July, pp. 22–4.

Schick, Irving. (1999) *The Erotic Margin*, London, Verso.

Sembene, Ousmane. (1995 [1960]) *God's Bits of Wood*, trans. by Francis Price, London, Heinemann.

Sène, Nar. (2001) *Djibril Diop Mambety: la caméra au bout du nez*, Paris, L'Harmattan.

Shaka, Femi Okiremuete. (2004) *Modernity and the African Cinema: A Study in Colonialist Discourse, Postcoloniality, and Modern African Identities*, Trenton, NJ, Africa World Press.

Sherzer, Dina. (2000) 'Remembrance of Things Past: *Les Silences du palais* by Moufida Tlatli', *South Central Review*, 17.3, pp. 50–9.

Sherzer, Dina, ed. (1996) *Cinema, Colonialism, Postcolonialism*, Austin, University of Texas Press.

Shiri, Keith. (1992) *Dictionary of African Film-makers and Films*, Westport, CT, Greenwood Press.

Shohat, Ella. (2003) 'Post-Third-Worldist Culture: Gender, Nation, and the Cinema', in Guneratne and Dissanayake, eds, *Rethinking Third Cinema*, pp. 51–78.

Shohat, Ella. (1992) 'Notes on the "post-colonial"', *Social Text*, 31–2, pp. 99–113.

Signaté, Ibrahima. (1994) *Med Hondo: un cinéaste rebelle*, Paris, Présence Africaine.

Smith, Murray. (1995) *Engaging Characters: Fiction, Emotion and the Cinema*, Oxford, Oxford University Press.

Spivak, Gayatri. (1996) *The Spivak Reader*, ed., Donna Landry and Gerald Maclean, London, Routledge.

Spivak, Gayatri. (1995) *Imaginary Maps*, London, Routledge.

Spivak, Gayatri. (1993) *Outside in the Teaching Machine*, London, Routledge.

Spivak, Gayatri. (1990) *The Postcolonial Critic*, ed., Sarah Harasym, London, Routledge.

Stam, Robert. (1999) 'Third World and Postcolonial Cinema', in Pam Cook, ed., *The Cinema Book*, London, BFI, pp. 120–34.

Taubin, Amy. (2001) 'Pregnant Pause: *The Season of Men*', *Village Voice*, 26 September–2 October, www.villagevoice.com.

Taylor, Clyde. (2000) 'Searching for the Postmodern in African Cinema', in Givanni, ed., *Symbolic Narratives/African Cinema*, pp. 136–44.

Taylor, Clyde. (1989) 'Black Cinema in the Post-aesthetic Era', in Pines and Willemen, eds, *Questions of Third Cinema*, pp. 90–110.

Thackway, Melissa. (2003) *Africa Shoots Back: Alternative Perspectives in Sub-Saharan Francophone African Film*, Oxford, James Currey.

Timberg, Craig. (2005) 'Portraits of Anywhere but Home', *Washington Post*, 27 February, A16.

Tlatli, Moufida. (2001) 'Sins of the Mothers': Interview with Peter Lennon, *Guardian*, 22 June, www.film.guardian.co.uk.

Tlatli, Moufida. (2000a) Interview with Olivier Barlet, *Africultures*, May, www.africultures.com.

Tlatli, Moufida. (2000b) Interview in Dossier de presse for *La Saison des hommes*, www.filmdulosange.fr.

Tlatli, Moufida. (1995) 'Moving Bodies: Interview with Laura Mulvey', *Sight and Sound*, 5.3, pp. 18–20.

Tlatli, Moufida. (1994) 'Stories of Women: Interview with Tahar Chikaoui', *Ecrans d'Afrique*, 8, pp. 8–11.

Tomaselli, Keyan. (1989) *The Cinema of Apartheid*, London, Routledge.

Tomaselli, Keyan, Arnold Shepperson and Maureen Eke. (1999) 'Towards a Theory of Orality in Afrcan Cinema', in Harrow, ed., *African Cinema*, pp. 45–71.

Trinh, Minh-ha. (1992) *Framer Framed*, London, Routledge.

Trotsky, Leon. (1966) *In Defence of Marxism*, London, New Park.

Ukadike, N. Frank. (2002) *Questioning African Cinema: Conversations with Filmmakers*, Minneapolis: University of Minnesota Press.

Ukadike, N. Frank. (1994) *Black African Cinema*, Berkeley, University of California Press.

Willemen, Paul. (1989) 'The Third Cinema Question: Notes and Reflections', in Pines and Willemen, eds, *Questions of Third Cinema*, pp. 1–29.

Williams, Patrick, and Laura Chrisman, eds. (1993) *Colonial Discourse and Post-Colonial Theory*, Hemel Hempstead, Harvester Wheatsheaf/Pearson.

Williams, Patrick. (2007) 'Black Looks/Black Light: Med Hondo's *Lumière Noire*', in Mpalive Msiska, ed., *The Black Gaze*, Trenton, NJ, Africa World Press.

Williams, Patrick. (2003) '"Faire peau neuve" – Césaire, Fanon, Memmi, Sartre and Senghor', in Charles Forsdick and David Murphy, eds, *Francophone Postcolonial Studies: A Critical Introduction*, London, Arnold, pp. 181–91.

Williams, Patrick. (2001) 'Entering and Leaving Modernity: Utopia and Dystopia in Mambety's *Hyènes* and *Touki Bouki*', in Wendy Everett, ed., *The Seeing Century: Film, Vision and Identity*, Amsterdam, Rodopi, pp. 124–34.

Wynchank, Anny. (2003) *Djibril Diop Mambety ou le voyage du voyant*, Paris, Editions A3.

Young, Robert J. C. (2001) *Postcolonialism: An Historical Introduction*, Oxford, Blackwell.

Index

Note: 'n' after a page number indicates the number of a note on that page